The Press in English Society from the Seventeenth to Nineteenth Centuries

Frontispiece. **Newspapers and readers: a scene in a coffee house in the City of London. Mezzotint print from a painting by Robert Dighton after 1780 (Guildhall Library).**

The Press in English Society from the Seventeenth to Nineteenth Centuries

Edited by Michael Harris and Alan Lee

Rutherford • Madison • Teaneck
Fairleigh Dickinson University Press
London and Toronto: Associated University Presses

Published for the Press Group of the Acton Society Trust

Associated University Presses
440 Forsgate Drive
Cranbury, NJ 08512

Associated University Presses
25 Sicilian Avenue
London WC1A 2QH, England

Associated University Presses
2133 Royal Windsor Drive
Unit 1
Mississauga, Ontario
Canada L5J 1K5

Library of Congress Cataloging-in-Publication Data
Main entry under title:

The Press in English society from the seventeenth to nineteenth centuries.

Bibliography: p.
Includes index.
1. Journalism—Social aspects—Great Britain—History. I. Harris, Michael, Dr. II. Lee, Alan J.
PN5124.S6P74 1986 302.2'322'0941 85-45535
ISBN 0-8386-3272-6 (alk. paper)

The paper used in this publication meets the requirements of the American National Standard for Permanence of Paper for Printed Library Materials Z39.48-1984.

Printed in the United States of America

Contents

Alan J. Lee
1943–1981

This book began as a joint project in which Alan was to have been responsible for the nineteenth-century section. His reputation as a historian of the press was growing rapidly, particularly following publication of *The Origins of the Popular Press, 1855–1914* and no one was better qualified to coordinate a collection of this sort. Tragically, soon after setting the project in motion, he contracted leukaemia, and though he was able to complete the preliminary editorial work and take part in a conference for contributors in the spring of 1981 he suffered a terrible relapse and died suddenly in July. The loss of a friend and colleague was a desperate blow and has not only delayed the appearance of the volume but also deprived it of the sort of lucid and thoughtful analysis based on a profound knowledge of the subject which would have given it greater substance. Alan had organized all the nineteenth-century essays and had discussed the material with the friends and colleagues who were involved. However, he left behind only a shadowy sketch of the way he intended to handle the introduction. Alan will continue to be greatly missed by everyone who knew him, and his death represents a serious setback to the study of newspaper history. He leaves a wife and three young children.

Michael Harris

This book was sponsored and funded by the Acton Society. The Acton Society Trust is an independent non-profit-making organization. It was set up in 1948 and is a recognized charitable trust. It has carried out or sponsored many research projects in social and economic fields.

The Acton Society Press Group was formed in 1974 in response to the setting up of a Royal Commission on the Press, with the object of studying the press industry and of providing a forum where problems could be discussed. Among its previous publications is *Newspaper history from the seventeenth century to the present day,* edited by George Boyce, James Curran, and Pauline Wingate (London: Constable/Sage, 1978).

THE EDITORS

Michael Harris	Department of Extra-Mural Studies, University of London
Alan J. Lee	Late of the Department of History, University of Hull

LIST OF CONTRIBUTORS

Virginia Berridge	Institute of Historical Research University of London
Louis Billington	Department of American Studies University of Hull
Jeremy Black	Department of History University of Durham
Diana Dixon	Department of Library and Information Studies, University of Loughborough
Catherine Hughes	Department of the History of Art Canterbury College of Art
Tony Mason	Centre for the Study of Social History University of Warwick
Terry Nevett	Faculty of Administrative Studies Polytechnic of the South Bank, London
Thomas O'Malley	University of Birmingham
William Speck	School of History University of Leeds
Richard Wilson	School of Economic and Social Studies University of East Anglia

The Press in English Society from the Seventeenth to Nineteenth Centuries

General Introduction

An introduction to a book appearing under such a comprehensive title inevitably faces the difficulty of establishing a clear-cut conceptual framework. Not only are questions about the interaction between newspapers and periodicals and the society in which they are produced and circulated notoriously hard to answer, but the study of the development of the press is still at a formative stage and much of the groundwork has yet to be completed. Not that there is any lack of interest in the problems. Because of their pervasive character, these forms of publication crop up in the context of a very broad range of disciplines. Quarried for material of all sorts, they have come under scrutiny by students of literature, bibliography, history, and social science. Each discipline has established a separate approach as well as a variable period emphasis, but although a good deal of useful research has been done, the advances made on each front have not always been fully integrated. Temperamental discontinuity between the disciplines seems to have aggravated the usual problem of time lag. The previous volume in the series Communication and Society, dealing exclusively with newspapers and published under the short title *Newspaper History,*[1] offered a collection of essays which reflected several of the different approaches and ideological interpretations and represented at least a gesture toward a general synthesis.

Partly because of the variations in method and interest within the overlapping disciplines and their multiple subdivisions, a number of long-term imbalances have been created in the available picture. Neglect of the publications of the seventeenth and eighteenth centuries is combined with a blurring of the relationship between the London and provincial press, as well as between those forms of output catering for the upper and lower levels of market. Similarly, the recurrent emphasis on a single line of political activity centered on the issue of "the freedom of the press" has tended to obscure equally important general issues. Much needs to be done before the dragons and elephants can be removed from the map and be replaced by an accurate topography.

As Alan Lee has pointed out in his brilliant study of the post-1855 newspapers, it is possible to approach the social history of the press from two directions.[2] Firstly from the production side, in which the publications are seen primarily as a business enterprise and in which the emphasis is placed on patterns of ownership and the processes of production and distribution. Much of the work on the development of the newspaper press during the eighteenth and nineteenth centuries has followed this line. Secondly from the demand side, in which the center of interest lies in the relationship between the newspaper or periodical and the readership. The distinction between the two approaches is not clear-cut, as the opinions and interests of readers inevitably impinged on the conduct of most publications and both approaches involve an examination of content. Although the essays in this collection are often concerned with production issues, the emphasis here is on the external relations of the newspapers and periodicals, and one of the main aims of the book is to indicate how the identification and analysis of selected content areas can open up the complex relationship between the press and society.

The investigation of content poses particular difficulties for the individual researcher. The bulk and range of the material entombed in the mass of surviving copies is bad enough. A view of the Burney collection of pre-1800 newspapers in the stacks of the British Library is in itself enough to deter any but the most obsessive. Equally the expanding range of materials charted in bibliographies of nineteenth-century periodicals provides vitally useful but daunting information.[3] But at the same time the need for specialist knowledge across a range of disciplines and over an extended period also makes demands on the researcher which it is particularly difficult to meet. These problems alone suggest the value of the sort of group enterprise represented in this book. In some respects the history of the press, like the history of crime and urban history, is at a stage in its development when group activity can sometimes achieve more than the struggling individual.[4]

The contributors to this volume consist of a group of historians of the eighteenth and nineteenth centuries who are not specifically historians of the press but whose specialist interests have led them to make extensive use of the contemporary newspapers and periodicals. Because of the variable starting points, the methodology is not altogether consistent between individuals nor, to some extent, between the chronological sections. The eighteenth-century section, for example, is concerned entirely with the newspaper press, while the nineteenth-century section takes in a broader spectrum of output. Nonetheless, the shared objectives and the common empirical approach have meant that in each of these specially written essays the contributors are dealing with an interconnected series of issues and problems focused on selected content areas. Inevitably the topics chosen, though picking up some of the major themes, touch the history of the press over this long period fairly selectively. Some topics, such as advertising and politics, are identified in one period but not in the other. Equally, while many potentially useful subjects are omitted altogether, it has not been possible in a collection of this kind to balance the representation of material from London and the provinces.

Two general points about newspaper content which predominate in this collection may need to be emphasized here. Firstly, specific influence can seldom be pinned down in a historical context. Contemporary efforts to come to terms with this problem have proved problematic enough, and the whole approach to "effects research" is being reconsidered.[5] None the less, at a rather different level it should be noted that even in the eighteenth century there are elements in newspaper content which can be linked to a precise sequence of cause and effect. Criminal advertising, for example, can be followed up through the depositions at provincial quarter sessions to provide a rare glimpse of the newspaper in action. Current research suggests that the dominant influence of the press in a politically advanced society lies in the reinforcement of existing attitudes and opinions, and this primarily integrative role is implicit in these essays.[6]

Secondly, there are the problems of overlap and definition which are consistently lurking in the background of any discussion of press content. The newspaper in particular has always displayed a peculiar volatility. Material appearing in separate forms was sometimes absorbed by the newspaper press, becoming part of its characteristic content. On the other hand, material developed in the newspaper itself sometimes spun off, assuming a life of its own in separate publications. Advertisements, commercial information, and popular fiction, for example, each separated from and merged with newspaper content over a very long period. At the same time, the newspaper formed part of a chain of publication. By a continuous process of republication or imitation, the sort of material circulating through the press was also made available by a variety of alternative means. Magazines, pamphlets, almanacs, serials, plays, ballads, and posters, as well as other types of ephemeral output, each formed a link in the complex process of transmission through society. Among the forms of recurrent publication embraced within the catch-all and sometimes confusing term *periodical,* a considerable continuity of approach existed, and it is difficult to isolate the newspaper from the ebb and flow of alternative forms. The problems of identification vary, but in general neither news coverage and topicality nor format and frequency of publication are entirely effective for the purpose. The inclusion here of discussion of content within the broad category of the periodical provides a crucial indication of the way in which the newspaper merged with or separated from the general output of the press.

The chronological division of the book represents an attempt to acknowledge the substantial changes in the organization and structures of the press, as well as within society at large, which form an implicit background to the collection. In the brief introductions to each section an attempt is made to bring together some of the general points which provide a setting for each of the contributions.

PART ONE

The Seventeenth and Eighteenth Centuries

Introduction

Within the shifting patterns of English society the newspaper held an ambiguous position. Closely associated with the crucial activities of commerce and politics, the press came to represent both stability and change in the community. The collapse of the tottering system of restraint in 1695 signaled the beginning of an erratic but long-term period of expansion centered in London and spreading continuously outward as printers set up in business in the main centers of commercial activity, first in the South and West and subsequently in the developing urban centers of the North of England. The burgeoning newspapers were based in form and style on the old model of the *London Gazette,* and to a great extent their content reflected the social attitudes of that establishment publication.

Throughout the eighteenth century the English newspaper remained locked into the dominant economic system. This was partly a reflection of the commercial circumstances of the newspapers themselves. In London, after a period of hectic competition, ownership of the press was concentrated in the hands of variably sized groups of booksellers to whom the newspaper was a subsidiary element in a broader range of commercial activity.[1] In the provinces, the papers almost invariably remained in the hands of individual printers, whose miscellaneous participation in the commercial life of their communities extended well beyond, and provided the setting for, their newspaper interests. In each case the predominantly commercial position of the press was emphasized by a continuous and increasing involvement in advertising. During the whole of this period newspaper proprietors and advertisers stood in a symbiotic relationship to one another. In the early stages the two roles were often combined, but the value of the newspaper as a commercial device and the growing demand for space soon introduced a separation of interest and, potentially at least, an element of tension. By the 1720s the major London dailies were entirely dependent on advertising revenue for their profits, and if the source of income was less than crucial to the other forms, its contribution was still of considerable value. The English newspapers needed advertising, not only to supplement income but also to balance their appeal and relate to the communities they served. The advertisers, on the other hand, relied heavily on the press for the marketing of a widening range of goods and services. It was through the advertising content, whether commercial, official, or personal, that many papers touched the lives of their readers most directly.

From this economic base the eighteenth century newspapers catered consistently for a readership focused in the middle and upper levels of English society. The subject of trade in particular provided a common denominator between all sections of the English press, and newspaper content was shot through with material of special interest to the trading community. The heavy emphasis on foreign news may itself, in part, have reflected the concerns of the merchant interest. At the same time, while the domestic news and advertising sections provide a very accurate image of the lives of the commercial and social élites, the supplementary content represented by essays and correspondence, real and imagined, seldom moved outside the areas established at the beginning of the century. Trade, party politics, religion, literature, and manners, the last-named aimed mainly at a female audience, remained the dominant components of newspaper content, reflecting the social and cultural preoccupations of 'respectable' readers.[2] The limited information available on the distribution pattern of the English newspapers underlines this social emphasis. The London weeklies and thrice-weeklies in particular maintained their sales by spreading geographically very widely but within a limited social range. Similarly, the regular drop in sales of the London-based dailies at the end of the social season and of the parliamentary session, when most of the upper and many of the middle classes left the capital, highlights the character of their readership.[3]

Few attempts were made through the English newspapers to cater directly for a popular market, though it must have been clear enough that such a market existed on a grand scale. The sale of the Stationers' Company almanacs reached an average of 400,000 copies a year by the 1660s,[4] and this rising figure in combination with a substantial street literature and chapbook trade suggests the existence of a vast popular readership. In London the ability to read was apparently very widespread by the early eighteenth century among both men and women,[5] and the concentration of literate and semiliterate working people whose skills were already underpinned by a regular supply of cheap material offered a considerable commercial opportunity.

The proprietors of some of the conventional London weeklies, which were largely reliant on sales rather than advertising revenue, seem to have made an attempt during the early eighteenth century to broaden the range of their appeal.[6] However, the first consistent attempt to open up a new area of readership was made by a number of low-level printer-entrepreneurs who created a stratum of newspapers in London which bridged the gap between conventional up-market publications and the more popular forms of output.[7] From the second decade of the eighteenth century, appearing both stamped and unstamped, these papers undercut their respectable counterparts in price and offered a style of content with more appeal to the lower levels of readership. Serialized fact and fiction, available cheaply to the publishers by simple piracy, and the sorts of criminal biographies and dying words which figured prominently in street literature rapidly became the content staples of this section of the newspaper press.[8] At the same time, the news cover, though cast in the established form and including much material lifted from the full-priced publications, was tailored to popular taste by the inclusion of jokes and accounts of the circumstances of low life. Even the advertising reflected the interests and needs of low-income groups. This formula proved highly successful, and the cheap London papers flourished through the 1730s.[9] However, by midcentury the entire range of 'popular' output had disappeared, providing a striking illustration of the way in which the relationship between the press and its readers was mediated by commercial interests buttressed by the law. On the one hand was the cartel of respectable booksellers holding shares in established newspapers and actively defending their general control of the publishing business. On the other was the Stamp Tax introduced in 1712 which, as well as keeping the price of the newspaper beyond the reach of many potential purchasers, provided effective protection to the proprietors of the legitimately stamped publications against competition from low-level interlopers. In combination, these vested interests squeezed the cheap newspapers out of existence—the unstamped by an Act of Parliament in 1743 (16 George II c2) and the stamped by a more obscure commercial process.

The collapse of the eccentric 'popular' press in London reestablished a uniformity of approach which remained largely undisturbed in the provinces. In some respects the provincial papers stood in the same relation to their full-price London competitors as the cheap publications in the capital itself. Relying on a lower cost to boost sales and increasingly using local material to attract new readers, their proprietors nonetheless made few attempts to broaden their appeal and move outside the accepted social limits. In a provincial setting the newspaper continued to help to define and integrate communities around the dominant social and economic groups and in this respect emphasized the primarily 'static' position of the press.

Paradoxically this integrative role was combined with a more 'dynamic,' even a potentially more radical, approach developed through the consistent involvement of sections of the English press in the workings of the political system. After 1695 the propaganda campaigns of politicians out of office were increasingly centered on the newspaper, which offered both continuity and a high degree of flexibility. Throughout the eighteenth century sections of the English press offered readers a torrent of abuse and criticism leveled at those in authority. There were few defenses against this. Though the idea of the reintroduction of some sort of general censorship lingered into the next century, in practice only *ad hoc* expedients were available. Prosecution under the law of libel could be modestly successful, and legal action could drive underfinanced papers out of business. At the same time it could be used to maintain the parameters of consensus and exclude material in direct support of such political outsiders as the Jacobites. But though able to disrupt the production and distribution of the politically sponsored papers, prosecution could not touch the principals and ironically gave a useful notoriety to the material under attack. Limited alternatives such as the interruption of supply through the Post Office proved little more than an irritant, and the authorities were continuously thrown back on the production of their own newspaper-centered propaganda, as pioneered in the *London Gazette.*

Throughout the century almost every major politician was involved at some stage in his career with the financing and distribution of newspapers. Successive administrations from the Queen Anne period onward poured large sums of public money into the press, while the establishment of a newspaper became the almost invariable accompaniment to the formation of an opposition grouping.[10] In each case the press filled the dual role of a channel of communication into the community at large and a means of establishing a link between the loose-knit groups of politicians themselves and their supporters. The London newspapers of the eighteenth century often contain the most fully worked out statement of political ideology that was committed to print.[11]

Only a limited number of London newspapers were under direct political sponsorship during the eighteenth century, and the influence of subsidies on newspaper finance generally, even in the early nineteenth century, has been greatly overstated. None the less, the very general distribution of these papers, artificially boosted by both ministry and opposition, gave their content a considerable currency, and the flavor of party conflict spread outwards into every section of the press. In the commercial London papers such as the *London Evening Post,* conventional news coverage and related material could easily be modified to express a consistent party view, and this was sometimes picked up and redirected through provincial papers. Toward the end of the century, perhaps after achieving a greater commercial self-confidence, the provincial press itself became more directly involved in the sort of politico-business dispute described by Richard Wilson in Chapter 4, and subsequently the issues of national and local reform became a recurrent theme in some of the principal papers published outside London.[12]

Political information and comment, whether concentrated in the sponsored publications or forming part of the miscellaneous content of commercial papers, was directed primarily at the 'parliamentary classes.' However, in practice the political material, for which there was always a substantial demand, filtered very widely through English society. The distinction between sales figures and the actual level of readership, which has often been shown to be important during the nineteenth century, was even more so during the seventeenth and eighteenth centuries when problems of supply and cost were more marked. Both in London, from early in this period, and increasingly in the provinces, readership was multiplied in various ways. Public houses of all kinds, by providing their customers with a selection of newspapers, became and remained the most important access points. At the same time, group purchase and reading, the hire and posting of copies, loan arrangements between business colleagues, neighbors, or families and their dependents gave a widespread experience of the press. Access shaded away through casual contact with papers used to line trunks, pad out wigs, and fulfill other low-key social functions so that a single copy of a London or provincial paper could reach a very large number of readers at a variety of social levels. Equally, as the communication networks and postal systems improved, few areas of the country lay outside the distribution pattern of a newspaper of some sort.[13]

Against this background, politicians attempted to use the press to achieve a series of practical and overlapping objectives. As well as attempting to influence voters at the elections, efforts were made through the press to bring pressure to bear on sitting M.P.s through their constituents. This two-stage process, focused in the major opposition papers, involved the publication of a range of political information which reflected on the actions of members and which included voting lists, addresses, and other miscellaneous details of political behavior. Similarly, attempts were made to exert a more general influence over public opinion which could be redirected against parliamentary targets. This approach was reflected in the profound but elusive involvement of the newspaper press in the outbursts of popular feeling over such issues as the Excise and Jewish Naturalisation Bills, as well as in the more coherent campaigns of the elder Pitt and, more importantly, of John Wilkes.[14]

In this way the English newspaper contributed to the gradual extension of the political nation, becoming in the process more than a passive reflector of the existing social order. Whether or not the fears or expectations of the politicians attempting to use the press to manipulate opinion were realistic, by emphasizing its involvement in politics they were helping to legitimize and extend the role of the newspaper as a channel of communication.

The first chapter in this collection are mainly concerned with the political role of the newspaper. Although focusing on the coverage of religious affairs, Thomas O'Malley, in an analysis of the content of the *London Gazette,* places the subject in a political setting. By examining every section of this government-controlled paper, including its advertising content, he indicates how religion was used in a far-reaching campaign to buttress the position of the later Stuarts and provide recurrent support for the establishment. His contribution highlights the way in which the newspaper, even at this early stage in its development, was involved in a quite sophisticated way in an attempt to rally support and influence public opinion. William Speck, on the other hand, focuses on a sequence of general elections during the first half of the eighteenth century and investigates the ways in which the newspapers were used by the fluctuating political groupings. Looking mainly at the London papers but also referring to local publications, he provides a valuable indication of the range of public debate and of the ways in which issues were used in an attempt to influence the electorate. The general election was the point at which the politicians, public opinion, and the press were in their most characteristic conjunction, and this chapter explores both the strengths and limitations of the newspaper in that context. Jeremy Black is concerned with the extensive coverage of foreign affairs in the London papers of the early eighteenth century. As well as considering the complex process by which information was transmitted through Europe, he also identifies the way in which its presentation in the press was linked to the political disputes of the period. His contribution underlines the extent to which the readership was kept very fully informed about events abroad and the depth of interest in what often appears to be very intractable material. Richard Wilson studies the role of a number of provincial papers in a long-running dispute over the export of wool. Although the press in the provinces is often written off as a pale reflection of its London counterpart, he indicates that the local papers, whatever their shortcomings, were actively engaged in coordinating action and arousing opinion well before the end of the century.

1

Religion and the Newspaper Press, 1660–1685: A Study of the *London Gazette*

Thomas O'Malley

The relationship between any society and the newspapers which serve it is highly complex. In this chapter the relationship is explored by examining the way religious issues were dealt with in the newspaper press of the period 1666–85. The focus of the discussion is the *London Gazette,* a government publication and the only paper which ran throughout most of these years.[1] It is not possible in this period (or perhaps in any other) to list accurately the effects of any newspaper's religious content on the society in which it operated; but it is possible to arrive at a general assessment of its significance.

After some opening remarks on the religious life of England between 1660 and 1685, it will be argued that the newspaper press in these years, in particular the *London Gazette,* was regarded as a crucially important medium of communication by the government of Charles II and by the various religious groups that existed in England. The *Gazette's* treatment of religious issues, it will be argued, was designed to exploit orthodox religious sentiment in the interests of the government and to signal changes in the government's religious policy to the nation. The paper, then, helped to bolster the Stuart regime by sanctioning it with religious orthodoxy and by directing 'public opinion' along the lines which government policy took at any one time. In short, the *Gazette* played an intimate part in the complex religious history of the period.

I

Religious life in England between 1660 and 1685 was dominated by the division between the state church, the Church of England, and those Christians who chose not to be coerced into practicing their faith within that body. After the restoration of the Anglican Church in 1662, the whole population of around five million was nominally included in its membership. In fact indifference and nonattendance at any type of church

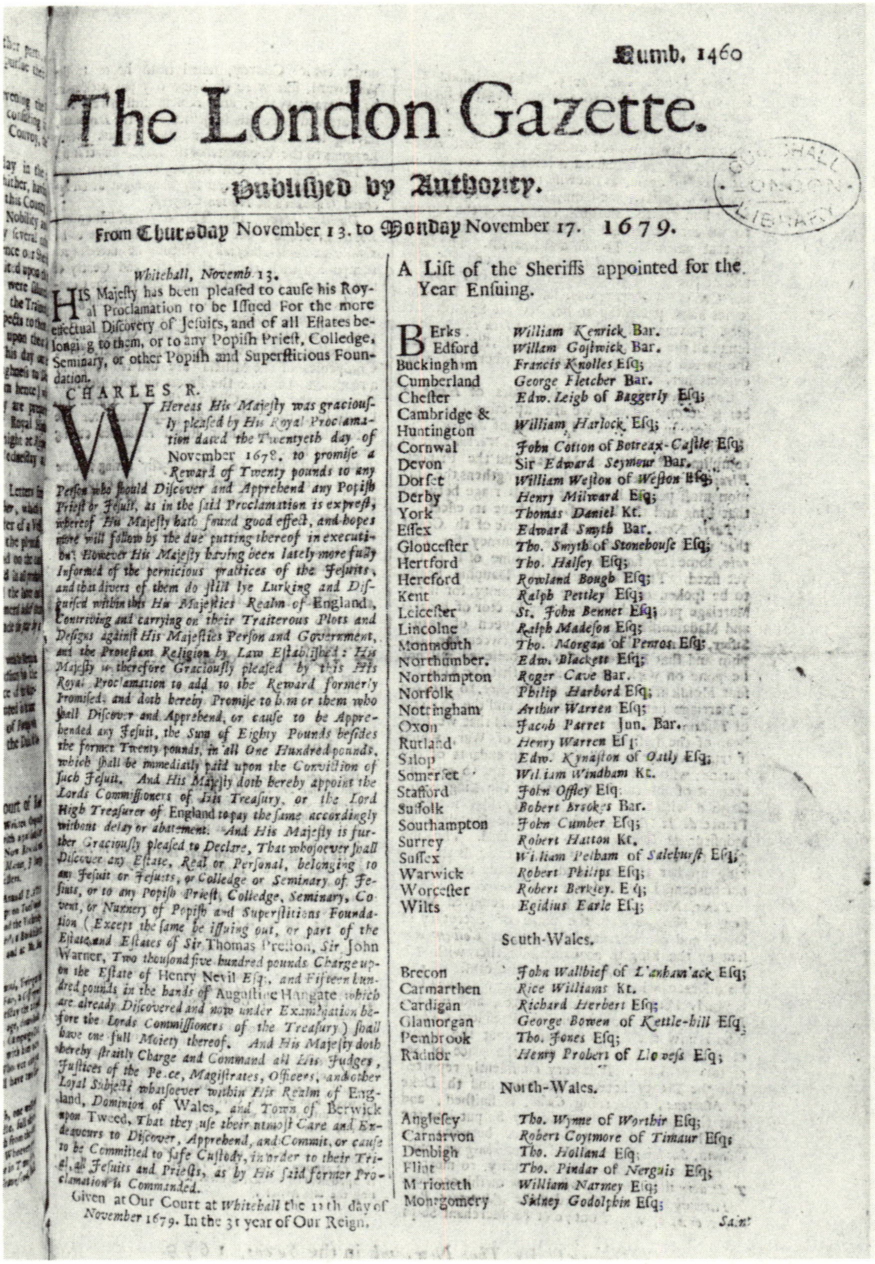

Numb. 1460

The London Gazette.

Publiſhed by Authority.

From Thurſday November 13. to Monday November 17. 1679.

Whitehall, Novemb. 13.

HIS Majeſty has been pleaſed to cauſe his Royal Proclamation to be Iſſued For the more effectual Diſcovery of Jeſuits, and of all Eſtates belonging to them, or to any Popiſh Prieſt, Colledge, Seminary, or other Popiſh and Superſtitious Foundation.

CHARLES R.

WHereas His Majeſty was graciouſly pleaſed by His Royal Proclamation dated the Twentyeth day of November 1678. *to promiſe a Reward of Twenty pounds to any Perſon who ſhould Diſcover and Apprehend any Popiſh Prieſt or Jeſuit, as in the ſaid Proclamation is expreſt, whereof His Majeſty hath found good effect, and hopes more will follow by the due putting thereof in execution; However His Majeſty having been lately more fully Informed of the pernicious practices of the Jeſuits, and that divers of them do ſtill lye Lurking and Diſguiſed within this His Majeſties Realm of* England, *Contriving and carrying on their Traiterous Plots and Deſigns againſt His Majeſties Perſon and Government, and the Proteſtant Religion by Law Eſtabliſhed: His Majeſty is therefore Graciouſly pleaſed by this His Royal Proclamation to add to the Reward formerly Promiſed, and doth hereby Promiſe to him or them who ſhall Diſcover and Apprehend, or cauſe to be Apprehended any Jeſuit, the Sum of Eighty Pounds beſides the former Twenty pounds, in all One Hundred pounds, which ſhall be immediatly paid upon the Conviction of ſuch Jeſuit. And His Majeſty doth hereby appoint the Lords Commiſſioners of His Treaſury, or the Lord High Treaſurer of* England *to pay the ſame accordingly without delay or abatement. And His Majeſty is further Graciouſly pleaſed to Declare, That whoſoever ſhall Diſcover any Eſtate, Real or Perſonal, belonging to any Jeſuit or Jeſuits, or Colledge or Seminary of Jeſuits, or to any Popiſh Prieſt, Colledge, Seminary, Covent, or Nunnery of Popiſh and Superſtitions Foundation (Except the ſame be iſſuing out, or part of the Eſtate and Eſtates of Sir* Thomas Preſton, *Sir* John Warner, *Two thouſand five hundred pounds Charge upon the Eſtate of* Henry Nevil *Eſq;, and Fifteen hundred pounds in the hands of* Auguſtine Hangate *which are already Diſcovered and now under Examination before the Lords Commiſſioners of the Treaſury) ſhall have one full Moiety thereof. And His Majeſty doth hereby ſtraitly Charge and Command all His Judges, Juſtices of the Peace, Magiſtrates, Officers, and other Loyal Subjects whatſoever within His Realm of* England, *Dominion of* Wales, *and Town of* Berwick *upon* Tweed, *That they uſe their utmoſt Care and Endeavours to Diſcover, Apprehend, and Commit, or cauſe to be Committed to ſafe Cuſtody, in order to their Trial, all Jeſuits and Prieſts, as by His ſaid former Proclamation is Commanded.*

Given at Our Court at *Whitehall* the 11th day of *November* 1679. In the 31 year of Our Reign.

A Liſt of the Sheriffs appointed for the Year Enſuing.

Berks.	*William Kenrick* Bar.
Bedford	*William Goſtwick* Bar.
Buckingham	*Francis Knolles* Eſq;
Cumberland	*George Fletcher* Bar.
Cheſter	*Edw. Leigh* of *Baggerly* Eſq;
Cambridge & Huntington	*William Harlock* Eſq;
Cornwal	*John Cotton* of *Botreax-Caſtle* Eſq;
Devon	Sir *Edward Seymour* Bar.
Dorſet	*William Weſton* of *Weſton* Eſq;
Derby	*Henry Milward* Eſq;
York	*Thomas Daniel* Kt.
Eſſex	*Edward Smyth* Bar.
Glouceſter	*Tho. Smyth* of *Stonehouſe* Eſq;
Hertford	*Tho. Halſey* Eſq;
Hereford	*Rowland Bough* Eſq;
Kent	*Ralph Pettley* Eſq;
Leiceſter	*St. John Bennet* Eſq;
Lincolne	*Ralph Madeſon* Eſq;
Monmouth	*Tho. Morgan* of *Penros* Eſq;
Northumber.	*Edw. Blackett* Eſq;
Northampton	*Roger Cave* Bar.
Norfolk	*Philip Harbord* Eſq;
Nottingham	*Arthur Warren* Eſq;
Oxon	*Jacob Parret* Jun. Bar.
Rutland	*Henry Warren* Eſq;
Salop	*Edw. Kynaſton* of *Oatly* Eſq;
Somerſet	*William Windham* Kt.
Stafford	*John Offley* Eſq;
Suffolk	*Robert Brookes* Bar.
Southampton	*John Cumber* Eſq;
Surrey	*Robert Hatton* Kt.
Suſſex	*William Pelham* of *Salehurſt* Eſq;
Warwick	*Robert Philips* Eſq;
Worceſter	*Robert Berkley* Eſq;
Wilts	*Egidius Earle* Eſq;

South-Wales.

Brecon	*John Wallbief* of *Llanhamlack* Eſq;
Carmarthen	*Rice Williams* Kt.
Cardigan	*Richard Herbert* Eſq;
Glamorgan	*George Bowen* of *Kettle-hill* Eſq;
Pembrook	*Tho. Jones* Eſq;
Radnor	*Henry Probert* of *Llovesſ* Eſq;

North-Wales.

Angleſey	*Tho. Wynne* of *Worthir* Eſq;
Carnarvon	*Robert Coytmore* of *Timaur* Eſq;
Denbigh	*Tho. Holland* Eſq;
Flint	*Tho. Pindar* of *Nergais* Eſq;
Merioneth	*William Narmey* Eſq;
Montgomery	*Sidney Godolphin* Eſq;

Saint

The *London Gazette*, Monday, 17 November 1679 (Guildhall Library).

services was likely to be the norm for the bulk of the lower ranks.[2] Nonetheless a substantial percentage of the population openly defied the provisions of the Act of Uniformity of 1662 and the Conventicle Acts of 1664 and 1670, as well as the older laws against Roman Catholicism, and continued their religious practice outside the Church of England. In doing so they were subject to the operation of these laws and many suffered heavy persecution.[3]

Those groups worshiping outside the state church included the Presbyterians, the Roman Catholics, the Independents, the Particular Baptists, the General Baptists, and the Quakers.[4] Charles II and his government would have preferred a more comprehensive church settlement than the one which emerged in 1662. They had to bow to the swell of pro-Anglican pressure emanating from the political classes, who saw the Church of England as the bastion of the state, monarchy, and social order after the social and political turmoil of the Civil War and Commonwealth years (1642–60). Until the 1680s Charles II was generally willing to listen to pleas for a measure of toleration and in 1672 actually introduced such a measure in the form of the Declaration of Indulgence. This policy, and in particular this measure, angered the pro-Anglican gentry on whose support the fate of the Stuart monarchy rested, and Charles was forced to withdraw the declaration. The Popish Plot and the Exclusion Crisis of 1678–81 badly shook the monarchy, not least because the heir to the throne, James Duke of York, was known to be a Roman Catholic. Charles rode out the storm and in fact was at his strongest as monarch when he eschewed attempts at toleration after 1681 and fell back upon the support of the Anglican establishment until his death in 1685. Over all, the religious history of the years 1660–85 was fraught with tension and conflict.[5]

II

In this section the *London Gazette* will be examined in order to show how important a means of communication it was to the government of late Stuart England. I have chosen to focus on the *Gazette* because of the unique position it held as the long-term voice of 'authority' in the period. The newspapers which appeared after the lapse of the Licensing Act between 1678 and 1682 are of great interest but as yet await in-depth study. The *Gazette* was in effect the only newspaper in England between 1666 and 1678 and continued in existence after the demise of the publications which appeared during the subsequent hiatus; it therefore merits special attention.[6]

Writing on the history of the newspaper press in the seventeenth century is relatively underdeveloped. A rush of work in the late nineteenth and early twentieth centuries by writers such as J. Williams and G. Kitchin was followed by a lull until the more recent work of Frank, Walker, and Crist.[7]

There has been no modern study of the newspaper press between 1660 and 1689, a circumstance owing more to neglect than to lack of evidence.

The *Gazette* has suffered from this neglect and has also received a "bad press" among historians. To George Kitchin it represented "the lowest state of degradation of the party press," and to Professor Kenyon it was merely a "tame government organ." Most historians concur, if only by silence on the point, with the judgments of J. C. Muddiman and J. R. Western. To Muddiman the *Gazette* was "almost valueless for domestick news," and Western felt able to assert that it carried "no home news."[8] Such opinions, however, are unfair, as even a cursory look at the paper's contents reveals that it does contain, in one form or another, quite a substantial amount of domestic news.

One reason why the *Gazette* has been neglected is that much writing on the history of the press has concentrated on the struggle for a "free" press—one free from government if not commercial pressures. In this analysis of press history the years 1660–85 are regarded as a dark period dominated by the efforts of the restored government to control all forms of printed material, including newspapers. The *Gazette* was the government-operated newspaper for most of these years, and as a consequence it has been assumed that the paper is of little intrinsic interest because it was not free from government control and was simply a dull mouthpiece of official views. No historian has seen fit to study the paper in depth, and as a result, although the *Gazette* has been used as a source, it has never been considered as an active force in late Stuart England. Nonetheless the *Gazette* should be investigated precisely because it was not free from government control. It will not do to dismiss it as an occasionally useful but largely 'contaminated' historical source.

Why then did Charles II's government seek to monopolize the newspaper press? Governments had tried to control the products of the printing press ever since the fifteenth century when the technique was brought to England, and Charles II's regime was no exception to the rule. Besides the obvious political reasons, the efforts of successive governments in late Stuart England to control the press were encouraged by the generally held belief that the reading public was easily duped. Readers would, it was assumed by the ruling classes, believe anything that was in print. A consequence of this was that it was necessary to ensure that the information which they did receive in print was authoritative. The philosopher Thomas Hobbes thought that "the Common-peoples minds, unlesse they be tainted . . . are like clean paper, fit to receive whatsoever by Publique Authority shall be imprinted in them." Richard Baxter too thought that " it is easie to deceive the common people if men have liberty and interest, and opportunity." Given these views, it is not surprising that the greatest Tory journalist of the age, Roger L'Estrange, felt that the people were "capable of being . . .

wrought upon by convenient hints and touches" through the columns of an official newspaper.[9]

This credulous public, so easily deceived, gleaned their misinformation from a variety of sources. Straightforward rumor and gossip played an important role, as too did private letters, almanacs, and illegal newsletters. Between 1678 and 1682 their information also came from the newspapers which appeared after the lapse of the Licensing Act, and throughout this period they could obtain a healthy supply of illegal pamphlets. It is not surprising that the government of Charles II, fearful that its loyal subjects should be misinformed about its aims and intentions, should take steps to eliminate unofficial sources of information. In 1662 it secured the passage of the Licensing Act designed to supervise the products of the printing presses. From 1663 Roger L'Estrange was appointed Surveyor of the Press, and he conducted a vigorous campaign designed to prevent the publication of unlicensed pamphlets.[10] In 1666 the *Gazette* reported that some people from Weymouth had been "sent up for to the Council for false news," and throughout the reign Charles's government issued proclamations which attempted to prevent the unauthorized dissemination of information. In 1672 a proclamation "to restrain the Spreading of false News and Licentious Talking of Matters of State and Government" was issued. One reason for the government's suppression of the coffeehouses in 1675 was that "in such Houses and by the occasion of the meetings of such Persons therein, divers false, malicious and scandalous Reports are derived and spread abroad, to the defamation of His Majesties Government." The proclamation for *Suppressing the Printing and Publishing Unlicensed Newsbooks and Pamphlets of News* issued in 1680 objected to the "unlicensed pamphlets of news . . . full of idle and malicious reports."[11]

As well as these negative devices used to stem the flow of misinformation to the credulous public, the government employed more positive means to ensure that reliable information was disseminated as widely as possible. Royal proclamations were issued, official newsletters were sent to subscribers, and loyal sermons were delivered and published with official sanction. In 1681 a diarist noted one method used to draw the public's attention to official information: "The order of the Justices of the peace of Middlesex against dissenters is since printed, and hath been affixed in divers public places." Another technique employed by the government to disseminate "correct" opinion was the use of the Judges. It was customary for the lord chancellor to address the judges before they departed on circuit, and they were expected to repeat the relevant parts of this discourse to the justices of the peace in the localities. Judges, though, had a dual role. Besides delivering political harangues to the local gentry, they were an important channel of information from the localities to the Crown.[12]

The *London Gazette* must then be seen in this context; it was a positive weapon in the government's armory, designed to combat the influence of seditious misinformation on the credulous public. In this sense the government was acting positively when it sought to monopolize the press. Although it obviously wished to prevent the spread of information which might threaten the stability of the regime, it was also responding to a real need for reliable, authoritative information in an age of rumor, gossip, and uncertainty.

Having established the context in which we must view the *Gazette,* we must now look more closely at the paper itself. The man who controlled it for much of this period was Joseph Williamson, under-secretary to Lord Arlington and ultimately, from 1674, secretary of state. Although he was the person who supervised the paper on behalf of the government, the actual editing was done initially by Charles Perrot and later, from 1671, by Robert Yard.[13] In spite of this it is clear that Williamson kept a close eye on the contents of the paper. In 1671 Yard wrote to Williamson seeking his approval for an item in the paper, and later in the same month Williamson was asked to review the *Gazette* in manuscript before publication.[14] In addition, Williamson was constantly receiving requests to insert notices or book advertisements in the *Gazette* from individuals like the lord mayor of London or the bishop of Oxford. It is fair to conclude that the content of the *Gazette,* down to the inclusion of notices and advertisements, was subject to careful scrutiny by Williamson's deputies, if not by the man himself.[15]

This task was all the easier because the paper was compiled with care from 'reliable' orthodox sources. The secretary of state had a network of correspondents in various parts of the British Isles and abroad who provided him with regular information for inclusion in the official newsletters and *Gazette.* Their social background was often highly respectable, including figures such as the duke of Ormond, the Archbishop of Dublin, and the bishop of Carlisle. Even Lord Arlington saw fit to abstract Prince Rupert's account of the naval battle off North Foreland in 1666 against the Dutch for inclusion in the *Gazette.*[16]

What kind of market was there for the *Gazette?* The habit of reading newsbooks become well established during the period of the Civil War among the upper and as well as the more humble social groups. The Quaker leader George Fox reports how in 1653 he heard the influential J. P. Thomas Fell "talking of the News Book of the Parliament," and we know that the more lowly Thomas Rugg obtained much of the information for his diary of public events from the newsbooks of 1649–61. The habit continued after the Restoration, and by the time the *Gazette* appeared in 1665 it had a well-established market to exploit.[17]

The size and distribution of this market is hard to assess accurately. Little is known about the paper's circulation before the 1690's, but it is now possible to estimate the numbers printed for one week in 1666. The *Gazette* appeared twice a week, and documents in the State Papers suggest that for one issue, No. 93 dated Monday 8th October, 12,960 copies were printed, and for issue No. 94 dated Thursday 11th October, 15,552. These figures accord with those available for the year 1705, when totals varying from 11,250 to 15,250 per issue were printed. This suggests that over a forty-year period, even after the competition provided by the lapse of the licensing law in 1695, the circulation of the *Gazette* was fairly high and constant.[18] Copies of the paper were sold at 1d each in London and were distributed sometimes free, or at other times for payment of 2*d.* or 3*d.* a copy, around the country.[19]

Given this large circulation, the *Gazette* must have been a profitable enterprise. "I have now to acquaint your Excellency that your concern of the *Gazette* goes very well", wrote Thomas Newcomb, the paper's printer, to Williamson in 1673, and indeed it did do well. Figures for the paper's profitability are sparse, but the remarks of people like Newcomb who were involved in its production are not, and they all suggest that the publication was a "standing source of profit." In spite of being a "tame government organ", there was clearly a market for this reliable mouthpiece of government policy.[20]

How then was the *Gazette* distributed? The producers of the *Gazette* inherited a system of "book women" from the previous newsbook producer Roger L'Estrange. These women sold the paper and were paid a salary. Under L'Estrange they were allowed one hundred free copies a month to sell for themselves. In 1666 one of these, a Mrs. Andrewes, took a "fourth if not a third" of the copies printed directly from the printer Thomas Newcomb. On this basis she might take anything from between 3,240 and 5,184 papers for distribution in London. These were no doubt sold in the streets of the capital. Copies of the paper were distributed through London booksellers to the provinces, as when Samuel Lowndes sent the paper to a provincial customer in the 1680s. It is also likely that booksellers in London obtained copies from Newcomb for sale within the capital. Others, not necessarily booksellers, sent copies to the provinces. Richard Coffin had a London agent who sent him written news and regular copies of the *Gazette* between 1683 and 1697. The paper was also available in taverns and coffeehouses where it could be read aloud. These methods of distributing the paper were supplemented by the use of the Post Office by government employees to distribute the paper, a practice still in regular use during the early eighteenth century. The clerks at the Letter Office in London used their privilege & free postage to circulate the paper for their own profit. Finally, many of Williamson's correspondents received the paper gratis in return for information: for instance, one tavern owner was persuaded to correspond with Williamson, in return for which "he would have a private letter of intelligence and a gazette or two free weekly which would bring much custom to his tavern." Hawkers, booksellers, agents, tavern and coffehouse keepers, and government officials, all were involved in distributing the paper either by direct sale or through the Post Office.[21]

There is some information which sheds light on the geographical distribution of the *Gazette*. Recent work has suggested that in the mid seventeenth-century London may have been "a uniquely literate environment" when compared to other parts of the country. The proportion of the *Gazette* distributed in London by the methods just described lends partial support to this view. London certainly consumed large numbers of the *Gazette*. A list of Williamson's correspondents in 1674 provides some more clues: there are 116 correspondents, each in receipt of one or more newletters a week, and they no doubt received a *Gazette* as well. The largest number of these, twenty seven, were resident at one of the major ports, reflecting the importance of commercial and shipping news in the paper. *Gazettes* also went to Newcastle, Carlisle, York, Hull, Boston, Oxford, Bristol, Gloucester, Poole and Rye, as well as overseas to Dublin and Paris. Although the list does not provide a valid sample, it does suggest that the majority of readers were likely to be found in the main centers of commercial activity, especially London.[22]

What then can be said about the composition of the readership of the *Gazette?* The paper appealed to and was read by the élites of society, in particular by government or local officials, merchants, and clergymen, and it is not surprising that the first number of the *Gazette* sought to address "merchants and gentlemen." It contained information of use and interest to this section of the community in the form of proclamations, shipping notices, information on local markets, and advertisements for quite sophisticated publications. The large number of advertisements for religious publications carried by the paper no doubt reflects, among other things, the importance of the clergy as readers of the paper; and among Williamson's correspondents there was an archbishop, a bishop, and two deans. Other government officials and local government officers received the paper. Williamson's correspondents included four army officers, at least three diplomats, and five mayors. Justices of the peace also figured among its readers. For instance, as early as 1666 it was assumed that "a few lines in the Gazette" would prompt "the Justices to keep strict watch to prevent seamen escaping."[23]

Although the *Gazette* was aimed at the upper strata of society, it is possible that people lower down the social order had access to the contents of the paper. Measurements of literacy are based on the capacity to write a signature, and as writing was generally taught after reading in Tudor and Stuart England, it is likely that the ability to read was more socially diffused than the ability to write. The practice of reading aloud to others not necessarily literate was also a means whereby the *Gazette*'s contents could be made available to people in less elevated social positions. If any of the lower orders did have regular contact with the paper's content over most of this period, they would have been presented with a "world picture", a view of social reality, which must have been a powerful persuasive to conformity. The paper consistently presented a world populated by a clergy, nobility, and gentry all loyal to the king, and in which any form of dissent which did appear was vilified. Although this point should not be overstated, it is important to bear it in mind when considering the relationship between the paper and the society in which it operated.[24]

Having looked at the *Gazette* and its readership, some examination of the potential impact of the paper can be attempted. This is a tricky subject to deal with in any period, and especially in the seventeenth century where the evidence is so piecemeal. A lot of this material tells us what effect people at the time thought or wished the paper to have, not what effect it actually did have in given situations. This must be borne in mind when considering what follows. Nonetheless, it is important to note that contemporaries *believed* the paper to have some force, even if they failed to specify exactly how this was manifested.

The paper was intended to be a reliable source of information. It was published "By Authority," and the information in it was meant to be regarded as official. It is in this context that the government used the paper to crush rumors and provide the readership with authoritative information. In 1678 Williamson inserted a notice to counteract a rumor about "great numbers of men" assembling on the Isle of Purbeck during the Popish Plot scare; and at another time attempts were made to contradict a "common rumor" about some dishonorable transactions among Oxford dons. Two items which further illustrate this role were published in 1682: the first was printed "for the undeceiving of the Publick" and the second was ordered to be "published in the Authorized London Gazette, for Satisfaction of His Majesties good Subjects in England, some whereof may perhaps be imposed upon by this infamous Libeller." In fact, the comments of some readers suggest that the paper was indeed regarded as a source of reliable information. One felt that "The Gazette carries the day", and Pepys liked the paper because it was "full of news, and no folly in it". Another reader wrote from Lyme in 1666 that he was "glad of the rational account of the fire [of London] in the Gazette, after such a diversity of reports."[25]

As well as being considered a reliable source of information, the *Gazette* wsa believed to be able to enhance the public image of a town or an individual. After peace was made with the Dutch in 1667, the people of Deal wanted an account of the celebrations conducted there to be included in the *Gazette* so as to enhance their "fame" or reputation. After the Duke of Buckingham had successfully completed some public business at York, Williamson learned that "It is wondered by this gentlemen that nothing is said of him publickly" and was asked to ensure that an account of his conduct "may be in the next Gazette."[26]

Items in the paper do occasionally seem to have had some observable results. A description of a man detained at Bristol which appeared in the *Gazette* on Thursday, 23 October 1679 was spotted by the brother of the recently murdered Archbishop Sharp of St. Andrews. He wrote to the Duke of Lauderdale, and as a result the king signed a warrant authorising the examination of the suspect. On another occasion Charles II told Sir John Reresby that a notice in the *Gazette* would be a cheaper and more effective way of catching a notorious thief than would the issue of a proclamation. He was proven correct. One correspondent noted how a report in the paper influenced the way a group of people disposed of their money, and in 1667 a "notice in the Gazette of the King's care for maimed seamen . . ." caused a meeting at Ipswich to enact that all lands given or bequeathed for the poor should be employed in their maintenance.[27]

The one area in which the *Gazette* and other newspapers in these years were clearly believed to have an effect was in the field of politics. One of Williamson's correspondents had confidence in the papers ability to "inflame all England against the Dutch" if a suitably worded notice were inserted in it with "some consequences being drawn out and added." M.P.s complained about a report in the *Gazette* from Holland in 1673 which suggested that some of them might be negotiating with the Dutch whilst Parliament was not sitting. In 1678 Monsieur Moranville, the man who translated the *Gazette* into French, was arrested and brought before the Commons for inadvertently mistranslating one of the royal proclamations connected with the Popish Plot. During the Exclusion Crisis the Whig Parliament of December 1680 launched an attack on the court which had fined the producers of opposition newspapers. As in the modern era, people firmly believed that the newspaper press had political influence.[28]

If then we take into account the information surveyed in this section, we can arrive at some reasonably firm conclusions. The *Gazette* was part of a general attempt by the late Stuart regime to control the flow of information to the reading public. This was not just a negative practice: it did fulfil a need for reliable information. The government kept a close eye on the contents of the paper and drew its information from safe orthodox sources. The paper had a large circulation, a circulation which seems to have been concentrated in urban/commercial centers, especially London. The paper was intended for the élites of late Stuart society, although it is likely that its contents were available to more humble folk. Clearly the government and the paper's readers believed strongly that the paper had influence. Given then that the *London Gazette* was an important means of communication in late Stuart England, we can now consider the reactions of one section of its readership to newspapers before assessing its content.

III

It is clear that those religious groups that refused to conform to the Church of England regarded the newspaper press as an active and influential mechanism in society. Religion was a constant theme of the newspaper press from the 1640s to the 1690s and, as we shall see, the *Gazette* was no exception. No newspaper operating in seventeenth-century England could avoid religious issues for very long, and it was inevitable that people of all persuasions would be included in the readership. Ralph Josselin, the vicar of Earls Colne in Essex, read the 'prints' of the 1650s and the *Gazette* in the 1670s. Some of more reformist sympathies than Josselin read the paper and were perhaps sometimes more skeptical of its contents. In 1667 "Charles Aland . . . a great fanatic, and former cornet in Lamber's army . . . bade his son advertise his friends to keep in readiness and not to believe the *Gazette* as to the number of men in arms in Scotland." The moderate Nonconformist Roger Morrice read the *Gazette* and occasionally noted its contents in his "Entring Book."[29]

The *Gazette* was, as we shall see, the voice of Anglicanism, and non-Anglican opinions were given no sympathetic coverage in its columns in this period. During and after the Exclusion Crisis of 1679–81 non-Anglican groups testified to the importance they felt newspapers had by being associated with the production of newsbooks. The Baptist stationer Francis Smith produced *Smith's Protestant Intelligence, domestick and foreign* in 1682. The Catholic sympathizer Nathaniel Thompson, who was regarded by Luttrell as a "printer and publisher frequently of popish news," produced the *Loyal Protestant and True Domestick Intelligence* from 1681 to 1683. Even the Quakers agreed in 1683 "That for a time half a sheet of most remarkable sufferings be weekly published." Although intricately connected with the heated political atmosphere of these years, these publications suggest how important the newspaper press was considered by those Christians who were not members of the state church.[30]

Why did these religious groups hold this view? Although many motives were involved, at root they were concerned about the possibly damaging effect of newspaper comment on their ability to worship freely. William Warwick, a Quaker, pinpointed this concern when he argued that the writer of a newsbook, in this instance Roger L'Estrange, "by insinuating and lying would incense both Rulers, Magistrates and People against an innocent and peaceable people, who in scorn are called Quakers." The power of the press to aid witch hunts, still with us today, was well appreciated in the seventeenth century.[31]

The Quakers in particular appreciated the power of the newspaper press. The governor of Jamaica was convinced that English Quakers read the newsbooks and felt that the inclusion of a certain report in one of them would "take much off the rude roughness of that Sects temper." He was in part right. During the 1650s the Quakers had paid close attention to the contents of the newsbooks, a practice which they continued after the Restoration. The Quaker William Bayly wrote "An Anser to (a) quere published in the Newesbooke" in 1663, a copy of which "was delivered . . . to ye hand of Roger L'Estrange who is ye publisher of ye weekly newes." The leader of the movement, George Fox, and the "mother of Quakerism," Margaret Fell, both read the *Gazette.* An influential committee of the movement, the Meeting for Sufferings, kept an eye on the *Gazette* for information about Judges' circuits, and it would appear that Quakers in the localities occasionally received copies of the paper from one of their number in London.[32]

Some Quakers shared the view that the *Gazette* could help suppress rumors. In 1682 an agent of the prominent Quaker William Penn inserted a notice in the paper concerning "a Report spread abroad of the Death of William Penn Esq; Proprietary of Pennsilvania, to the great prejudice of his Affairs," assuring readers that "there is no manner of ground for it." They also kept a watchful eye on the *Gazette's* more polemical sister paper the *Observator* which appeared in April 1681. When that paper carried an accusation that a Quaker printer had produced the Declaration of the rebellious Duke of Monmouth in 1685, they rushed out a reply denying the charge. The Quakers were particularly sensitive about their public image, but their concern about the potential effects of reports carried in the *Gazette* and other newspapers is indicative of the overall concern felt by dissident religious groups. So we must add to the picture of the *London Gazette*'s audience the smaller detail of a section of its readership, the non-Anglican Christians, who were susceptible to its influence and who were well aware of its power.[33]

IV

The religious content of the *Gazette* was of special importance in post-Restoration England. The Stuarts were restored in 1660 on a wave of reaction among the gentry against what they saw as the political, religious, and social instability of the Interregnum. In restoring Charles Stuart the gentry looked for the assertion of social and political stability, and stability in their minds was inextricably bound up with the restoration of the Church of England, a body which was regarded as one of the bulwarks against a return to disorder. In 1660 they restored not only a king but also a church. Charles took a long time to appreciate the necessity of full cooperation with the pro-Anglican gentry on religious matters, but his government was nonetheless concerned from the outset to present him as loyal to, and protector of, the Church of England. This was calculated to enhance his image in the eyes of the pro-Anglican gentry on whose support his regime relied. The religious content of the *Gazette* must be seen in this context if it is to be fully understood.[34] The paper not only reflected popular religious attitudes but was also used to bolster the Stuart regime by propagating an Anglican orthodoxy which was consistently associated with the monarchy. At the same time it guided its readers through the forests of religious controversy along paths chosen by the government. At all times it should be remembered that the religious content of the *Gazette* was constantly being manipulated in the interests of the regime.

The *Gazette* operated in a society steeped in religion. It reflected the assumptions of that society, as when, for instance, it mirrored the widely held belief in Providence, or the doctrine that God intervened in everyday life. As Keith Thomas has written, people in these years "happily collected stories of the judgements which had fallen upon blasphemers, cursers, perjurers, murderers, adulterers and sabbath-breakers, and they were confident that the Lord would avenge himself upon their political opponents." It is not surprising then that the *Gazette* should often refer to Providence nor that given the decline in the fashion for such belief, also identified by Thomas, that the number of stories in the *Gazette* referring to its workings were clustered into the first five to ten years of the paper's life. The inclusion of providential stories in the 1660s may partly have been intended to combat the tactic employed by the more radical wing of Dissent of compiling a sensational and partly fictitious collection of anti-Royalist prodigies, issued in three parts in 1661–2 as *Mirabilis Annus.* The government went to considerable lengths to suppress this publication, demonstrating their feeling that such stories in the wrong hands could have an adverse effect. With such a problem in the air, it was to be expected that the *Gazette* should carry references to Providence in the 1660s, if only to reassure its readers that when God intervened in the world he was, by and large, on the Royalists' side.[35]

In general, then, references to the direct intervention of God, or implying his intervention, have a positive tint to them when they appear in the *Gazette.* After a storm at Deal in 1665 it "pleased God to preserve those ships of His Majesties and Merchants that are here." The plague visited Sherborne in the same year because "it pleased God," and God saw fit to free Cambridge from infection the following year. A sea victory in 1666 was greeted as "Blessed News," and a naval skirmish in January 1667 involved heavy gunfire, but "by a wonderful providence not one of our men [was] hurt." God was also involved in the Great Fire of London, for as the *Gazette* explained, it was a mark of "the heavy hand of God upon us for our sins, showing us the terror of his judgement in thus raising the fire, and immediately after, his miraculous and never enough to be acknowledged Mercy in putting a stop to it." The paper was tapping deeply held assumptions when it interpreted events in this manner and thus harmonized with the outlook of many of its readers.[36]

The *Gazette* reflected and supported the fact that the Church of England was the only state church. It carried regular items which tacitly ackowledged and enhanced the Church's status. The first issue of the paper carried an announcement about the election of Walter Blandford to the see of Oxford, and such items were a regular feature of its news coverage over the years. Another regular item was the list of Anglican preachers who would deliver sermons to the king during Lent. This sort of material was included without comment and testified to the privileged status of the Church of England in the eyes of both the government and the paper's readers. Needless to say, notices relating to the formal activities of other religious groups were never included.[37]

The Church of England appeared in the *Gazette* in another guise. It was constantly in attendance at major events of public ceremonial, and its presence was diligently reported by the paper. One writer has noted that the power of the gentry in the eighteenth century was closely allied to its use of public ritual or "theatre," and it would be doing Charles Stuart and his regime an injustice to suggest that they undervalued the importance of public ceremony for maintaining social and political order. On such occasions the Church was on hand to give the proceedings spiritual credibility and to receive in return the sanction of political authority.[38]

One such occasion when the link between the regime and Anglican orthodoxy could be underlined in public and in the pages of the *Gazette* was the funeral of an important officer of state. George Monk, Duke of Albemarle, the man who had been largely responsible for the return in 1660 of Charles Stuart, and by implication the restoration of social and political order, died in 1670. Charles made sure that he had a pompous if somewhat belated funeral in April 1670. The body was taken in procession to Westminster Abbey where it was received by "Deans, Prebends and the whole Quire in the Copes and Formalities . . . the Service of the Church read, an excellent Sermon was preached on the occasion by the Lord Bishop of Salisbury."[39] Civic ceremonies conducted with the Church in attendance were reported accordingly. The mayor, common council and aldermen of Yarmouth heard a sermon before going to the market cross to hear the proclamation of peace with the Dutch read in 1667. The celebrations commemorating the restoration of the king in Edinburgh in 1677 were preceded, according to the *Gazette,* by "several learned and pious Sermons adapted to the design of that day." The *Gazette* rarely failed to report the activity of the Church of England at such ceremonies, giving more publicity to the important link between Church and state.[40]

This link was reemphasized when the Church of England was engaged in some event of public import. The *Gazette* reported the confirmation of the daughters of James Duke of York by the Church of England in 1675. Two years later it carried an account of the wedding of the Princess Mary with William of Orange. The paper recorded royal christenings as well as the fairly regular installation of Knights of the Garter in a church on St. George's day. In recording such ceremonies the *Gazette* served to make public the role of the Church of England in legitimizing the public ceremonial of the élites and in particular of the monarchy.[41]

As well as underlining the link between the monarchy and the Church of England, the *Gazette* promoted the idea of kingship as sacred. Besides frequent references to Charles as "pious" or "sacred," the paper carried many items on the miraculous healing power attributed to the monarchy, the power to cure the King's Evil by touch.[42] Throughout the period the paper carried regular notices indicating that the king would take a summer break from the arduous task of touching for the Evil.[43] Belief in the king's power was widespread and popular, and these notices were directed at ministers and churchwardens whose job it was to direct sufferers to the king.[44]

In this coverage the *Gazette* illustrates some points made by Thomas about the way the Stuarts manipulated the popular attachment to the idea of the king as a repository of healing power, and also about their sensitivity to the maintenance of the prestige of the ceremony. In 1677 the paper reported a visit of the king and his brother, the Duke of York, to Plymouth where they, "with the reiterated Acclamations of the People, went to St. Andrew's church, where His Majesty after Divine Service, was pleased to heal for the evil." Here the readership of the *Gazette* would see the king in a dual role, as "miraculous" healer and as cementer of the body politic, binding the masses to the Church and king by this public display of divinely inspired healing. Both king and gentry understood the power of this belief, and the *Gazette* reflected and promoted that understanding.[45]

A ceremony so important was indeed exploited to the full. Charles II is said to have "touched" at least 90,000 people during his reign, the peak coming between May 1682 and April 1683 when he touched 8,577 people. The *Gazette* reflected this pressure, printing notices to ensure that "the persons granting Certificates to such as come to be Touched . . . take great care in the Registering of them, and that before they give such Certificates they do well inform themselves that the Persons have the Evil." Hints in the notices of this time, during the post-1681 Tory Reaction, about the ceremony being "abused" and how the King's surgeons wished "to prevent His Majesties being defrauded" suggest that the government was highly sensitive to the public image of the event.[46] The upheavals of the Popish Plot had possibly unleashed popular criticism of the King's healing power and the systematic attempts to make churchwardens use certificates, attempts in which the *Gazette* played an important part, were in part designed to forestall such criticisms of the ceremony. In 1684, whilst efforts were still being made to promote the use of certificates, the Presbyterian Thomas Rosewall was indicted for high treason for allegedly "casting aspersions on the reality of the royal healing power." He was found guilty and the *Gazette* carried notice of his conviction, although Richard Baxter maintained that "no such words were spoken." In all, the *Gazette* keenly promoted ceremonies of the élites, as well as exploiting popular ideas about the healing powers of the King, and in doing so helped to legitimize Church, State and Monarchy.[47]

V

Another aspect of the *Gazette's* content which is of particular interest in this context is advertising. As in so many other areas, the paper has not been properly studied to see what its advertising can reveal about the period 1665–85.[48] Although Williamson is thought to have discouraged the carrying of advertisements in the paper, over the years it included a growing number of items.[49] The rate of increase accelerated during the 1670s and 1680s the bulk being concerned with lost or stolen property, runaway servants, or books. In a sample of over 78 percent of the issues published in these years, 273 advertisements or official notices with a religious content were noted, 246 of which were for books. The bulk of these appeared at times when political tension was high, and this reflects, as will be seen, a general preoccupation of the *Gazette* with guiding its readers along officially acceptable lines. Nonetheless we should bear in mind also that commercial pressures from booksellers wishing to gain access to the medium of the paper would have played a part in the appearance of many advertisements.

Some of the miscellaneous advertising had a religious flavor which reflected, often unconsciously, assumptions about the status of churches, churchmen, and religion. The paper noticed thefts from churches, like the one from Westminster Abbey in 1675, and it often alluded to the clerical members of its readership when it carried a notice about the annual feast of the sons of the clergy without further remark. Secular books were promoted by associating them with the name of a famous divine, while auctions of the libraries of deceased clergymen were considered safe and worthy projects to promote.[50] Advertisements also reflected the individual belief in Providence. In 1666 Jeremiah Snow, whilst giving the public notice of his solvency, declared that "it hath pleased God to bless his Endeavours with some small Estate." A physician in 1668 stated that he had arrived at his skill "by the blessing of God," and the City of Lincoln thought it wise to insert a thankful "blessed to God" when in 1677 it denied rumors that it was plague-stricken.[51] However the majority of the religious advertisements carried by the paper were for books, and this accords well with the view that 'religion was the main concern of the English reading public' in these years.[52] The majority of these books were written by clergymen of the Church of England, or by lawyers or gentlemen supporting it. Among those whose works were advertised in the *Gazette* were such famous Anglican divines as John Wilkins, James Ussher, Edward Fowler, John Tillotson, William Lloyd, Gilbert Burnet, and a host of other less illustrious figures. That Church of England clergymen should figure so prominently in this area is not surprising, given the official status of the paper. All the same, the significance of these advertisements is that the *Gazette* with its heavy commitment to the established church could not be rivaled as a means of promotion: an advertisement in this paper was special indeed. No other religious group, even the Quakers with their highly sopisticated press organization, could match the promotional potential of the *Gazette*.[53]

Such advertisements went further than simply enhancing the position of the Church of England. Closer examination of the *Gazette* reveals that advertisements were inserted to harmonize with the position of the government on the various religious crises of the years 1665–85. This is not surprising, given what has already been noted about the close supervision of the paper's contents by Williamson and his deputies. In June 1670, in the face of pamphlet attacks by Dissenters on the second Conventicle Act, which came into force the previous May, the *Gazette* carried a notice about a book called "Toleration Disapproved . . . wherein the nature of persecution in general, and the unjust complaint of the dissenting parties . . . are distinctly considered."[54] Late in 1673, after Charles had been forced to withdraw the Declaration of Indulgence and whilst the government was still sympathetic to the cause of toleration, the *Gazette* carried advertisements for books by the Nonconformist divines Joseph Caryl and John Owen.[55] From 1678 onward, when the Popish Plot broke, the paper, probably in part because of the force of parliamentary and public interest, carried a host of advertisements for books associated with the Plot. Israel Tonge's book *The Jesuit's Morals* and Lloyd's best selling sermon delivered at the funeral of Sir Edmund Berry Godfrey were advertised in December 1678. In 1679 the paper, among a mass of other items relating to the plot, carried advertisements for the narratives of Titus Oates, Miles Prance, and William Bedloe. In allowing these advertisements to be carried in the *Gazette* the government was possibly trying to sanction some publications and not others, but it was certainly lending credence to the Plot by promoting such material.[56]

One consequence of the Plot was that there was renewed parliamentary agitation for the relief of Protestant Dissenters. In what was no doubt a further attempt to show its firm commitment to Protestantism, the government allowed the *Gazette* in 1679 to carry advertisements for books by the Nonconformists John Owen and Richard Baxter. Baxter, one of the most prolific religious writers of the century, appears only once in a favorable aspect in the *Gazette's* advertising columns, and in this case the book suited the times and the government's ends: *Which is the true Church? The Whole Christian World, as Headed only by Christ, (of which the Reformed are the soundest Part) or the Pope of Rome and his subjects as such.*[57] After the dissolution of the Oxford Parliament in 1681 and the collapse of the agitation for the exclusion of James Duke of York from the throne, the government launched a full-scale attack on its Whig opponents and their dissenting allies. In 1682 the *Gazette* carried an advertisement for a book by William Saywell which *attacked* Baxter and Owen, and other books attacking papists and Dissenters alike were advertised with such titles as *A Discourse of Prayer: Wherein this great Duty is stated to oppose some Principles and Practices of Papists and Fanaticks; as they are contrary to the publick Forms of the Church of England.*[58]

So, the advertisements in the *Gazette* performed a dual role. They enhanced the status of religious orthodoxy and in particular of the Church of England in oblique as well as in more overt ways. They were also used to harmonize with and promote the government's position at any given time on the sensitive religious issues of the day.

VI

Although important, the manipulation of advertisements was not the only way the government dealt actively with religious issues in the *Gazette.* In this section an examination is made of three other devices: the deployment of straightforward news items, proclamations, and finally addresses. These materials tend to overlap with each other, but they can illustrate the various ways in which the government used the *Gazette* to guide the political nation along the lines it wished.

Straightforward 'news' items about papist or Nonconformist groups are rare, but when they do occur it is possible to detect a reason for their inclusion. The paper recorded, with some smugness, the illness of the radical Dissenter Vavasour Powell in 1665, and likewise when the prominent ex-Quaker Anthony Pearson died in 1666, it was at pains to note that he did "upon his Deathbed very solemnly confess his former Errors . . . declaring that he now dyed a true Son of the Church of England."[59] The government at this time was still nervous about the potential power of the Nonconformists and was anxious to dishearten and weaken them in any way it could. Thus it was pleased to be able to report from York in 1666 the recent conformity of "eleven Ministers, who had been great leaders in the late times." Four years later, after the passage of the second Conventicle Act, it reported the murder of a jailer by one of his Nonconformist inmates. One feels that when in 1682 the *Gazette* carried a report about William Penn sailing from Deal for Pennsylvania "with a great many Quakers who go to settle there," it was trying to encourage the rest of them to go along too![60]

Of more significance are the various official government pronouncements concerned with religion which were printed in the *Gazette,* often in the form of royal proclamations. Proclamations were generally printed and circulated around the country as separate items, but inclusion in the *Gazette* gave them a wider currency. They were used to inform people of forthcoming days of public fasting or thanksgiving, or, as noted above, to promote the capture of criminals[61] But when printed in the paper their main function seems to have been to inform people of certain events and to direct their interpretations of these events along appropriate lines.

Before the Popish Plot of 1678 the government had printed proclamations in the *Gazette* against Roman Catholics, but it was that event which sparked off a flood of antipopish official pronouncements which were published in the paper. The status of a proclamation and of the *Gazette* must have lent authority to the stories of a Jesuit-inspired design upon the life of Charles II and upon the Protestant religion as by law established in England. Although, as Professor Kenyon points out, the public could only rely on government actions and rumors about the plot from the autumn of 1678 until the publication of Oates's narrative in April 1679, any reader of the *Gazette* would have had a good idea of what was going on in these months. The issue of October 1678 carried a proclamation informing people of a "Horrible Design against His [Charles II's] Sacred Life"; and by the next issue another proclamation had made it clear who was responsible: "the Bloudy and Traiterous Designs and Popish Recusants against His Majesties Sacred Persons and Government and the Protestant Religion."[62]

This latter proclamation and many of the others which crowd the pages of the *Gazette* in 1678 and 1679, prompted by Parliamentary pressure, lent weight to and promoted the idea of a Popish Plot. The language of some of these proclamations could only aggravate an already tense situation. In November 1678 a proclamation declared that "Jesuits are at this time secretly disguised and lurking within this Realm." As if this "lurking" was not sinister enough, by May 1679 Catholics had "[out of their detestable and barbarous Malice] conspired and agreed together to set on Fire the City of London." Reluctant as the crypto-Catholic Charles Stuart may have been to fully believe the Plot, the *Gazette* presented government policy as wholeheartedly enthralled by the stories of Oates and his like. No doubt the government wished to control the flow of information on the subject and direct opinion along manageable lines, but it was under considerable pressure from Parliament to appear convinced by the Plot, and so its efforts in the *Gazette* can only have inflamed the anti-Catholic hysteria of these years.[63]

To Catholics, then, the *Gazette's* coverage of the Plot must have been unwelcome. Protestant Dissenters cannot have been too happy with their treatment either. In 1668 the paper printed the King's speech to Parliament which reflected the tolerationist views of the new "cabal" ministry, asking M.P.s to "beget a better Union and Composure in the minds of my Protestant Subjects in Matters of Religion." Again in 1672 the paper carried a small notice about the Declaration "for indulging of Nonconformist and dissenting persons . . . in matters of Religion." Both of these modest attempts to redirect religious policy failed and the overwhelming number of official pronouncements which mention Dissenters in the *Gazette* were hostile.[64]

The most sustained attack on dissent in the *Gazette* came at the time of the government's counterattack against the Whigs and their dissenting allies after 1681. In these years the government pursued a policy of ousting Whig opponents from positions of power in local government and crushing their Dissenter allies by ordering the strict enforcement of the penal laws against Dissent. In this process, sometimes known as the "Tory Revenge," the *Gazette* was a key link in the public campaign waged by the government against its enemies. The paper carried a host of Loyal Addresses, news items and proclamations which egged the gentry on to prosecute Dissenters, with such effect that, along with the other measures described, it "brought the realm nearer to total outward conformity than at any time since the collapse of Laudian 'Thorough'." By continually presenting such items in the paper, the government could have left local officials in no doubt whatsoever about its intentions. At times addressers seem overly anxious to achieve public recognition of their conformity in this matter by publication of their Address in the *Gazette.* They seem worried lest late publication might affect their standing with the government. For instance, in 1683 the "Ancient Corporation" of Poole addressed the King, begging him "to accept this our most hearty and sincere Mite, which (like the poor Widow) we do cast in the Treasury of Addresses; being heartily sorry we have not done it sooner." Publication of such material in the *Gazette* was designed to have a snowball effect, each new Address which was published prompting others to appear.[65]

Throughout 1682 and 1683 Addresses were printed from towns, counties, companies, and corporations praising the wisdom of the king and deploring the activities of the Earl of Shaftesbury, the Rye House plotters, and rebellious Dissenters. Most of the Addresses were repetitious and encouraged the association of Dissent with rebellion. The sentiments expressed in "The humble Address" of the Justices of Middlesex printed in July 1683 were typical of those encouraged by the government through the *Gazette:* "We . . . have for several years last past, observed the unquiet Spirits of this sort of men [Dissenters from the Church of England]; and have presumed in our frequent Addresses to Your Majesty . . . to acquaint Your Majesty with our Apprehensions of those Conventicles. . . . We are humbly of opinion that those dangerous Meetings, the Conventicles, are not to be suffered, nor the persons who frequent them, trusted.[66]

The government deliberately encouraged these Addresses so as to pressure local opinion along the correct lines. In 1680 Charles himself ordered the publication of an Address in the paper, and in 1682 the *Gazette* informed its readers that "His Majesty is very much satisfied with the Loyal Addresses that are daily presented to His Majesty."[67] Some contemporaries, like the diarist Luttrell and Sir Samuel Clarke, saw them for what they were, propaganda. Henry Care, a writer for the opposition paper, the *Weekly Pacquet of Advice,* saw this too. He claimed that one Address published in the *Gazette* in 1681 was part of a design to keep "up the Hubbub against the Presbyterians" by insinuating that the treacherous designs of Popery were "some small close doubtful business," whereas the attempts of "Schisms and Faction" were "more open and dangerous." In spite of its all too obvious role, the government saw fit to cram the paper with material of this kind.[68]

In 1683 the *Gazette* carried two major items which were clearly intended to be statements on the government's attitude to Dissent and were obviously meant to gain the widest possible publicity by inclusion in the paper. The first appeared in July and was a decree of the University of Oxford "against certain pernicious Books and damnable Doctrines Destructive to the Sacred Persons of Princes." In this, statements by the Nonconformists Baxter and Owen were condemned along with pernicious doctrines from other sources like the work of the poet John Milton and the Nonconformist publication *Mene Tekel.* The other statement was a full disclosure of the Rye House Plot in the form of a proclamation which appeared in August. In it the "Malevolent Party" responsible for the Plot was firmly identified with those who met in "Seditious Conventicles," and some of the wanted men were further identified as Nonconformist preachers. Through statements such as this in the *Gazette* and the encouragement given to Loyal Addresses, dissent was firmly allied with sedition and rebellion in the eyes of the paper's readership—an association which served the ends of government policy.[69]

VII

The religious life of post-Restoration England was complex and politically sensitive. In this chapter an attempt has been made to demonstrate the way in which the major newspaper of the period interacted with the religious life of these years. It has been shown that the *Gazette* was an important means of disseminating information in late Stuart England. The government's concern with the paper, its large circulation and profitability as well as reader reaction, all testify to its importance. Religious dissidents too, as has been shown, recognised the power and influence of the newspaper press and of the *Gazette* in particular. It follows that the religious content of the paper was of real significance to the society in which it circulated. This coverage was complex. From simply reflecting the fact that it appeared in a spiritually orientated society, it went on to present only one form of spiritual orthodoxy to its readership, that of the Church of England. It helped to bolster the Stuart regime in the eyes of the pro-Anglican gentry who had been instrumental in bringing about the Restoration in 1660, by presenting the monarchy as ecclesiastically orthodox, at times even sacred. In all of this it was in accord with the sentiments of the ruling groups in society, reflecting and reinforcing their ideas on how the world was structured. But it went further than that. At times, mainly through the use of advertisements, addresses, and proclamations, it not only informed the readership of such events as the Popish and Rye House Plots, but sought to guide their interpretation of them. The *Gazette* certainly contributed to the hysteria surrounding the Popish Plot and to the savagery of the 'Tory Revenge'—in both cases it helped to promote a climate of persecution.

The *London Gazette* was a newspaper which played a significant part in the complex religious history of late Stuart England and, difficult as it is to assess, it is a good example of the way early newspapers interacted with society. Indeed, the example of the *Gazette* suggests that newspapers could and did play an active part in the history of late Stuart England.

2
Politics and the Press

William Speck

After the lapsing of the Licensing Act in 1695, when formal censorship of the press came to an end, publication came to play a more vital part in politics than ever before. Of course, poems on affairs of state, woodcuts or engraved prints, broadsides, and pamphlets had been exploited before for political purposes, especially during the civil war and the Exclusion Crisis. To sustain a protracted campaign, however, required periodicals and newspapers, which had not been practical when the government could control their publication. Once the controls were lifted, the press really came into its own. Within a decade there were no fewer than twelve papers appearing in London, and by the end of Anne's reign the provincial press had been established in Norwich, Bristol, Worcester, Liverpool, Newcastle-upon-Tyne, Nottingham, and Stamford.[1]

Several papers had Tory or Whig party colours. The first London daily paper, the *Daily Courant,* was a whig organ, as were George Ridpath's *Flying Post* and John Tutchin's *Observator,* while Abel Roper's *Post Boy,* William Pittis's *Heraclitus Ridens,* and Charles Leslie's *Rehearsal* were Tory publications. A third force in politics, however, the government itself, also made its voice heard in the press. At first this could only be done through the official *London Gazette,* but in Anne's reign, as Alan Downie has shown, Robert Harley augmented it with 'unofficial' publications, creating a propaganda machine which by 1711 employed four other periodicals, among which Defoe's *Review* and Swift's *Examiner* were outstanding.[2]

In dealing with the political content of the press in Anne's reign, a distinction has to be made between newspapers and periodicals. Newspapers proper had very little by way of political copy. They were smaller than modern papers for one thing, which left them with little room for editorials. The *Flying Post,* for instance, was roughly the size of two modern A4 sheets, printed on all four sides in double columns, while the *Daily Courant* was one foolscap sheet, again printed on both sides with two columns, which closely followed the format of the *London Gazette.* Papers even followed the layout of the official organ, with foreign news being reported first from such places as Berlin, Bern, Cadiz, Hamburg, Paris,

Utrecht, Venice, and Vienna, with often only brief entries for London, Edinburgh, and Dublin at the end. Indeed, some papers 'lifted' copy wholesale from the *Gazette.*

Periodicals, on the other hand, contained hardly any news at all, consisting mainly of an essay. The classic examples of this, were the *Tatler* and the *Spectator.* Although produced under Whig auspices, they kept their partisanship down to a minimum, deliberately seeking to avoid the party political battle. There were, however, overtly political periodicals, whose essays were concerned with current affairs from a decidedly partisan point of view. Defoe's *Review,* and the *Examiner,* were the more distinguished in this genre, but it could also include the *Observator,* the *Rehearsal,* and the *Medley.* The *Observator* took the form of a dialogue, usually between the "Observator" and a "Countryman," Roger. This was parodied by the *Rehearsal,* the full title of which was the *Rehearsal of Observator, etc.,* in which the two characters also appear, though uttering very different opinions. Thus where Tutchin had 'Observator' keeping Roger on the Whig straight and narrow, and vilifying the Tories, Leslie shows him to be a villainous Whig hack. The two papers kept up a running commentary on each other in the early years of Anne's reign, as did the *Examiner* and the *Medley* between October 1710 and August 1711. The *Medley* was a Whig paper which succeeded the short-lived *Whig Examiner* in the task of rebutting the Tory Weekly.

By the reign of George II the picture was more complex. In the mid-1730s, for example, there were about nineteen London papers, including three dailies and four "Evening Posts." They tended to be bigger than those published under Anne, most having four three-columned pages. The earlier distinction between periodicals retailing news and those which contained mainly essays was no longer as clear-cut, for many carried a 'lead article' or 'editorial.' It is therefore necessary to distinguish three main types: the plain newspaper; the essay; and the composite. The first type included all four Evening Posts—the *General, London, St. James,* and *Whitehall,* together with the *Daily Journal, Daily Post,* and *Daily Post Boy.* These were no longer as dependent upon the *London Gazette* as their predecessors had been even for foreign news. The *Daily Journal,* for example, published reports 'from our particular French correspondent.' Those which contained primarily an essay were the *Corncutter's Journal,* the *Craftsman* in its earliest form, the *Free Briton* and the *Hyp Doctor.* Among the composites were the 'Weeklies' such as *Applebee's, Fog's,* and *Read's,* and the modified *Craftsman* as well as the *Daily Courant.* The provincial press had also become well established. By 1758 twenty-eight towns had their own papers, while Bristol and Newcastle-upon-Tyne boasted three each, and five other centers maintained two apiece.

The political affiliations of the press had altered too. Whereas in Anne's reign one can detect Whig, Tory and government periodicals, under

George II they tended to divide into government and opposition papers. In the early 1730's the main government organs were the *Daily Courant,* the *Free Briton* and the *London Journal.* To them was added in 1733 the *Corncutters' Journal,* for which "£1, 104. 16s. 8d. of Treasury money was expended on its circulation during the eighteenth months of its existence."[3] The *Daily Courant* was written by a team of writers, including Matthew Concanen and Barnham Gould, while the *Free Briton* was largely the work of William Arnall and the *London Journal* that of James Pitt. These men are now chiefly recalled in footnotes to Pope's *Dunciad,* Arnall and Pitt especially, with their pseudonyms of Walsingham and Osborne, the latter of which was twisted to "Mother Osborne" in opposition writings.

Opposition papers included *Fog's Weekly Journal,* the *London Evening Post* and the *Craftsman.* "Fog" was in fact Nathaniel Mist, a Jacobite journalist who tried to sustain a press campaign for the Pretender's cause although by the 1730's, he had been forced into exile. Popular Jacobitism as measured by ephemeral publications had largely disappeared by this time, as much on account of the disdain of James for the medium as to the vigilance of the ministry.[4] The *London Evening Post* was a more moderate Tory organ, while the *Craftsman* tried to construct a genuinely Country platform on which Tories and opposition Whigs could stand. Moreover, judging by surviving lists of known subscribers it was by no means unsuccessful in its appeal, since the politicians who were identified represented "a very broad spectrum of opinion, including high Tories and moderate opposition Whigs."[5] In 1737 *Common Sense,* a new opposition weekly subtitled the *Englishman's Journal* began publication, partly replacing the *Craftsman* as the main organ of those who were opposed to Walpole. It was joined in 1739 by the thrice-weekly *Champion.* Meanwhile in June 1735 the ministry merged all its subsidised papers into a single publication, the *Daily Gazetteer.*[6] The provincial press was likewise polarised into Court and Country newspapers. As G. A. Cranfield concluded "it is extremely difficult today to make any distinction between the true Tory papers and those which belonged properly to the Whig opposition. . . . it is probably more satisfactory—and certainly simpler—to regard them all as simply 'Opposition' papers."[7]

The contrast between the reign of Anne and that of George II can be illustrated from a study of the coverage by the press of the general elections of 1705 and 1734. These elections have been chosen not because they were 'typical,' but because they were fought over issues which brought out most clearly the role of the press in politics.

The issue in 1705 was the "Tack." This was the word used to describe the notorious occasion in November 1704 when a number of high church Tories had tried to persuade the Commons to append, or tack, the Occasional Conformity Bill to the Land Tax Bill in order to force it through the Lords. Occasional conformity was a practice whereby Protestant Dissenters took communion in the Church of England in order to qualify for local or

"The Coffehous Mob." From Edward Ward, *Vulgus Britannicus* (1710), part 4, frontispiece (British Library).

national offices, as stipulated by the Corporation and Test Acts, but thereafter attended their own conventicles. Since this violated the principle of the Acts, which was to secure a monopoly of power for the Anglican Church, the Tories had introduced bills to outlaw the practice in 1702 and 1703. Both had been abortive because of opposition from Whigs in the Upper House. On the third occasion, therefore, some of their sponsors determined to overcome this opposition by attaching the bill to a measure for raising revenue, since the peers could not alter or amend money bills. The 'Tack' had, however, been defeated by 251 votes to 134. The government had achieved this majority with the help of a substantial number of moderate Tories who had either abstained or even voted with the Whigs against the "Tack," rather than jeopardize supply. This combination of moderate Tories and Whigs enabled the government to control the Commons on most occasions until the end of the session.

Ministers hoped to maintain this combination to sustain them in the new parliament which would emerge after the general election to be fought in the spring of 1705. They therefore employed the press to try to keep up the distinction at the polls between moderate Tories and Tackers. The Whig press, on the other hand, attacked all Tories, Tackers and moderates, indiscriminately, while the Tory press closed ranks in the face of Whig criticism.

Daniel Defoe began the ministerial campaign in support of moderation in the pages of the *Review* for 17 April 1705.[8] "The author of these sheets," he declared," without vanity or affectation, declares himself sincerely desirous of the general peace, abstracted from the prejudice of parties; he abhors, from his soul, all the remains of that spirit of strife, *be it on which side it will,* that hinder a general union of charity and love among Christians, Protestants and Englishmen of all sorts." Advising the "Gentlemen freeholders, who to choose in your approaching elections," he recommended "Men of Peace." He indicated the ministry's preference for moderate Tories by admitting that he desired "the Government should be in the hands of Churchmen, 'tis our free choice, that we should have a Church Parliament, only let them be men of peace; other qualifications may be requisite, but this is absolutely necessary." He therefore urged the electorate to "choose men of peace, men of moderation, men of morals, men of estates, men of the Church." In his *Review* essay for 28 April, he defined men of peace as those "that wisely hold the balance between contending parties, and prevent the eagerness of hot men, on either side, running us to irrecoverable confusions."

Despite his alleged impartiality, and advocacy of moderate men between the extremists on either side, the only partisans he explicitly condemned were the Tackers. "These are the hair brained gamesters," he wrote, "that venture their whole inheritances upon the cast of a dye." On 1 May he characterized the division on the Tack as being one over such issues as whether "the French be let in, and the war be thrown up, or shall it not?" or "shall the Queen be deposed, and the Prince of Wales brought in, or no?" or "Shall the Protestant Religion be abdicated, and Popery restored or no?" or "shall the Toleration be repealed and persecution succeed or no?" "You must not choose a Tacker," he warned the voters, "unless you will destroy our peace, divide our strength, pull down the Church, let in the French and depose the Queen." When, despite his advice, Tackers were returned in some early elections, he predicted that not half of the 134 would get back into Parliament. Later, as results showed that over half were being returned, he complained that they were for the most part coming in for rotten boroughs such as Bramber, Gatton, and Marlow. "Were it not for this monopolising of votes, commanding and managing of burroughs," he complained to the Tackers, "I am of the opinion very few of you would get into the House." When notwithstanding this assertion some of them were returned for county seats, he blamed the high church clergy for leading the forty-shilling freeholders astray. He noted on 29 May that "of 318 parsons in the county of Kent, above 250 of them, in conjunction with the papists, nonjurors and Tackers, gave their votes for" a Tacker.

In his attempts to denigrate the popular support for the Tackers in some constituencies, Defoe asked the question, "If a Hot Churchman, if a Tacker, be set up for a member of parliament, on one side, and a moderate churchman, whig, or call him what you will stands on the other, on which side shall the papists, the atheists, the drunken, swearing and most vicious of the people vote?" and answered by asserting "that all these generally are for the high churchmen, Tackers etc." This provoked Charles Leslie to reply in the *Rehearsal,* "Let the cause then be determined by this. And to begin our reckoning give in your list of any atheist deist Socinian Jew or Gentile in England that is not against the Tackers and the Bill which they tacked." Leslie insisted that the Tackers were supported by "the body of the principal gentry, both for estates and reputation. The other by tag, rag and long tail, the refuse and scum, the beasts of the people."[9]

His defense of moderation brought Defoe into the firing line between the partisans of the Tackers and of their Whig opponents. Thus he was assailed by Tutchin in the *Observator* as well as by Leslie in the *Rehearsal.* In the *Review,* Defoe criticized the violence perpetrated by both side in the Coventry election, and urged that if the peace were not kept there then troops might have to be used to preserve law and order at the polls. Tutchin took the occasion to accuse him of advocating military rule, which was the last straw as far as Defoe was concerned. In the *Review* for 22 May he gave vent to an accumulation of dissatisfaction with Tutchin. "The author of the Observator having treated me in a most scurrilous manner in several of his papers," he fulminated, "but without all bounds in his last; I cannot but think myself obliged to examine the reason of his behaviour, and the truth of his allegations, and exposing the falsity shall be answer enough for me."

He was particularly hurt by Tutchin's haughty dismissal of him for his lack of learning. "He says, I have read but little: I believe I may pretend to have read more than himself, and yet make no great pretence to books."

The spectacle of the two Whig authors mauling each other in print was a diverting one to other journalists. The *London Post,* for instance, referred to it in its issue for 28 May. Benjamin Harris, the editor, was a Whig himself, and was concerned that their quarrel would help the Tacking cause. His editorials during the election consisted of dialogues between Truth and Honesty and a high church parson, who exchanged the following views on the fracas.[10]

> *Parson* Why here has been a terrible battle between the Observator and the Review.
> *T and H* Well, and which has got the better of it?
> *Parson* Why the Church . . .

When the parson referred to the strong language employed by the participants, Truth and Honesty replied, "Why the Observator us'd to call himself a gentleman; sure he won't call names . . . and what says the Review? Does he call names?" "He does not directly thunder roar and below, as t'other does," riposted the parson, "but he's damnably sly and cutting by the way of innuendo, and retort, calls as many rogues by craft as t'other does in coarser terms."

> *T and H* This is excellent sport for you is it not?
> *Parson* Ay, we have been striving to loose these two mastiffs at one another for a long time, and at last we have set them on, and I am for making a ring for them, fight dog, fight bear . . .

Another curious observer of the dogfight was the *Wandering Spy,* a paper which appeared in June and took the form of whimsical essays based on prospects from the top of the Monument. Thus in number three the author claimed that from that vantage point he saw

> two men hard at work beating of an ill look'd, odd, dishap'd fellow in a mortar; but after all they could do, his limbs were so stiff, and his bones so hard, that if they had gone to beat the mortar to powder it might have been as soon done as to beat this fellow into the shape of other Christians; they thump'd him, maul'd him and pummelled him heartily, that he cried out like a cat roasting, but no alteration wrought in him; then came that saying of Solomon into my head, (viz) if you take a fool and bray him in a mortar, yet will he not turn from his folly. And immediately it was whispered in my ear, that this was the Moderator and Daniel Defoe taking fruitless pains to make the Observator an honest man.

The *Moderator* was another ministerial paper which appeared during the elections, with a "line" so close to the *Review*'s that some thought it too was written be Defoe, an impression which the real author was at pains to correct in the fifth number. Like the *Review* it claimed to be published "for promoting of peace; for reconciling differences between parties; to shew wherein every one misses it, and for uniting the hearts of the people to Her Majesty and Government."

Despite the efforts of the government, however, the parties were not to be reconciled. Besides attacking the *Review,* Leslie and Tutchin kept up a running battle with each other throughout the election. Their differing accounts of the same events show how partisanship could distort press reports in his election. The *Observator* for 11–14 April reported that at Ipswich

> . . . the people of the town met at their hall, where one of the bailiffs began a health to the honest Tackers, which so disgusted those honest gentlemen that were in the company (who were lovers of their Queen and Country) that they all departed and left the Tackers to themselves. I need not tell you that no honest true-hearted Englishman is employ'd in the publick offices of the town, that follows of course; but just before the rising of the last parliament, in order to support the Tacking cause, the bailiffs made a certain eminent Tacker and eighty other country gentlemen freemen of the said corporation.

The format of the *Observator* was a dialogue between Observator himself and Roger, a so-called "Countryman." These words Tutchin put into the mouth of "Countryman," having him conclude his account of affairs in Ipswich with the question "Now Master, is this fair?"

Leslie answered the question in the *Rehearsal* for 21–28 April under the headline "The Observator's lies about Suffolk and Ipswich." The *Rehearsal,* too, took the form of a dialogue between Observator and Countryman, only Leslie put the words into the "foul mouth" of Observator, "which lapps slander like sweet milk, and being destitute of all shame or morality cares not for truth or falsehood, but throws dirt and bespatters, like a postillian in armour of leather." "Countryman" in fact refuted the story. Thus he contradicted the account of all honest men leaving the hall when the health to the Tackers was proposed by asserting that only one man left, a coachman to a Roman Catholic, and "an impudent fellow like John Tutchin." As for the bailiffs of Ipswich making eighty country gentlemen freemen of the town, he rebuked Observator, insisting that "it was not the bailiffs (as thou impudently liest) but they were chosen freemen by the body of the freemen present at several Great Courts (as the Common halls are called) and not all at once, just before the rising of the last parliament as though put'st it. It was done in about two years time."[11]

Tutchin and Leslie also clashed in their reports of events in Northampton on 23 April, the queen's coronation day. According to the *Observator,*

> In that city there are two coffee houses followed by two parties; those few Jacks and Tackers that are there (and very inconsiderable people too) but now especially the black robe have supported a woman whose husband is a Frenchman but who has left her in keeping a coffee house; she's one of no extraordinary character but keeps her coffeehouse table covered with Dyer's news letter, the Rehearsal and papers of that sortment.

Dyer's was a manuscript newsletter which vigorously defended the Tackers in this election. It prophesied that "very few of the 134 will miss of their elections, notwithstanding the senseless clamours of Whiggish libellers."[12] According the Tutchin, guests at this Tory coffeehouse in Northampton failed to attend a celebration planned for 23 April there because they were downcast at receiving the news that the navy had successfully repulsed a French attack on Gibraltar. The *Rehearsal* rejoined:

> Now I am to tell thee that this is an errant lie . . . there was but one person in Mrs. Laforce's coffee house that night and he a whigg, several clergy and gentlemen her friends being at the Rose and Crown that night to drink the Queen's health being the day of her coronation by an appointment made the 6th of February last, being the day of her birth. . . . The Observator says the women marry'd a Frenchman insinuating . . . a Papist, who tis well known her husband was a Hugonot. The Observator would insinuate as if only very mean people came to her house tho' the present Knights (of the shire) most of the gentlemen and I believe three parts of the clergy in the county was at her house this election; And I believe at no other coffee house.

Leslie explained why he had bothered to refute a story which seemed "of no great consequence in it self." It was because several libels against the Tories could be inferred from it, such as that they were disaffected from the Queen and in the interest of France, and that they could only maintain one coffeehouse in the town. "But the election in North Hampton which followed," he concluded, "wherein true churchmen were chosen, is a full confutation of all that this story was contrived to suggest. And shews that the malice and industry of a certain party is indefatigable."

The biggest clash of all between the two in this election occurred over their reporting of the Suffolk county contest.[13] According to the *Rehearsal,* on 9 May,

> . . . about ten in the morning came the Lord Dysert and Sir Robert Davers [the Tory candidates, both Tackers] ushered into the town by such a body of all the chief gentry and most reputable yeomanry of the country, as enlivened the reputation of the Church party. When presently they were succeeded according to custom by Sir Samuel Barnardiston and Sir Dudly Cullum [the whig candidates]. But to see what a rabble had espoused that faction! You never beheld such a scoundrel medley . . . the rout of Presbyterians, Independents, Anabaptists, Quakers, who ap-

> peared in a body, Papists and moderation brothers . . . began such a noise of No Tackers, No French Shoes Hear the Queen etc. that you would have thought Hell had been broke loose. But when my Lord Dysert and Sir Robert Davers appeared (those noble Tackers) I was surprised to see how all that glorious appearance was transported and presently entertained with the grateful music of No Forty Eight, No Presbyterian Rebellion, Save the Queen's White Neck. . . . But you would have rejoiced to see how the clergy went unanimously in a body . . . to the place of polling and polled above 200, which so dispirited the adverse party that we heard no more of them. . . . The enemy brought in the lame and the blind and all that could but speak yet we outpolled them by 573.

Observator retaliated by asserting that Leslie's "account is so notoriously false in every particular that . . . no persons can justly give any credit to that scandalous paper." Tutchin insisted that, so far from being accompanied by a rabble or a mob, the Whig candidates were escorted by

> nine baronets, three knights, upwards of twenty gentlemen from £500 to £1000 per annum, and a great many other gentlemen from £200 to £400 per annum, besides several of the most eminent clergy of the county, and the generality of the best trading people, masters of ships and farmers. . . . As to the 200 clergymen which the said paper insinuates to have come in a body and poll for the other candidates, I am assured . . . they did not amount to 50.

Leslie challenged Tutchin to name the nine baronets who were with the Whig candidates at the polls, and repeated his assertion that two hundred clergy had polled in a body for the two Tackers.

Such discrepancies indicate a serious weakness of the press as a prime souce for politics in this period. The accounts are so shamelessly biased in favour of one side or the other that it is impossible to take any of them at face value. They are scarcely even pretending to report occurrences objectively or accurately. Any historian who relies on them for what actually happened at the polls in 1705 is bound to be seriously misled.

Yet if they are useless as records of actual events, or at least have to be used with the utmost caution for their factual information, they are unique records of how events were perceived by men attempting to influence and shape public opinion. The government at this time was trying to persuade people to vote for moderate men, Tories as well as Whigs, to keep out Tackers and other zealous partisans. The Whigs, on the other hand, were out to maximize their strength in the new Parliament, and denigrated all Tories, whether they had supported the Tack or not, as high church bigots. The Tory press, at the same time strove to unite the party and to eliminate the distinction between Tackers and moderate Tories. Dyer and Leslie even represented the Tackers as heroes fighting to save the Church.

In the event, the distinctions which the government had tried to keep alive through the election campaign virtually disappeared. The Tories returned to Westminster were not divided between Tackers and moderates as they had been in the previous Parliament, but rallied behind William Bromley, a leading Tacker, in a dispute for the Speaker's chair. The government could not sustain a majority with moderate support alone, and had to lean increasingly on the Whigs. How far this closing of the Tory ranks during the general election was due to the press is now impossible to ascertain. That it did play a role, however, and probably a major one, in this process seems to be indisputable.

Just as the defeat of the Tack set the scene for the general election of 1705 so the defeat of Walpole's Excise scheme prepared the ground for that of 1734. Sir Robert's attempt to shift the duties on tobacco and wine from the customs to an inland excise gave the opposition to him their best chance during his long ministry. Although the bill to give the scheme effect was not actually defeated on the floor of the House of Commons, the resistance to it in Parliament and throughout the country was so strong that the Prime Minister felt it to be preudent to withdraw the measure. The M.P.s who opposed it consisted of 106 Tories and 98 dissident Whigs. Opposition leaders strove to keep this combination together during the election campaign in order to present a united front in the new Parliament. They played down the distinctions between Tories and Whigs in their ranks and presented themselves as a single Country party. During the election campaign, for example, the *Craftsman* claimed that nothing was "more demonstrable than that the court whigs of this age are exactly the same kind of creatures with the court tories before the Revolution; that vice versa the body of the present tories have adopted the spirit of the old whigs, and by acting in conjunction with the independent whigs of our times, have in a great measure abolish'd those silly appellations, and made court and county the only prevailing distinction amongst us."[14] The government, on the other hand, sought to split the opposition by playing on the divisions. Thus it described the Tories as Jacobites, dismissed the dissident Whigs as a self-seeking faction, and discredited the notion that together they formed a united Country party. So far from perceiving the contest in terms of Court and Country, the government claimed that it was one between their supporters, who upheld true Whig principles, and Tories who were Jacobites and apostate Whigs who were Jacobite fellow travelers. At the general election the *Free Briton* poured scorn on the opposition's boast that it was united into a Country party by observing that "the dissatisfied whiggs, having too slender a strength of their own, adopt every veteran Tory, and quondam Jacobite, to join in those measures of opposition; whilst the motley mixture of irreconcilable parties is called a Country Interest."[15]

The press began the election campaign in earnest by publishing lists of those MPs who had been for or against the Excise scheme. These appeared not only in London periodicals but were either printed in provincial papers, such as the *Suffolk Mercury,* or advertised for sale in them. As Paul Langford observes, "the publication of these lists represented the most determined and effective attempt by any eighteenth-century opposition to attract electoral support on a national basis."[16]

As in 1705, reports of the same contests in government and opposition papers were very different. According to an epigram in the *Grub Street Journal,*

> Told by court whigs, or country whigs and tories
> Of most elections there are different stories;
> Corrupt or clear we see each party made
> As Grub Street writer is inclined or paid.[17]

The *London Evening Post* of 4–7 May "corrected" a story published in the *General Evening Post* and the *Northampton Mercury* about the electioneering of the Country candidates in Stamford. "It is plain the author of the paragraph in the above mentioned papers has not considered the truth," it concluded, "but followed the impulse of his own corrupt thoughts; His inventions have always been very awkward and whoever is capable of believing his legends may be imposed upon without any great difficulty, and if this least had not exceeded those of the common run, we should no more have set about to confute it, than we should call an owl to account for hooting." There were owls on both sides, as Dr Langford notes: "where there were competing local papers the results were bizarre. In Norfolk, for example, the Jacobite *Norwich Gazette* and the Whig *Norwich Mercury* disputed every inch of the ground. Their reports of the same event bore little resemblance to each other, and neither could make a claim to the political disposition of any locality without being flatly contradicted."[18] Where there was only one local paper the coverage of the election varied. Some, like the *Newscastle Courant,* contented themselves with the barest reports and the minimum of comment. Presumably, as G. A. Cranfield has argued, they were anxious not to alienate half their customers, and perhaps encourage the launching of a rival paper, by displaying strong partisanship.[19] Others, however, were less circumspect. The *York Courant* was flagrantly in favour of Country candidates and against the Court throughout the polling. It regularly opened with extracts from the *Craftsman,* and championed the opposition candidates in the Yorkshire election.

Although the papers were no less biased under Walpole than under Anne, the rise of a provincial press in the meanwhile did lead to the reporting of events in the localities which made the papers a repository of facts as well as a record of propaganda. For example, there was no contest in York itself in 1734, a fact which could be obtained from the London papers. The *York Courant,* however, contains information on the state of the parties in the City not to be gleaned elsewhere. On 7th May it reported that "Sir William Milner Bart declined standing candidate for this City at the ensuing election, so that Sir John Kaye Bart and Edward Thompson Esq will be chosen on Wednesday next without opposition." Milner and Thompson had sat in the previous Parliament as ministerial supporters, while Kaye was an opponent of the court. In the event, therefore, thanks partly to Milner standing down, a government and an opposition member were returned for York without a contest. After the election, on 7 July, a curious advertisement appeared in the *Courant:*

> Whereas a list of all those tradesmen who are said to have promised their votes to Sir William Milner and Mr. Thompson . . . hath been printed and distributed, and as it is apprehended with an intent not so much to expose the weakness of the said gentlemen's interest as to keep up divisions and animosities amongst the citizens, and prejudice them in their different trades and callings as if their support and maintenance depended solely upon one set of people: This is therefore to give notice that whoever will inform against the author or publisher of the said list, shall receive the hearty acknowledgments of the injured citizens.

A week later the anonymous advertiser received a public reply in the columns of the *Courant,* telling him that the list "was published by those who were true friends and faithful subjects to his Majesty King George and sincere well wishers to the Protestant succession in the House of Hanover." The author of the previous advertisement riposted in the next issue,

> . . . that the list was published to let the world know what freemen were grateful to their old members, in hopes that all persons in the same interest would make them useful returns. Surely every citizen in a contrary interest can readily understand by this, that he is to be sacrificed to their resentment (or caprice) whenever time permits, or humour prompts. If this is not keeping up divisions and animosities amongst us, I don't know what is; but it unfortunately happened to those snarling malecontents that a majority hath lately declared for the Country Interest; and if such extream particularity must be shewn by one party, we are capable of making equal returns.

The advertisement columns of the *York Courant* thus indicate how bitterly divided the City was under the apparently tranquil surface of an undisputed return.

The press remains, however, more useful as a source for how events were shaped than for what events took place. Although the Court won the general election of 1734, it was notorious that it did so by virtue of its interest in small boroughs, the counties and cities going overwhelmingly for its opponents. Since it was in the large constituencies that public opinion could make itself felt, it appears that the opposition won the propaganda war, even if it lost the election. The government virtually conceded this at the time. The *Daily Courant* for 30 April conjured up an opposition politician whom it called "the Political Upholsterer" and imagined him planning his campaign. It had him say:

> Another of my schemes for the propagation of patriotism was to secure a set of newspapers for the insertion of particular articles to answer any immediate designs, give a proper turn to a foreign or domestic occurrence, and keep up the spirit of the party thro' the nation; The Daily and Evening Posts, Fog and the Craftsman have answered all these views, as well as we could desire; and as long as we have these vehicles for political slander, we shall never despair of governing the passions of the people as we please.

The *London Journal,* reflecting on the election results, bluntly observed, "supposing it true that the Majority of the people are against the Ministry, what doth that prove? The people are sometimes right and sometimes wrong." The *Corncutter's Journal,* in a pathetic attempt to offset the impact of the opposition press, published "A Dialogue between Dick and Tom about parliamenteering." Tom is upbraided by Dick for accepting treats from two county candidates in his borough, and dissuaded from voting for them. When Tom says the court candidates were for the excise scheme, a standing army, the Riot Act and the Septennial Act, Dick asks him, "Pray Tom do you understand what these things mean?" Tom replies, "No, not I, but *Fog* and the *Craftsman* make it as plain as a pikestaff." Dick comments that "their weekly seditious and treasonable writings whereby they inflame the people, and give them false notions of things, make it necessary to have an army, to keep the enemies of the Government in awe." This was a blatant admission that the opposition had won the campaign for the hearts and minds of the voters.

The opposition press was beside itself with frustration, for though it could claim that the sense of the nation was in favor of the Country rather than the Court, it had not succeeded in toppling Walpole. In this respect the press was less influential in 1734 than it had been in 1705. At the previous general election the government's electoral strategy had not succeeded, largely because more Tackers got back into the House of Commons than it had bargained for. One reason for this appears to have been that the electorate was less amenable to control and more susceptible to public opinion in Anne's reign than it was to become in George II's. By 1734 the growth of oligarchy in the constituencies rendered a majority of them impervious to public opinion and much more vulnerable to ministerial control and influence. The result was that Walpole won the election even though public opinion was overwhelmingly against his government.

A final fruitful comparison between the two elections which a study of the press brings out is that they were fought in very different ideological circumstances. In 1705 the Church in danger was the main battle cry of the Tories, while the Whigs attacked their intolerance toward dissenters. In 1734, Excise provided the main source of discord. *Fog's Weekly Journal* summed up this change on 13 April 1734:

> There are some words in our language the sound of which are of such malignant efficacy that they are seldom pronounced but they put the people in a ferment and alarm them with idle fears. . . . These are Liberty and Property; Religion was a word once altogether as pernicious, but . . . that is happily banished.

The notion that editors of some local newspapers consciously struck a balance between sales and politics can be well illustrated by developments in Newcastle-upon-Tyne during George II's reign. As we have seen, there was only one paper published there during the 1734 election, the *Newcastle Courant,* and this reported contests almost entirely as news, with little or no political comment. Presumably this was a deliberate policy to avoid giving offense to government supporters among its readers, for it was biased in favour of opposition candidates. At the next general election, however, held in 1741, Court candidates could count on a new paper, the *Newcastle Journal,* which had been launched in 1739. The two papers consequently came out on opposite sides during the campaign. The campaign got under way early in October 1740, six months before the election, when Walter Blackett and Nicholas Fenwick, the sitting members for the City, took out joint advertisements in both newspapers to announce that they would be standing together, and desiring the votes and interests of the free burgesses. Within days of this announcement Matthew Ridley also advertised in the *Courant* and the *Journal* that he too would be a candidate. Thereafter both advertisements regularly ran in both papers right up to the polls, being joined in January 1741 by another from William Carre, denying rumors that he was not intending to stand. Although both local papers carried their advertisements, as the campaign developed the *Courant* came out for Blackett and Fenwick, while the *Journal* supported Ridley. Neither adopted Carre, and perhaps this, as well as his late entry into the lists, helped to place him at the bottom of the poll when the votes were eventually counted.

The two papers were also rivals for readers, however, and the newsworthiness of the electoral campaign sometimes overcame political considerations. For instance, the *Courant* carried a much fuller report of the celebration of Ridley's birthday on 14 November than did the *Journal.* Where the latter succinctly reported that "yesterday being the birthday of Matthew Ridley Esq., one of our worthy aldermen and candidates, the same was celebrated by his friends with all imaginable demonstrations of joy," the former elaborated on the form which the celebrations took,

> viz. ringing of bells, firing of guns, and displaying of flags by the ships in the river; and to conclude the rejoicing of the day, many gentlemen met at the summer house of Capt Johnston in the Close which hangs over the river and was elegantly illuminated upon the occasion when his Majesty's

> health was drank, attended with a royal salute of guns, beating of drums, musick and loud huzzas, the Prince and Princess of Wales, and the rest of the royal family; Alderman Ridley's health with many returns of the day, and success to him at the next general election . . . Liberty and Prosperity to the freemen of Newcastle upon Tyne; and each with a proper salute of guns etc.

This doubtless roused more local interest than the *Journal's* coverage of the same events, even though it also publicized Ridley's election campaign.

Perhaps Blackett and Fenwick protested to the *Courant* about this, for it ran an even more elaborate story of the celebrations for Blackett's birthday on 18 December.

> The day was usher'd in with the greatest demonstrations of joy entirely proper for so zealous a Patriot for Liberty etc.—in the morning all the bells of the several churches were rung, and continued till late at night; at ten o'clock the British flag (notwithstanding the severity of the season, yet the love of the freemen for the worthy alderman and member and the honour of his day, engaged them to it) was displayed on the highest spire of St. Nicholas's church by M.T. and proclaim'd the day; the ships at the Key also in honour of it hung out their flags; on the sight of all which, every hour after the guns in the high and low parts of the town were discharg'd, till night. In the afternoon some of the friends of the conjunction made a grand procession through the several streets with cocades of purple ribbon gilded preceeded by the French horns, hautboys etc, which considering the few at first setting out, the unexpectedness of it, and the numbers that were every minute adding to them, shew's the zeal that animated them. The procession ended at the house of that ever memorable gentleman, the subject of the day, amidst the discharge of loud guns, etc. when was drunk his Majesty's health, the Prince and Princess of Wales and the rest of the royal family. . . . Health on the present occasion and success to him and his fellow our worthy representative at the next General Election, was the repeated toast. At night great numbers of bonfires were kindled, and at many of them hogsheads of liquor were set out for the populace. The whole affair was carried on with much decorum, and so little disturbance, as was really, all circumstances considered, very surprising; for there was not one window broke, nor any one knock'd down.

The *Journal,* by contrast, contented itself with a bare mention of Blackett's birthday celebrations, but reported a parade organized by Ridley's supporters through the streets of Newcastle on 26 December. Significantly the *Courant* was silent about Ridley's demonstration. Both reported a rally for Blackett and Fenwick on 1 January, though where the *Journal* estimated the crowd at between 1,000 and 1,200, the *Courant* claimed that it was 'the most numerous and grand that ever was seen here on any occasion; which is a fresh instance of the electors great respect to our present members for their faithful services in parliament.'

Although the two papers refrained from making partisan comments about the actual polling in May, they glossed the result very differently.[20] Blackett polled 1,453, Fenwick 1,231, Ridley 1,131, and Carre 683, which prompted the *Courant* to comment: "Whereupon the two former gentlemen in the Country interest were declared duly elected. On which occasion there were great rejoicings, as firing of guns, ringing of bells, and other publick demonstrations of joy; and the whole concluded with the greatest harmony and quietness that has been known here on such an occasion." The *Journal,* on the other hand, observed that "there never was so many persons polled at an election here before, or was it ever known that any candidate who polled the number of legal votes which Mr. Ridley did, failed to be return'd the second member, being 200 more than ever was known to miscarry." After the result was announced Blackett and Fenwick thanked their supporters with an advertisement in the *Courant,* Ridley his with one in the *Journal,* while Carre advertised in neither. These were a fitting final comment on the roles which the two papers had played during the election campaign.

By contrast with the hurly-burly of the contests of 1705 and 1734, the campaign in Newcastle-upon-Tyne in 1741 was a very gentlemanly affair. Indeed, elections throughout England were very much in the doldrums by the middle of the century after the heat and excitement of the first third. There were fewer contests for newspapers to report for one thing, the number of constituencies going to the polls dipping sharply after the 1734 election. Of the 245 constituencies in England, 107 were contested in 1734, compared with only 65 in 1741, 52 in 1747, 60 in 1754, and 46 in 1761.[21] It was not until the rise of radicalism, starting with the Wilkite campaign in 1768, that popular interest in elections picked up again, to be exploited by a more broadly based press than the earlier campaigns had known.

3
The British Press and Europe in the Early Eighteenth Century

Jeremy Black

News concerning foreign affairs constituted a large portion of the news reports carried by British newspapers in the early eighteenth century. This was the case for both printed newspapers and manuscript news letters whether the item in question was a daily, a triweekly, or a weekly. This chapter seeks to deal with two aspects of the newspaper reporting of European events in the early eighteenth century. Firstly, the sources of press reports will be considered. Secondly, some tentative comments will be advanced as to the impact of the press upon the conduct of foreign policy during the administration of Sir Robert Walpole.[1]

Whereas the most common source for modern newspaper reports of foreign countries is that of the foreign correspondent, this was relatively uncommon in the early eighteenth century. Some newspapers drew attention to the fact that they had procured a particular source of foreign correspondence, usually in the United Provinces, though sometimes in France or Italy, but these were never named, and it is difficult to know whether they were anything other than an attempt to personalize foreign newsletters. The major source of foreign news was plagiarism from other newspapers, either British or European. This applied equally to reports of domestic events, and was considered to be quite acceptable. The derivation of reports concerning foreign countries from other newspapers was a common European phenomenon. The chancellor of Denmark, in replying to an inquiry from the British envoy, Lord Glenorchy, about an item of news in a Danish newspaper, said "that he supposed that paragraph was copied out of some other paper, which the news writers here often do,"[2] and Glenorchy informed Lord Townshend with reference to a Hamburg paper, "The Copenhagen news writers generally take their account from this paper."[3]

Some British newspapers acknowledged their sources. Thus, the *Evening Post* of 13 June 1727, acknowledged debts to the *Amsterdam Courant* and the

Amsterdam Gazette, and in the issue of 4 July to the same papers with the addition of the *Paris à-la-Main.* However, most newspapers did not acknowledge the sources of their news, and the *Evening Post* was relatively unusual in this respect. In the *Evening Post* for 5 August 1727 appeared an article acknowledged as "from the supplement to the *Amsterdam Gazette* 8th August N.S. . . . describing two plans being canvassed at Vienna, one for a free communication of the Danube with Fiume and Trieste, the other an attempt to joyn the Danube with the Elbe." The same article appeared in the *Flying Post: or, Post Master* for 3 August, but without any attribution. Again, the *Evening Post* for 28 September 1727 carried an article, reprinted from the *Boston Gazette,* about a shipping disaster in the Atlantic, wherein the survivors owed their subsequent escape to cannibalism. The same tale was retold in other newspapers without attribution. The *Post Boy* of 7 May 1728, in a piece priding itself on the quality of its printer's foreign news, complained of plagiarism by other newspapers:

> . . . the extraordinary expense he is at in furnishing a Hague letter, which gives the best account we have of transactions in the different courts of Europe, the interests of Princes . . . transplanted and repeated by so many other newspapers, some in part, and some in whole.

The *Craftsman* of 17 July 1734 complained that

> . . . when a piece of false intelligence gets into one paper, it commonly runs thro' them all, unless timely contradicted by those who are acquainted with the particular circumstances.

It is clear that the provincial press received their European news from the columns of the London press, or from the handwritten newsletters sent from London. Thus, the *Northampton Mercury* of 12 June 1727 acknowledged debts to the *Evening Post,* the *St. James's Evening Post* and the *General Post Office Letter.* The London press drew heavily on the European papers, but especially on those of Paris and the United Provinces. Dutch newspapers were readily available in London in Queen Anne's reign[4] including those published in the United Provinces, but written in French.[5] Amsterdam, The Hague, Leiden, Utrecht, and Rotterdam all possessed French language newspapers. These had the best correspondents in Europe, and frequently received information about secret negotiations, a facility owing much to the propensity of Dutch bureaucrats for corruption. Use of these journals was not uncritical. The *Daily Post Boy* of 9 May 1729 reported:

> The Dutch Gazette tells us, the late Bishop of Rochester is gone to reside at Marseilles; but we believe their intelligence from that Quarter is not good enough to be rely'd on.

The same paper reported, on 12 October 1734:

> The *Paris à la main* which came by yesterday's mail, says they have letters at Paris, which place the King of Prussia in extremis . . . it would be a little odd, if we shall receive any real news from Berlin by way of Paris.

The *St. James's Evening Post* of 30 July–1 August 1730 alleged that the Dutch Gazettes were filled with "the common idle reports" of Paris. The *Daily Post Boy* of 4 January 1735, complained that "our Dutch correspondents . . . often pretend to know more of our affairs than we do ourselves."[6]

There is no doubt of the pervasive practice of plagiarism, nor that the major sources of foreign reports, whether of northern or of southern Europe, were Dutch. What is unclear is the extent to which material was actively filtered by a process of conscious editorial selection. In the case of newspapers arguing a particular political line it could be expected that such a process of selection would be most active. This is indeed the case with such leading opposition stalwarts as the *Craftsman* and *Fog's Weekly Journal.* In March 1731 the Walpole ministry claimed to have brought peace to Europe, and to have solved Britain's diplomatic problems by means of the second Treaty of Vienna. Both the *Craftsman* and *Fog's* challenged this over the next few months by stressing signs of continued tension, such as the continued construction of Spanish fortifications near Gibraltar.[7] The European news that these newspapers printed was deliberately used to challenge the ministry and to discredit its achievements,[8] and events that might have supported the ministerial case were played down or simply not reported.

Alongside such specific interpretations of the news, of which another instance can be seen in the skepticism displayed by these two newspapers about the efficacy of British negotiations at the time of the Polish Succession War,[9] may be set the more discursive essays that were printed at the beginning of these two newspapers. These tended to discuss not so much the news, as the general situation and served as a form of editorial. Many attacked arbitrary government upon the continent in order to warn their readers about the dangers from the Walpole ministry, which they represented as seeking to establish such a form of government.[10]

Reading the *Craftsman* and *Fog's,* it would be possible to argue that there was a distinct treatment of foreign affairs in the opposition press, a treatment that threw doubt both on the success of the government's foreign policy and on its underlying objectives. However, it is important to note that such is not the case with several other opposition newspapers. The *London Evening Post,* for example, tended to print foreign news without comment. Most newspapers followed this latter course of action, and the newspapers that regularly commented upon their foreign news formed a distinct minority.

In the handling of foreign news there is evidence of editorial selection that owed nothing to political partisanship. There was a vast amount of information available about European affairs. Foreign newspapers and newsletters were readily available in London coffeehouses.[11] Each post from the continent brought a mass of information. Far from uncritically printing this material and using it simply to fill newspaper space, the editors made a great effort to select what appeared accurate and to explain the basis of unlikely reports.[12] This was as true of some provincial publications as of those published in London. Thus the "London" report in the *Newcastle Courant,* a provincial newspaper with a very high standard of reporting, noted on 1 June 1734:

> Tuesday there was a current report of the death of King Stanislaus, the foundation of which it seems, was a letter wrote by the Postmaster of Emmerick, that a courier had passed thro' that place, and declared he was going to the French court to carry that news.[13]

Six years earlier, in the tense period of political jockeying that preceded the opening of Parliament, the "London" report in the *Original Mercury,* published in York, noted:

> The report of great armaments by sea at Corunna, pretended to come from Captain Cowper of the Townshend packet boat, appear to be notoriously false; for the said Captain has wrote . . . that the Spaniards . . . talked much of peace.[14]

The same newspaper, reprinting an account from a London paper of recent Catholic miracles in Europe, added the proviso that

> The *St. James's Evening Post* has always strange stories of the Catholicks; whether invented, or real, either way, the Readers are to judge.[15]

Plagiarism was not therefore incompatible with relatively high journalistic standards. Newspapers accepted that in printing news from abroad they had to combat the formidable problem of printing fresh news that was also accurate, in an age when it was usually impossible to check immediately the accuracy of recent information. In addition, the press faced the problem of the closed nature of most European politics. In most of Europe public political debate was muted and the convention that foreign affairs and the conduct of diplomacy were a mystery of state enjoyed a large degree of reality. This posed a major problem for the press, and led to some debate as to the extent to which the press could properly understand developments. A theme developed at length in the governmental press concerned the way in which the Opposition newspapers ignored these customary limits. The *Comedian, or Philosophical Enquirer,* one of the more interesting of the early London magazines, noted, in 1732,

> The study of Politics is of that intricate nature, and the secret springs by which the wheels of state move so difficult to be discerned, that it requires

> no slender genius, nor a small share of knowledge, to gain an insight into this science.

Several newspapers, in their reporting, recognized the problem. The *Post Boy* of 30 November 1727 reported a conference of envoys at The Hague, and commented:

> It is not to be expected, that we without Doors should be able to give a detail of what passed in that conference, or furnish out the precise contents of Monsieur de Fenelon's dispatches.

Eleven days later the *Evening Journal* noted with reference to the Council being held in Madrid:

> But everything which passes is kept so secret, that there is no diving to the bottom of which is transacting.[16]

Such a situation conflicted with the need for news, and newspapers adopted various attitudes in dealing with the problem. Most never explained the basis upon which they selected reports to print, and only a small minority of newspapers ever resorted to an editorial statement. One of the most interesting can be found in the *Free Briton* of 4 Feburary 1731. The *Craftsman,* a month earlier, had printed a "Hague letter" revealing and condemning the government's secret attempts to create an Anglo-Austrian alliance. This touched off a sustained debate about the legality of such articles[17] and it also led to discussion of the correct foundations for the accuracy of newspaper reports. The position of the author of the *Free Briton* on the legitimate basis of foreign coverage was comparatively modest:

> As to secretaries or Ministers of state being the only evidence in such cases I think differently. I think concurrent and repeated advices, previous to such insinuations, are an honest justification in the eye of reason and conscience.

And also, he might have added, the law. The only newspaper that entirely relied upon "secretaries or ministers of state" was the *Gazette.* As a source for foreign news this has been consistently underrated. There is no doubt that its circulation slumped during the first half of the eighteenth century, and it was clearly not the most interesting of newspapers nor the best written. The Duke of Newcastle, secretary of state for the Southern Department, in ordering the envoy at Paris, Horatio Walpole, to send regular reports for use in the *Gazette,* admitted that the paper had been going through a bad patch:

> The London Gazette being published by His Majesty's authority, is the only paper in the hands of the Government to be made use of for giving

> true relations of affairs abroad, and for discrediting the many false and often malicious accounts that are daily spread in other papers; and therefore it is of great importance to H.M.'s service, that it be supplied with all proper intelligence to induce the publick to have the more regard to it; and it being impossible for the writer of it to raise and keep up its credit, unless he be constantly furnished from abroad with authentick advices, from those places particularly, where H.M. has ministers or consuls residing (which was formerly regularly done, but has for some years past been too generally neglected), I must beg your Excellency will direct your secretary to collect the occurrences at the court or place where you are, and the advices that come thither from other countries, and to form a relation of such as may be proper to be made publick, to be sent every post, directed to Mr. Buckley at my office. I shall write in the same manner to all the king's ministers abroad that are in my province, as my Lord Townshend has done to those in his.[18]

Similar orders were indeed dispatched to other envoys,[19] as they had been on several occasions over the previous decade. It is clear that Professor Hatton's suggestion that a circular letter to all ambassadors abroad in 1714 constituted the last attempt to get more regular and more vital news for the *Gazette* is inaccurate.[20] What is unclear is how important these reports were.[21] It seems that the *Gazette* served as the principal source for reports in other British newspapers about ceremonial occasions in Europe, such as coronations, and about official statements or protests by other powers. Thus, most of the declarations produced by the combatant powers in the War of the Polish Succession were printed in the *Gazette*, and then in the other newspapers. As a weapon of persuasion the *Gazette* had virtually no impact, and indeed it did not appear in the *Hyp Doctor's* list of pro-government publications,[22] but it was not intended as a vehicle for debate. Government ministers felt that the importance of the newspaper was rather that it should serve as an unchallengeable statement of what had occurred, particularly in Europe.

This was felt to be of considerable importance because of the frequency with which reports were held to be influenced by foreign diplomats or opposition sympathizers. Several foreign diplomats, such as the Saxon agent Zamboni, had close links with newspaper figures, and attempts were made by diplomats to insert material that was judged helpful to their cause.[23] It was frequently alleged that a major source of foreign news was information fabricated in London and inserted into the newspapers as coming from abroad, usually from The Hague.[24] The opposition press accused the government of this tactic, and in October 1741 the London correspondent of the *York Courant* noted:

> We are this day informed in a sub-M-st-L Paper by way of Hague letter, that our merchant ships being took by Spanish privateers, and privateers by British ships, is all a joke; that this is only a trick between the Spanish and English privateers.[25]

Denying the report, the writer accused Walpole of being "the Great Patron of those Hague letters." It does appear to be the case that the place of origin of many reports were fabricated, and that a lot of this information was false.

Such information was usually intended to discredit the government's foreign policy. Thus, the summer of 1727 was marked by great uncertainty as to the preliminary articles that would lead to a congress for the pacification of Europe. Several copies of such articles were printed, some reporting that the British government was willing to concede points on such sensitive subjects as the retention of Gibraltar, and the restitution of ships seized by British privateers. The *Flying Post; or, Post Master* of 10 June reported, in an article headed "Paris June 14th N.S." [New Style]:

> We have had a very surprising copy of Preliminary Articles handed privately about there this week, they are said to be sent from London, by some Persons Disaffected to the Administration there, who had paid for their being inserted by the Writers of the *Paris à la Main,* in order to come back to you; they are exploded here as fallacious . . . the Author of the *Paris à la Main* will be severely punished.

The same newspaper, in its London section, noted that

> Several Persons concern'd in Publishing a translation of Preliminary Articles out of the *Paris Gazette à la Main* are examin'd in order to find out who were the contrivers of them; they are in several Particulars false and very scandalous; such as are highly injurious to conduct of the Hanover Allies and the British Administration; and so disadvantageous for England, that had we been constantly beaten in a Ten Years War, we might have hoped for Peace upon better Terms. They sunk our stocks to detriment of a multitude of Families; and a general uneasiness and dissatisfaction began to appear. . . .

Zamboni reported that the publication of the article led to a terrible uproar.[26] The government took the matter sufficiently seriously to make diplomatic representations in Paris:

> We hear that orders will be sent to His Excellency, Mr. Walpole, at Paris, to complain of the author of the *Paris Gazette Alamaine,* for inserting certain scandalous propositions in his Paper, and imposing them on the world for the Articles of Pacification lately signed.[27]

The Duke of Newcastle wrote to Horatio Walpole:

> We have been forced to print in the *Daily Courant,* but in an article from The Hague, so that it can't be charged upon the Government, a true translation of our Preliminary in order to remove the impression the publication of the false one may have given here; and indeed it appears from the intercepted correspondence of almost all the Foreign Ministers, that bringing of the affair of Gibraltar to the Congress was so far misunderstood, that it was necessary to set that matter right.[28]

Frequent attempts were made to control the reporting of events affecting Britain in various European newspapers, largely because, once they were reported, it was safe for British newspapers to reprint them, as long as a rider was attached to the effect that they did not believe them. Thus the *Suite des Nouvelles d'Amsterdam du 24 Octobre 1727,* in a London letter, reported a project to settle Anglo-Spanish differences by razing the fortifications of Gibraltar. Action was swift. On 18 November N.S., William Finch, the British envoy, wrote to the under secretary, Tilson, that

> The Amsterdam Gazeteer has been reprimanded for the Article relating to Gibralter. . . .[29]

In May 1728 Townshend was forced to take note of the Danish press:

> The King took notice with great surprise of the Article of the 16th of April from London, inserted in the *Copenhagen Gazette* of the 30th of that month, the contents of which are wholly false and groundless. His Majesty wonders the more that such an article should be allowed to be printed at Copenhagen, when that Court know very well the strong representation I made to Mr. de Sohlenthal upon the first news of the erection of the Altena Company. I have complained to that minister of the publishing such notorious untruths, who I doubt not will write to his Court accordingly, and you will take some proper opportunity of waiting on the Great Chancellor to let him know the evil tendency of printing such falsitys, which, if spread here by ill-disposed persons, are enough to inflame the Parliament and the nation, as if the King were indifferent in point which so nearly concerns the trade of his subjects, and you will leave it to his consideration whether such proceedings are not very unfriendly, when H.M.'s sense as to that company, must be very well understood at Copenhagen.[30]

Although the British diplomats refused to accept liability for the attacks of the British press, pleading the British law as their excuse, they believed that all foreign newspapers could be readily controlled and therefore should be.

The foreign coverage of the British press was worldwide. News was carried about South America, Africa, and the Far East. However, there were very few correspondents in those areas, and most non-European news concerned the British North American Colonies, North Africa and Persia. In the case of North America, news varied from trivial accidents to the constitutional deliberations of provincial assemblies. It was frequently reprinted from the American newspapers.[31]

North Africa, Persia, the Ottoman Empire, Russia, and, to a certain extent, the Carpathian Principalities, provided news that was recognizably different in type from that of lands nearer to Britain.[32] There was, in those reports, an element of the exotic, and at times, mysterious, similar to the impression made on the few British travelers who ventured so far, such as the diplomat George Woodward who attended the Polish Diet at Grodno in 1728.

The news from these areas presented a political world of decapitation and emasculation, massive armies endlessly contesting for mastery of the trans-Caucasian steppes and the Mesopotamian desert. Turkey, Persia, and Russia were involved in a major struggle for control of the Caucasus, the southern shores of the Caspian, and Mesopotamia. In addition, both Persia and Turkey were extremely unstable during the period. Their rebellions and conspiracies were followed with great attention in western Europe. In part, there was an element of the fantastic and incredible in the doings of potentates with such names as Tamas-Kuli Khan, the Bashaw of Bendar, the Khan of Crim Tartary, and the Hospodar of Wallachia.[33] In part, the warfare of the region was of direct political interest for western Europe. Whilst Turkey was engaged in conflict with Persia, Russia and Austria were free to play an active role in western Europe. The frequent changes of government in Persia were also marked by reporting that reflected on the nature of good government. The literary vogue for Persian Letters, displayed most effectively in the works of Montesquieu and Lyttelton, drew on a sizable body of factual reporting of Persian events. These reports created a surprising amount of interest in the country. The *St. James's Evening Post* of 17 April 1735 claimed that

> Thursday next being the anniversary of the birthday of Kouli Kan, the great deliverer of the Persian monarchy, a great number of gentlemen, friends of Universal Liberty, design to have an ox roasted whole at Mr. Jones.

With respect to the rest of Europe, coverage was fairly comprehensive. News was printed about all countries including those with which Britain had no diplomatic representation. The content of the news was also very extensive. The political plans of foreign courts were freely commented on. Military and naval developments received much coverage, and great attention was paid to the number of ships each power had at sea and under construction.

In reporting the European economies, news was devoted to "Events", and these tended to be economic legislation, such as sumptuary laws or import prohibitions, or trade. Trade received much attention. The whereabouts of British merchantmen was a staple of news, and great interest was shown in the success of other European powers trading to the Indies; the cargoes they returned with were enumerated in full, and as Dutch, or French, or British, ships moved from the Indies to Europe, their fates along the route were reported as fully as possible. A corresponding interest was shown in the movement of bullion from America to Iberia, and, as the stability of the European fiscal system depended upon these movements, much attention was, perforce, directed to hurricanes off Bermuda and peculation at Cadiz.

No newspaper specialized in financial news, but most British papers noted the prices of the French "India actions" and the successes of the Dutch lotteries. Dutch newspapers reported the prices of the British stocks with regularity. As with the French India actions, these were both a potential investment and an indicator of the stability of a fiscal and political system. There was much less British investment in Europe than European in Britain, and there is no equivalent in the British archives of the interest in British stocks shown, for example, by the Genoese and French residents.

This press coverage has not received a particularly favourable treatment from British historians. J. R. Jones in his recent work, *Britain and the World 1649–1815*, comments:

> Wilful misrepresentation of facts, sensationalism and pandering to popular prejudices, partisanship and appeals to xenophoia characterised most parliamentary debates, as did the treatment of foreign issues by the press. . . . Newspapers published a good deal of information about events in Europe, much of it biased or inaccurate.[34]

Such a view is incorrect. The press treatment was often xenophobic, and it was rare for the Catholic Church to receive favorable coverage, but the predominant impression is one of a measured treatment of European affairs that was on the whole accurate and attempted to discern the "true springs of policy". A major reason for this was that reporting of European affairs took place within a context of partisan rivalry between newspapers. Thus in 1718–20, when Britain was at war with Spain, there was a considerable difference in the coverage of this war, and of European affairs, between opposition newspapers such as the *Weekly Journal or Saturday's Post,* and ministerial papers such as the *St. James's Weekly Journal or Hanover Post-Man.* Reports were frequently challenged by rival papers, and considerable maturity was displayed by both sides in the evaluation of contradictory reports of what was a very confusing conflict. During peacetime, a further barrier to the free statement of xenophobic material was the willingness of the British government to aid in the suppression of reports that angered foreign governments or their envoys.[35] Thus, in 1735 the *Daily Post Boy* was subjected to intensive legal action as a result of its criticism of Dutch corruption. When the Swedish envoy complained in 1738 about the *Daily Post's* attack upon Swedish war supplies to Turkey, the British government responded with legal action. In 1727 the *Post Boy* was reprimanded by the government in response to Dutch pressure. The British government's attitude was best summed up by Andrew Stone, who noted in 1737:

> You know very well the unbounded license of our press; which, I think, is in no case more to be lamented, than where the persons injured are strangers to us. . . .

Thus, governmental action served to reinforce the prevalent tendency toward sober comment about European countries. Foreign envoys might, and indeed often did, bewail the liberty of the British press, but in general standards of reporting were high, and Spain and France in this period were treated with about the same degree of impartiality as that with which modern British newspapers report Russian developments.

British papers had a widely diffused readership, and it is interesting to note that cheap papers carried nearly as much foreign news as their more expensive counterparts. The headpiece of the *London Farthing Post* depicted four hawkers, the first shouting 'Great News', the second 'From Spain', the third 'From France', and the fourth 'From Holland.' There are many glimpses of foreign news being read by men of unexalted social status. The *English and French Journal* of 12 September 1723 referred to a tobacconist reading press reports about Russo-Swedish relations in a coffeehouse.[36] The *Comedian or Philosophical Enquirer* of August 1732 attacked 'these mechanical Machiavilians' (*sic*), the 'inferior tradesmen' who assiduously read the press, although it did not specifically refer to reading about foreign affairs. A year earlier the *Weekly Register* depicted the coffeehouse bore who "raves most vehemently about Kings, Parliaments, Ministers, Treaties, fortifications, trade", and a thousand other things, that "tis easier to talk of, than understand."[37]

It is impossible to say how wide this readership was, though there are a few glimpses into the interests of the readers. In 1726 the *St. James's Evening Post* reported that

> on Monday night a Barber and a Porter being discoursing of the present posture of affairs in Europe, at an alehouse in Chancery Lane, they Quarrelled; . . . the Porter stabb'd his antagonist . . . so dangerously, that his life is despair'd of.[38]

It is perhaps significant that in general when the newspapers sought to advertise their value and to obtain more readers, they stressed the quality of their foreign news. Announcing that it was to become a daily, the *Post Boy* stated in August 1728 that this new paper would include,

> as usual, the Original Hague Letter, confessedly superior to anything extant to that kind; which has never fail'd to give general satisfaction, and which can be procured by none but the proprietors of this paper.[39]

Three months later the new paper printed a letter supposedly sent in by an enthusiastic reader who claimed that

> Your Hague letter I always read with pleasure. The writer of it is an able, and, what is more, an uncommon and impartial man. His observations on the present state of affairs in Europe are curious, judicious, and useful; and his intelligence is as remarkable for veracity, as for its superiority in every other respect to anything of that kind extant.

THE

LONDON FARTHING-POST.

Great News
From France,
Spain,
And Holland.

MONDAY, *February* 5, 1739.

The Trial *of* Christopher Layer, *Eſq; at the* King's-Bench *for High Treaſon*, Nov. 21, 1722. Mich. 9 Geo. I.

AFterwards, in *June* laſt, Dr. *Murphey* carries *Lynch* to the Priſoner's Houſe, who propoſed to them to go to the *Griffin Tavern* in *Holborn*. Thither they went, and the Priſoner ſoon came to them; and you have heard in what Manner *Murphey* preſented *Lynch* to the Priſoner, as being the Gentleman he had before ſpoke to him of, and what Propoſals were made at that Meeting by the Priſoner to *Lynch*. That there was to be an Inſurrection in the Kingdom in favour of the Pretender, in which they ſhould be ſupported by a great many of the Army and the Guards, as well as by ſeveral of the Nobility and Gentry; and that he wanted a fit Perſon to take one of the firſt Steps in it by ſeizing the Perſon of ſome General, or other great Man.

It may be proper here to take notice of an Objection which was made to this, which is the very beginning of our Evidence; That *Lynch* being an abſolute Stranger to the Priſoner, it is very extraordinary that the Priſoner ſhould make a Propoſal of ſo dangerous a Nature to him at firſt ſight. But this is plainly accounted for by the Witneſs, who tells you he was intimately acquainted with Dr. *Murphey*, and *Murphey* was very intimate with and introduced him to the Priſoner, as a Friend who might be confided in. Agreeably to this you obſerve that the firſt Thing the Priſoner accoſted *Lynch* with, was that he had had ſuch ſtrong Recommendations of *Lynch*, that he was fully ſatisfied in him.

This Witneſs goes on to give you an Account that in a Day or two after, in purſuance of the Directions he had received from the Priſoner, he went to the ſame Tavern, and ſent for the Priſoner. They had ſome further Converſation about a Riſing, and the Inclination which appeared in the Nation for a Revolution. And now it was that the Priſoner informed *Lynch*, that there was a great Man at the Head of this Affair, who neither wanted Wit, Courage, or Reſolution, and would at a proper Time give *Lynch* Orders to effect ſomething conſiderable. At this Meeting the Priſoner particularly engaged *Lynch* to ſeize the Earl *Cadogan*. The Reaſon of this Attempt the Witneſs gives you, that it was in order to diſcourage the King's Party, and animate the Pretender's. And, Gentlemen, the Meaning of this is plain and obvious; for if an Inſurrection was begun, what could be more likely to create a Confuſion in the Army, and diſpoſe the Soldiers to revolt, which appears to have been a main Part of this Deſign, than the ſeizing of their General?

There were ſeveral other Meetings both before and after the Priſoner's going into the Country, where the Witneſs told you he had ſtaid ſixteen or ſeventeen Days. At thoſe Meetings they diſcourſed concerning the Conſpiracy; and at one of them it is remarkable the Priſoner told *Lynch* that if they once made a beginning here, they ſhould want no Aſſiſtance from Abroad. And at laſt *Lynch* tells you, that he being under Neceſſities, expreſſing great Uneaſineſs at the Delay of the Project, and, as I remember, talking of going beyond Sea, the Priſoner actually advanced to him a Sum of Money, no leſs than eight or ten Guineas at different Times, in order to engage him to ſtay in *England*, and to aſſiſt in the intended Deſign of a Revolution. This is one Proof of the Overt-Act laid in the Indictment of liſting Men.

(*To be continued.*)

FOREIGN AFFAIRS.

Madrid, Jan. 19.

BY the new Convention enter'd into between the King of Great Britain and his Catholick Majeſty, the latter of theſe Princes, amongſt other Things, promiſes to pay in four Months after the Ratification thereof, the Sum therein ſtipulated for indemnifying the Britiſh Merchants for the Damages they have ſuſtained by the Capture of their Ships; and in order to gain time, the Courier diſpatch'd the 14th to Don Thomas Geraldino, carried the Ratification of his Catholick Majeſty, that the Exchange might be immediately made in London. The King of Spain refus'd to ratify the Convention, ſign'd the 9th of September at London, becauſe of the Article therein relating to the South-Sea Company; every Thing that relates to that Company being to be diſcuſs'd and determin'd in a private Negociation.

Letters from Lisbon inform us, that Magnificence in Furniture and Dreſs prevails there to as high a Degree as at the Court of Spain, particularly upon the Anniverſary-Days of the Royal Family; and that Cardinal de Motta and Silva is dangerouſly ill.

PORT NEWS.

Southampton, Feb. 1. Arrived Charming Betty, and Mary, from Jerzey; Willing Endeavour, from Marabella; Helena, of this Place, from Lisbon; Four Brothers, and Saliſbury, from Roan. Wind S. W.

Deal, Feb. 1. The Ships remain as per laſt. Came down ſince and remains, the Mary-Anne, Cuite, for Lisbon. Arriv'd the St. Peter, Emptage, from Lisbon; the Mary, Watſon, from Maryland. Wind W. S. W.

The Sally, Webb, from Gibraltar, bound to London, is forc'd into Briſtol Channel.

The *London Farthing Post*, Monday, 5 February 1739 (Guildhall Library).

In fact, the paper's circulation appears to have suffered in this period,[40] but other newspapers clearly regarded reports about foreign affairs as of the greatest importance to their circulation. The first number of the *British Observator,* a London paper founded in 1733, proclaimed,

> Our constant care shall be to procure the best foreign advices, to digest them into a proper method, and to cloath them with a convenient stile.

Twenty-four years later, the first number of another London paper, the *London Chronicle: or, Universal Evening Post,* noted:

> The first demand made by the reader of a Journal is, that he should find accurate account of foreign transactions and domestick incidents.

The volume of foreign material was, as has been suggested, maintained at a very high level. Assessing the contents of the previous day's papers the author of the *Grub Street Journal* of 12 December 1734 noted that

> In the *Daily Advertiser* . . . there are but eleven lines of domestic news; in the *Courant* and *Daily Post Boy* not one.

This may have been too much for some readers who, as the newspaper proprietors recurrently discovered, had very miscellaneous interests.[41] However, the inclusion of such a mass of foreign news suggested a consistently high level of involvement and it seems unlikely that the proprietors would have prejudiced their sales by continuing to offer unwelcome coverage. A reader of the *Newcastle Courant* in 1733 may have indicated the inclinations of a large cross section of his fellows when he urged the author to

> By no means let a rapsody upon the Test Act, justle [*sic*] the Emperor and his dominions out of your comment.[42]

A certain amount of press interest in foreign affairs clearly arose from domestic political circumstances and the general unpopularity of Walpole's foreign policy. The progovernment *London Journal* referred in 1731 to,

> the close alliance with France, which the writers against the court own to be the chief cause of their Papers, and that which gave rise to their numerous productions.[43]

Whether these papers had any direct influence upon the "close alliance with France" or other elements of policy is impossible to establish. Until 1733 the opposition to Walpole, both within and without the ministry, concentrated its attacks upon issues of foreign policy. The interminable negotiations of the 1720s, the indecisive and expensive armaments of the late 1720s, the confrontation with Britain's old ally Austria, the alliance with the former enemy France, and the supposed challenge to national interests presented by the government's alleged failure to stand firm over Spanish depredations, Gibraltar, and French works at Dunkirk, all provided issues upon which the government could be challenged in Parliament, Council Chamber, and in the broader area of public opinion. The opposition publicists displayed great skill in selecting those foreign policy issues in which the government could be made to appear weak, unsuccessful, foolish, and dishonest. Bolingbroke's knowledge of foreign affairs might be held to account for the particularly sophisticated handling of foreign policy in the *Craftsman,* but in fact it did not prove to be necessary to have any deep knowledge of foreign affairs in order to attack the obviously vulnerable foreign policy of the government.

The government press argued that these attacks, and the more general feature of press criticism of the government, harmed British foreign policy by presenting a picture of a divided and disloyal nation. It is certainly the case that the leading opposition newpapers were regularly forwarded to their courts by several foreign diplomats.[44] There is a large collection of such newspapers in the French archives.[45] Some foreign diplomats cited savage press attacks upon the ministry as partial evidence of its impending fall, and this was particularly marked at the time of the Excise Crisis, when envoys such as the French Chavigny and the Sardinian Ossorio believed that civil war was imminent.[46] It is possibly the case that foreign governments misunderstood the nature of British politics, and underrated the country's stability.[47] The standard conception of Britain, a conception partly propagated by Whig publicists, was of a state responsive to the will of a wide political nation. This was seen by some as conducive to a state of instability, of a government dependent on the popular whim. Whether regarded as praiseworthy or reprehensible, the role of public opinion was very difficult to measure in eighteenth-century England. It was appreciated that the press did not represent too accurate a measurement, but in the absence of anything else (and addresses are notoriously easy to manipulate), a lot of attention was perforce devoted to it.

Through their interception of the mails, the government was well aware of the importance attached by foreign envoys to the press,[48] and throughout Europe diplomats were frequently provoked to remonstration and action by news reports.[49] Responses to such reports varied. Some politicians were very skeptical. Molesworth, the British envoy to the King of Sardinia, was startled by a report in the supplement of the *Amsterdam Gazette* about Sardinian intentions toward their Protestant minority. He demanded an explanation from the Sardinian foreign minister, who,

> told me he did not doubt but I understood the world better than to give credit to a newspaper.[50]

Cardinal Fleury, the French prime minister was, on the other hand, deeply disturbed in the summer of 1733 by press reports about British diplomatic intentions, and questioned the British envoy very actively on the matter.[51]

In general, however, it is possible to state that in the Walpole period, foreign powers were not usually guided in their actions by reading British newspapers, however much they may have been influenced in their perception of British politics by the existence of a vocal press. The British government was not dependent for information or ideas upon the press, but it had to take into account the possibility of the press being used to mount a campaign whose consequences might inconvenience them in Parliament. News items which suggested that British policy was dependent upon foreign influence were of particular danger. The press could suggest that British policy was dictated by Hanover or France. In October 1729 the *Original Mercury* in York produced the sort of report that was most unwelcome in the period before the opening of Parliament:

> The *Utrecht Gazette* of the 15th instant, N.S. in the article from Paris of the 8th, says, it was reported there, that Cardinal de Fleury had declared to the Plenipotentiaries of England, that the most Christian King would regard as an open rupture, any attempt that should be made against the Gallions, or to hinder their return into Spain.[52]

Ultimately the attempt to use issues of foreign policy to precipitate the fall of Walpole failed. The major attacks mounted upon the French alliance in 1728–31, and upon Britain's Spanish policy in 1738–39, did not provoke the fall of the minister. However, it could be argued that Walpole's awareness of the political vulnerability and unpopularity of the French alliance led to his decision in 1730 to break with France. To ascribe such a decision to the press would be inaccurate. The press was only the most obvious method by which public opinion could be both manipulated and expressed.[53] Public opinion was efficacious usually only if it could be expressed in Parliament, and foreign policy was, with the army, the sphere in which the monarch proved to be most impervious to outside pressure. It was only when Britain drifted into war with Spain and France that debate over foreign policy became of major importance, particularly in the vexed question of "continental" versus "oceanic" policies. But the press of the 1720s and 1730s, by its interest both in coverage of foreign events and in diplomatic activity, had helped to develop among the political nation a strong interest in and knowledge of the outside world. Such a development was not solely due to the press, nor did it begin in the Walpolean period. The experience of two major European wars in which Britain had been directly involved, and the linkage between these wars and the strife of British political groups, had done much to develop an interest both in foreign affairs and in foreign policy, and this interest was encouraged by the accession of continental princes to the throne of Britain. The role of the press was in spreading these interests throughout Britain and in sustaining them in the period of relative peace that followed the accession of George I. The hyperbolic claims of the *Flying Post; or, Post Master* of July 1729 cannot be dismissed:

> . . . all the three kingdoms have reason to rejoyce that the darkest corners are illuminated with the works of celebrated news writers, and that there is no part so obscure, but every week or oftener, it is illustrated with some rays of these shining lights.[54]

Thanks to the press the diaries of Derbyshire ministers and Somerset doctors could include references to European affairs,[55] and the political nation became fairly well informed about the affairs of the greater world and the issues of British foreign policy. If this process did not regularly bear political fruit it was nevertheless of the greatest importance in the education of the political nation. Britons may have been xenophobic but they were increasingly well-informed xenophobes.

4
Newspapers and Industry: The Export of Wool Controversy in the 1780s

Richard Wilson

Eighteenth-century provincial newspapers are, at first sight, a marvelous source for the economic historian interested in the growth of those business communities that created the Industrial Revolution. Although, like all newspapers, they were of an essentially ephemeral nature, destroyed or used for some other purpose each week, you can be confident that, for whichever one you are looking at, the businessman of the region in which it circulated, whether merchant, small master, or shopkeeper, read and discussed their contents at home or in his inn, coffeehouse, or club. This in itself makes them a unique type of record and endows them with an unparalleled immediacy. But at the same time you are uncertain what these men, poring laboriously over the minute print, made of the digest of foreign, London, and local news and how it influenced the conduct of their affairs. In this respect we know much more about how business communities–whether in an enfranchised borough or the unrepresented towns of the Midlands and North–developed a political consciousness in the great national contentious issues of the eighteenth century–the conduct of war, the Jacobite rebellions, the Wilkite Crisis, the American and French Revolutions, and the local working out of the perpetual puzzle of patronage and religion.[1]

But when you study in detail the eighteenth-century provincial press to provide a guide to the economic and social evolution of key towns and industrial areas, the newspapers are less helpful. This stems from the nature of the newspapers themselves and the ways in which these big

I am most grateful for the help I have received in writing this chapter. John Styles gave good advice, suggested additional sources and, not least, read through and commented on this essay. Harold Carter kindly lent me his printout of Sir Joseph Banks's papers in the Sutro Library, California (see note 15 below) so that I was able to peruse them in the comfort of my study rather than attempt to read a score of microfilms in the Natural History Museum Library, and, as will be seen, I also made great use of his invaluable compilation, *The sheep and wool correspondence of Sir Joseph Banks.* Mrs Jane Fiske, a research student of the University of East Anglia, working on the diaries of James Oakes of Bury St. Edmunds, provided me with information about Oakes's activities and the Suffolk newspapers.

subjects were covered.[2] For eighteenth century newspapers carried, almost without exception, no editorials, and they never presented, or even briefly focused upon a detailed view of the state of an industry or a town's prosperity, or commented on social developments in the ways newspapers did after 1830. Especially in the golden age of the provincial press, between 1870 and 1914, these themes were handled superbly, in serious and extended reporting. However, any view of an industry or community derived from the Georgian provincial press has to be built up slowly by a painter's *pointillist* technique. Scores of these studies use this method, selecting advertisements and making sense of succinct stray references, and all their compilers would admit the limitations of these sources in their labors. The historian of the eighteenth-century provincial press concluded, "Reports of such major developments in agriculture as the rotation of crops, improved techniques of farming and breeding, enclosures, and all those advances which history textbooks dignify with the proud title of 'The Agrarian Revolution' are not to be found. Nor would one guess, from reading these newspapers, that anything in the nature of an 'Industrial Revolution' was taking place. The local section of a country newspaper was brief and extremely uninteresting."[3]

G. A. Cranfield was writing about the pre-1760 period and it would be unwise to apply his conclusions too rigidly to the rest of the century. In a sense his views express historians' frustrations two hundred years later. In fact the newspapers gradually filled out. As roads were turnpiked, and the postal service transformed by Ralph Allen, they provided a more up-to-date service of news, gossip, and advertisements. Their numbers increased. By 1770 there were four London dailies and eight or nine triweekly evening papers. In the provinces there had been a similar expansion. Between 1714 and 1725 twenty-two provincial papers were founded; by 1753 there were thirty-two; and by 1782 around fifty. There was an exchange of newspapers between the metropolis and provinces, with the balance of trade very much in favor of the former. As the system of distribution improved, however, some of the provincial press had circulations as high as two thousand weekly. The majority were confined before 1770 to a few hundred, but in most cases they were increasing. What we know even less about is their readership outside London. But we should not suppose that they were purchased solely by the landowners, clergy, merchants, and professional men of any district. In every county town and industrial and market center newspapers were to be found in the inns, coffee houses, and clubs, which were ubiquitous in Georgian England. There, as John Brewer has shown, after the 1760s an increasingly wide readership feasted themselves upon the accounts of George III and his ministers, Wilkes, and the control of our American colonies. Provincial papers had always supplied a political diet, hashed up by country printers from the London press. When the local press was able to attract a more socially extensive readership after the 1760s it could improve its fare. This also reflected the fact that as country newspapers became more numerous their circulations were restricted to smaller, and therefore more economically homogeneous, territories. To expand readership they had to include more local news and material about the trade and agriculture of their regions. As towns like Birmingham, Liverpool, Leeds, and Newcastle hummed with activity, their newspapers began to comment upon it and inculcate a fierce local pride.

Printers canalized these various changes in three main ways. Firstly, they were able to expand the amount of advertising, some much more successfully than others. Of course, as every student of the eighteenth-century press knows, many advertisements concerned runaway apprentices and stolen horses. Yet most were about the sale and letting of land and houses. Property provided essential collateral for loans, marriage portions, and settlements, and was still the basic outlet for that minority of the population which accumulated savings. Although these advertisements probably only record a minority of transactions involving property—for most were of a private nature in the eighteenth century—the newspapers became increasingly crammed with them. Land and investment property were of central interest to businessmen as much as the landed interest. After 1760 a wider range of advertisement begins to appear in the provincial press—notices for journeymen about supplies of coal, timber, bricks and lime, wine and beer; upholsterers and shopkeepers whetting the appetites of a growing consumer class; attorneys seeking outlets for money placed with them. Their variety delights the historian—professional and amateur alike.

Secondly, there was an extension after 1760 of the services which the newspapers had always provided often in an incomplete fashion, for merchants and shopkeepers. These were the lists of bankrupts, prices of stock, the assize of bread, corn and malt prices (local and at Mark Lane), coal prices, shipping news and, by the late eighteenth century, London prices of meat, leather, tallow, and wines. Some newspapers gave this material in greater detail than others, and it is clear that everywhere traders and manufacturers were relying increasingly on this information and the snippets of news that printers picked up from the London press about trade in the metropolis and provinces. Yet, although these services were improving—and they now provide historians with invaluable price data and comments about the state of trade—businessmen still relied on the news and specialized information they picked up in the markets and, above all, in correspondence with their suppliers, agents, and customers. Moreover, some prices, such as sorted wool, were so complex that the newspapers could not handle them satisfactorily. And not until much later, not really until the great age of the trade journal in the second half of the nineteenth century, did businessmen obtain in printed form the detailed comment, predictions, and annual résumés of prices and trade which were essential for their calculations. For before 1790 the provincial printer had his limitations when it came to offering a more sophisticated business commentary. In general he had poor access to information, lacked expert reporters, had to carry out general printing tasks, and was often stationer and dealer as well.

The third direction in which newspapers underwent a transformation for the business community was the way in which for the first time in any extended detail they began to focus opinion about politico-business issues. Disputes with our American colonies were crucial here. The repeal of the Stamp Act campaign in the 1760s, the conduct of the War after 1775, and its acute economic effects sparked off a whole range of criticisms from many different interest groups, not only about the military and economic strategy of Lord North's ministry, but also a more fundamental questioning of the entire political system. The newspaper, which in the provinces were, in many ways, still in their infancy until the 1760s, fed on these great issues to gain maturity. To give this chapter focus, I have chosen one of these debates—the controversy about the export of wool in the 1780s—to demonstrate the increasingly important role of the press, both in London and the provinces, in a key issue, and show the ways in which the warring factions of clothiers, merchants, and wool staplers on the one hand, and landowners and wool growers on the other, used the press to conduct a spirited national campaign in 1781–82 and 1786–88.

I

Although the demand for a limited exportation of combing wool from the Lincolnshire growers blew up unexpectedly in the summer of 1781, the history of the conflict between the wool growers and cloth manufacturers was a long and complex one. It stemmed from Tudor and Stuart mercantilist legislation, which totally banned the export of all English wool. Latent distrust between the two chief interest groups in the country's leading industry was easily fanned, especially by extremes of wool prices. When they were low the growers bitterly lamented the manufacturers' "monopoly."[4] There were rumblings in 1710, in the 1730s and early 1740s, and in the 1760s. In all these disputes it is clear the provincial press played little part. The controversy about the false winding of wool and marking of sheep with pitch and tar in 1752 is instructive because it was in many ways a full-scale rehearsal of the better-known struggles of the 1780s. Yet it reveals that the clash between the manufacturers and growers was organized on traditional lines, with the nascent provincial press playing a minimal role. It provides a marked contrast to the style of campaigning thirty years later.

Early in 1752, the House of Commons was inundated with petitions from no fewer than thirty-six centers of cloth and stuff manufacture throughout England, claiming that in the past ten years sheep, especially on the commons and open fields, were becoming more and more grossly marked with pitch and tar.[5] As the graziers soon pointed out, the controversy rested on the manufacturers' concern at the sharp advance of wool prices—some 70 percent it was claimed—in the past seven years. Nevertheless, the clothiers were able to demonstrate that daubing sheep to distinguish ownership meant, for them, heavy cleaning costs and dyeing problems. And what was worse was that the growers, in spite of legislation to the contrary, were "false" winding their fleeces by including, "cotts . . . large lumps of Dirt, which hang upon the skirts of the Fleece, Skin-Wool of very inferior Quality, Mort-Wool, coarse Shank Locks, Tail-Locks and several Sort of Refuse, Dirt and sometimes Sand," when they made up their fleeces into packs of 240 lb. weight. The problem was particularly bad in the wrapping of packs of long combing wool produced largely in Lincolnshire. The Yorkshire stuff makers reckoned—making those dubious calculations which all observers of the great wool textile industry delighted in—that £425,000 was lost to the nation by these malpractices. As was usual, problems in the wool textile industry were treated extremely seriously by Parliament. The committee of the House of Commons which examined the petitions from Leeds and Norwich, the two chief centers of manufacture in 1752, took evidence from stuff manufacturers, looked at some fleeces, and concluded that a strengthening of the laws was necessary.[6] A bill was quickly prepared after consultations with M.P.s and, above all, Lord Rockingham. The Yorkshire manufacturers, who were most active in the business, hoped to rush it through Parliament before the Lincolnshire landowners and growers organized their opposition. But the latter were not so somnolent as the manufacturers supposed. At first, they pressed delaying tactics both in the Committee and the House, and on 14 and 16 February the Lincolnshire M.P.s went on the offensive and argued successfully (by 86 votes to 79) that the existing laws, dating from Henry VIII's reign, were sufficient, and that the whole thing was an elaborate conspiracy of the manufacturers—"a collected Body put together by the Circular Letters sent from London with a Design to oppress the Wool Growers"—to beat down the price of wool.[7] David Stanfield, a Halifax manufacturer closely involved in directing the clothiers' case in London, concluded, "[I] shall only observe that by the Load of the Scotch members and those out of the West of England who look with a jealous Eye on the rising Manufacture of Yorkshire we were outvoted but I cannot say outdone in Argument."[8] Lord Rockingham, with an eye cocked at his own political interest, encouraged the Yorkshire manufacturers to issue a challenge to the Lincolnshire M.P.s to meet them the first day of the next session. But reluctantly the manufacturers had to admit defeat.

What is interesting in this discussion is that the press played so little part. The correspondence of the West Riding campaign survives, and it is clear that it was conducted on the traditional lines. Petitions were taken round the market centers, M.P.s canvassed, and a handful of the most competent merchants and manufacturers went up to London to push the Bill, lobby more members of both Houses, and give evidence before the Commons' committee. There were six weeks of feverish activity after the Yorkshireman arrived in London on 8 January. Other manufacturing centers operated similarly, some far more supinely than others, and an attempt was made to provide information and coordinate action by correspondence. It was in this area that the press later performed its most significant role. All, except the few principals closely involved in 1752, knew little of what was going on beyond secondhand knowledge gained from market gossip. Attempts to secure legislation were made by a few committed leaders in any industry. The rank and file remained largely ignorant of events and issues. It is significant that not a mention of the controversy appeared in the *York Courant,* the newspaper with the widest circulation in the North and which served the important West Riding manufacturing region. The *Leeds Mercury* has not survived for 1752. It was probably ailing, for the *Leeds Intelligencer* was founded two years later to provide a better news service for the textile area. And the Lincolnshire landowners and wool growers were little better aided. Of course, the more active amongst the former saw the London papers, although their digest of parliamentary affairs before 1772, especially about regional economic matters, was cursory. Otherwise they had to rely on the *Stamford Mercury,* which in 1752 provided no more adequate coverage of the controversy than the *York Courant* did for the Leeds and Halifax merchants and stuffmakers.

II

There were three events in the late 1760s and 1770s which transformed both the London and provincial press: George III's relations with his ministers, the Wilkite Crisis, and the breakaway of the American colonies. The London press was totally reinvigorated by the Wilkes affair. At its core was the struggle between the City, the tap root of Wilkes's support, and Parliament. For three years from 1768 it dominated the London press, and some of the bigger issues like the role of the executive in the constitution, as well as its constant scurrilous asides, spilled over into the provinces to give its press a new focus in political commentary.[9] Although the Wilkes crisis had links with the rebellion in America, it was later completely overshadowed by the outbreak of hostilities in the colonies in 1775. From the outset many trading interests, with proven connections in this the fastest growing sector of our foreign trade in the third quarter of the eighteenth century, were deeply divided about the causes and necessity of military action. Their profound misgivings were further confined by the course and misconduct of the war. In one important manufacturing area, the West Riding of Yorkshire, which was very badly hit by the collapse of exports of cheap cloth to America, the district's newspapers achieved maturity in the crisis. Before 1775, the *Leeds Intelligencer* (founded in 1754) and the second *Leeds Mercury* (1767) had both been overshadowed even in the industrial centers of the wool textile region by the *York Courant*. With the beginning of the war the two Leeds newspapers acquired a sharper political involvement. The *Intelligencer* spelled out, with increasingly lack of conviction, the Corporation's official line of government support, whilst the *Mercury* propounded the views of those merchants, often Dissenters, who pressed for peace, stressing the incompetence of the government's handling of the war, the depth of the economic recession at home, and the unconstitutional nature of the Volunteer Corps. There was a regular and lively correspondence in both newspapers which adequately reflected, for the first time, the different views of the commercial classes in West Yorkshire, although it had been foreshadowed to a degree during the Wilkes affair and the controversy over the Stamp Act and other economic conflicts with America in the 1760s.[10]

It was the mishandling of the American War that was responsible for the famous Yorkshire Association. Political historians have paid too much attention to the political implications of its petitions—placing the movement in the slow unfurling of the reform flag—and the association's struggle with the Rockingham interests in Yorkshire.[11] For underneath, the association had great support from the county's landowners and the West Riding's important commercial and manufacturing communities. It was a powerful and unique alliance forged by the mismanagement and disastrous economic consequences of the American War. A letter in the *Leeds Mercury*, stating the necessity for a county meeting in December 1779, caught the frustration of both the landed and commercial sectors with the government: "the Empire dismembered; Trade ebbing fast away, never (it is feared) to flow back into its former prosperous channels; Landed Property reduced one-third of its Value, with the universal scarcity of money everywhere complained of and everywhere felt."[12] The association had its origins in the worst recession of the eighteenth century.[13] Its development and the extension of its aims in London and those counties that quickly followed its lead in petitioning for "economical reform," triennial Parliaments, and an additional hundred knights for the shires to restore the 'purity' of the legislature, depended a good deal upon the London and provincial press.

The ideas behind the Rev. Christopher Wyvill's Yorkshire Association were part of a wider movement in the 1770s to achieve various stated aims by extraparliamentary means.[14] Its most popular form was the Volunteer movement. Wyvill's scheme for moderate political reform went beyond this into the much more constitutionally dangerous territory of political engagements, yet like the others it depended for its very existence upon widespread publicity about aims, subscriptions and members. It was in these areas that the newspapers played a new and vital role. They allowed the Yorkshire Association to achieve the status of a seminational political organization. Whereas legislation for the prosecution of the marking of sheep with pitch and tar in 1752 was hamstrung by the inability of a handful of interested West Riding manufacturers to whip up sufficient interest amongst the generality of their brethren in the other centers of production, in 1779–84 the aims of the Yorkshire Association were powered by a constant fuel of notices, subscription lists, resolutions of the committee in York and the delegates in London, and above all letters in the press. When Wyvill mounted a campaign of petitions during each parliamentary session after 1780 he initiated the procedure by asking the clerk of his great Yorkshire committee to dispatch a volley of letters and notices to the York, Leeds, and London newspapers, criticizing the role of the government and pressing for moderate reform to rekindle interest in the affairs of the association.[15]

It is necessary to stress the role of the Yorkshire Association as a background to the export of wool because it is clear that many of the procedures and the economic causes of the two movements share a good deal in common. The lessons that the committee members of the association had learnt about the use of the press, something very recent in the provinces, were not lost on the merchants and manufacturers of the West Riding and Norwich and, to a much lesser extent, the Lincolnshire landowners, when they became embroiled in the great issue about the export of wool in 1781.

III

Although the news of the disastrous surrender at Yorktown did not reach England until November 1781, it was already clear, by late summer, that the British government's prosecution of the war in America was going extremely badly. But landowners and wool growers, especially in the long combing-wool areas of which Lincolnshire was much the most important, were far less preoccupied with events across the Atlantic than with the collapse of wool prices. Since 1776 they had slid downward. In the summer of 1781 they plummeted. Fleeces, some as many as three years old and fast deteriorating, piled high in the farmers' barns and wool buyers' warehouses.[16] Landowners faced the prospect of large arrears in rents and all were worried that the value of land had declined by as much as one-third over the past five years.

On 6 September the Lincolnshire landowners met and, in a somewhat leisurely way, called a county meeting at the White Hart in Lincoln on the last day of October. That autumn day the city's inns were crowded with the carriages and horses of the Lincolnshire gentry and graziers. Already there had been some provisional organization of opinion that reflected even in remotest rural Lincolnshire the structure of the association movement. A petition was on the table from those growers who had met five days previously at Thetford, and eighty-one delegates, nominated mostly from the marshland parishes, were prominent at the meeting. The resolutions which were passed seemed moderate enough. A large and overselect committee of peers, M.P.s, landowners, and gentlemen was formed to seek ways of introducing "temporary" legislation to allow a limited export of long wool and the prohibition of Irish yarn imports.[17] The committee was asked to report on their progress at the end of the parliamentary Christmas recess at the St. Alban's Tavern. Copies of the resolution were dispatched to M.P.s in the other—chiefly East and South Midland—counties which were long wool-producing areas and to the London and Stamford newspapers. Then the newspapers suggest a curious lull in activity in Lincolnshire itself. It is clear from the extensive papers of Sir Joseph Banks, the president of the Royal Society and himself a considerable Lincolnshire landowner, recently but deeply committed to the wool question, that action depended a good deal upon himself, Henry Pacey, the Recorder of Boston, and another great landowner, Charles Chaplin of Tathwell.[18] They organized the distribution of pamphlets and the collection of data about prices and the amount of wool clip that was unsold. The facts were chilling. Moreover, they were invariably underestimated because the cautious Lincolnshire farmers were hesitant to supply any information that might be used against them by their landlords and the tithe-owners. In the Holland division 83,610 tods (of 28 lb each) were unsold; in nine parishes in Kesteven, 45,688 tods. Prices of Wold, High Walk, and above all Marsh wool (the longest staple) had fallen by over 50 percent in some instances since the 1776–77 season,[19] the latter from 18*s.* to 8*s.* for some Lindsey farmers.

But the Lincolnshire committee made such little concerted use of the newspapers that some graziers were convinced they were doing nothing. Only two letters appeared in the *Stamford Mercury*.[20] One decried the leisurely collection of statistics from the graziers and the tardy parliamentary progress of their petition, the other suggested that only the marshland graziers were deeply involved, and that there were divisions between owners and farmers and between the upland and lowland districts. Otherwise the *Stamford Mercury*—there was no Lincoln paper at this period; the *York Courant* and Leeds newspapers circulated on the northern fringes of the county—covered this vital issue very inadequately. It carried no editorial comment and provided an incomplete account of the subsequent meetings in London in early 1782. Parsons in far-flung Lincolnshire parishes would not have known that the wool export business was a subject of key interest from reading the *Stamford Mercury* in the winter of 1781–82. Of course, a great deal of information circulated at markets, both by word of mouth and handbills. The world of the Lincolnshire landowners and farmers was an old-fashioned and intimate one. And the gentry themselves read the pamphlets of Sir John Dalrymple, the writings of Thomas Pownell, Dean Tucker, and especially the Rev. John Smith, advocating a limited export of wool.[21] Sir Joseph Banks ordered down from London several hundred of the two editions of Dalrymple's pamphlet—*The Question Considered, Whether Wool Should be allowed to be Exported, when the Price is Low at Home, on paying Duty to the Public?*[22]—to be distributed in Lincoln, Louth, and Boston. The pamphlets written by a Scottish judge were not the best statement of the Lincolnshire case; and it is doubtful that they made much impact on the Lincolnshire graziers. Yet Sir Joseph and Charles Chaplin were both convinced of their efficacy. In February 1782 the latter wrote to Sir Joseph, "What is Huntingdon, Leicestershire, Derbyshire, Nottinghamshire etc. about that they do not join us? I wish some Pamphlets of each sort were sent down to some leading Men in every long wool growing County, as nothing wou'd be more likely to rouse them."[23] Both highly articulate, they were perhaps unaware that their landowning brethren, and even more the Lincolnshire farmers, were less adept than themselves at digesting this complex issue from Dalrymple's dry pamphlets. Certainly it is strange that Sir Joseph, who very clearly realized the uses of newspapers in focusing political and economic campaigns, for his papers contain countless press cuttings from the London, Yorkshire, and other newspapers on the wool question throughout the 1780s, did not get his lieutenants in Lincolnshire to make better use of them in summarizing Dalrymple's pamphlets and providing regular progress reports of the graziers' case. His correspondence frequently refers to the impact of a pamphlet or letter in the press, but at least in 1781–82—this was less true of the 1786–88 campaign—he seems to have despaired of ever shaking the Lincolnshire landowners from their lethargy. He wrote in 1782 of the landowners "battening at home in Idleness and apathy," and in 1787, when he wrote a pamphlet on the export of wool, he significantly recalled a homely maxim of Sir Robert Walpole who "likened the Country gentlemen to their sheep. Like them sayde he they layd down to be Taxd at Quietly and complain no more than they when they are shorn but touch only a bristle of the hog of Trade and he is sure to squeal and bite till all his neighbours believe him ill treated whether in reality he is or not."[24] The dilatoriness of the Lincolnshire landowners was a principal factor in their failure even to present an effective petition in 1782. The poor coverage of events and issues in the *Stamford Mercury* and other newspapers was a symptom but not a cause of their defeat. As Banks hinted in his quotation of Walpole's parable, the merchants and manufacturers were far better organized.

IV

Those in the West Riding were immediately alert to schemes of the Lincolnshire growers. "A committee of principal tradesmen of this country" attended a meeting on 30 October in Lincoln, and copies of the resolutions with the manufacturers' adverse comments on them were circulated.[25]

From the outset a more extensive use of the press was made. Some of the correspondence was quite independent of the manufacturers' organization. A letter of a Heptonstall stuff maker, Theophilus Sutcliffe, reducing the whole affair to a biblical simplicity, fell into this category. In his letter "To Lincolnshire Farmers" he reminded them that the Yorkshire clothiers "eat a vast sight of your large boned Lincolnshire mutton which helps you to pay rent as well as your wool." The American war was the cause of the low price of wool. The only solution was peace. In the meantime the Lincolnshire grazier should live more abstemiously like the West Riding clothiers: "Be content with milk, potatoes and a little of your excellent bacon and leave off roast beef, plum-pudding and strong beer only for three or four years."[26] Another correspondent asserted that Lincolnshiremen behaved "like Nabobs." He pointed out that the manufacturers were both more numerous and very much worse off.[27] These sentiments echoed the practical views of the Yorkshire clothiers.

The more urbane and "respectable" merchants met at the New Inn in Leeds, on the first day of December, to consider the resolutions of the Lincolnshire wool growers.[28] They called for a general meeting of both merchants and manufacturers throughout the West Riding under the chairmanship of the mayor of Leeds, William Smithson. Notices advertising the meeting were placed in the York, Manchester, and Leeds papers, and the resolutions agreed on 19 December were ordered to be printed in "such of the public papers the Committee thinks proper." They maintained that the export of wool and the repeal of the import of Irish yarns—in fact, little used in the West Riding—would be highly injurious to trade, that the merchants and manufacturers must write and correspond with the other textile regions, and that "the Landed Interest be applied to for their Assurances and Support," for the meeting was convinced that its prosperity depended upon the healthy state of industry.[29] Repeal the export laws and the landowners would be as much injured as the manufacturers themselves.

This was the opening salvo of the West Riding merchants' and clothiers' case. The next few weeks revealed the extent to which they expanded and coordinated their campaign by the use of the newspapers. They did so in three ways. The first was the provision of information to demonstrate that the American war was hitting them as badly as the Lincolnshire growers. Many of the facts were admitted *pari passu.* Readers could form their own view when they read the swollen lists of Yorkshire bankrupts and perused the sales of their property and possessions. They were also pointed to the figures for cloth exports and cloths milled in the West Riding. The position of worsted stuffs, not included in the cloth figures, was in fact far worse, for it depended more on exports. These were badly hit by the closure of the Spanish and Dutch as well as the American markets, and the government's inability to provide adequate convoys barred effective trade with Italy.[30] The three main markets for stuffs were virtually closed after the autumn of

1779. The Yorkshiremen were also careful to show how the processes of manufacture and sale multiplied five to six times the original value of the raw wool, and the Norwich manufacturers, making the finest of all stuffs, reckoned it was ten times. Diminished cloth output and increased unemployment were inevitable consequences of the Lincolnshire graziers' demands. If Parliament agreed to these, the landowners throughout the kingdom would be faced with horrendous poor rates. And in the background of the controversy were fears about the spectacular advance of the cotton industry in the 1770s. Even the Lincolnshire landowners were well aware that the demand for worsted stuffs used in clothing, especially the lining of clothing, and for window and bed curtains, and hangings was dwindling in the face of cotton's competition, although Sir Joseph Banks, arguing in a way which suggests he was an early precursor of that other Lincolnshire political economist, Margaret Thatcher, drew very different conclusions from the Yorkshiremen. He reasoned that cotton thrived on a totally imported raw material, whereas the wool textile industry ailed because it had grown lethargic upon the monopoly of the British wool supply.[31] It needed this prop kicked from under it.

Having established the facts of their own position,[32] the Yorkshiremen attacked the graziers' own case through the press. They did so not in theoretical arguments about monopoly and economic policy. Throughout they assumed that England had benefited enormously in prosperity since an ever-wise Parliament had conferred the monopoly of the country's wool supply upon its greatest industry. It was a trust that the industry had repaid handsomely to the great benefit of the whole country. Nor was there any discussion about the point, made over thirty years earlier by John Smith, that the continental producers had no need of English combing wool to mix with their own before they could produce comparable stuffs. All manufacturers clung blindly to this fiction throughout the 1780s. The attack was on a far lower plane than either monopolies or Smith's arguments. The difficulties of the Lincolnshire graziers were the consequence of their own folly and greed. They had only themselves to blame. Enclosure had meant an improvement in feed and this together with the graziers' experiments in interbreeding meant that fleeces were longer, heavier, and coarser. Whereas, within living memory, 8–10 fleeces had formed a tod of 28 lb, now it composed 3–4 and from the richest marches 2–3 only.[33] Wool was so coarse that it not unnaturally commanded a lower price, especially since output had risen sharply. In no other area producing combing wool had fleeces deteriorated to this extent. The example of Richard Brumfit of Leeds was cited. He was employing weavers, who formerly made "drawboys," to make carpets from the coarse wool. In reality he prospered, as did other carpet manufacturers in the 1780s, because the price of coarse wool was so low that they could market reasonably priced carpets for a wide market for the first time. The Lincolnshire growers were looking for "an extra-ordinary mode of redress." Their schemes were simply a maneuver by the landowners to retain their tenants. All that was necessary was that they reduce their rents, and the wool growers improve the quality of their fleece. Peace alone would restore prosperity. The export of wool was, even as a temporary measure, totally unnecessary.

Thirdly, the Yorkshiremen used the newspapers to organize opinion in the county and extend their case to the other manufacturing areas. There was a round of notices and printed resolutions, invariably inserted in the York, Leeds, and London papers, about meetings at Halifax, Huddersfield, and Rochdale, which quickly followed on the Leeds meeting of 19 December.[34] Resolutions of the separate committees of merchants and manufacturers were summarized and a full report of the support given by the grand jury at the West Riding Quarter Sessions. And Sir James Lowther made a novel use of the press to show that he was canvassing the opinion of his Cumbrian interests about the export of wool question on the basis of the Leeds resolutions of 19 December.[35]

It is also clear that manufacturers in East Anglia and the West Country were spurred into action by the Yorkshiremen. All the West Riding meetings concluded with the intention that the committees which instigated them would correspond with each other, and the manufacturers in Norwich and the West Country. At first any action was undertaken behind the scenes by leaders of the industry in the principal manufacturing centers. In all the areas except Yorkshire there was little immediate reaction to the Lincolnshire graziers' demands. The West Country, never involved in worsted manufacture, was especially inactive. Its problems were quite different, depending on heavy imports of the finest Spanish combing wool and experiencing high prices for the finer English short wools.[36] Even in Norwich, which in the 1770s still sparred with the West Riding for the leadership of the worsted industry, there was little comment in the papers, at least before notices for a meeting on 22 January began to appear.

In December 1781 the *Norfolk Chronicle* began to involve its readers in the controversy. There were no reports of the Lincolnshire meetings, but attention was drawn to the decay of manufactures and commerce in the city, the fact that the House of Commons had moved for accounts of the movements of woolen and worsted goods, yarn, and raw wool over the past seven years, and on 29 December there appeared a tart editorial about the Lincolnshire graziers and the king's conversation with the Lincolnshire M.P.s. It concluded, "Now having brought the evil upon themselves, they expect a measure nationally wrong, to remedy their own ill-conduct." The meeting on 22 January under the chairmanship of the mayor, Robert Partridge, approved a similar set of resolutions to those passed five weeks earlier in Leeds. Those of a meeting in Colchester, four days earlier, were both fuller and more rousing.[37] Four delegates were nominated to attend a meeting in London of all those who opposed the export of wool, and the meeting concluded that the Lincolnshire landowners and farmers suffered "only in common with every other interest in this country." In early February there were meetings in Sudbury, Stroud, and Frome bringing together many of those involved in the Suffolk, Wiltshire, Gloucestershire, and Somerset textile industries. On the first day of February, the Cambridge, Bedfordshire, and Hertfordshire yarn makers and wool staplers met at Potton, and appointed a committee of six to transact business. Again the resolutions were printed in the newspapers. And even though the Gloucestershire clothiers were never deeply involved in the controversy, they ordered the minutes of their meeting to be placed in the London, Bristol, Gloucester, Oxford, Hereford, York, and Wiltshire "papers as necessary."[38] All these meetings in Norfolk, Essex, Bedfordshire and the West Country indicated the work of a national committee, coordinating opposition and activity in London, and showed that interested M.P.s were being canvassed. Not surprisingly, John James recalled in 1857, "No adequate conception can be formed of the commotion which this movement caused among the manufacturers of the Kingdom."[39] His impression is confirmed from the *Cambridge Chronicle:* "this wool business" had in January 1782 "become a subject of almost universal conversation." The printer of the *Leeds Intelligencer,* Griffith Wright, thought the whole thing had gone too far. In a curious editorial, not untypical of the whimsy of the eighteenth-century provincial press, he invented a petition from the Linen and Cotton manufacturers to the queen, who as the fount of virtue, should give encouragement for the use of cotton drawers, "intended as a guarda costa, against the incursions and posterior attacks, of a set of freebooters, infesting the streets and alleys of most cities and large towns in the kingdom." Then came the disparagement of the self-importance of the West Riding manufacturers and the Yorkshire Association. "Committees of ladies from several Manufacturing towns in the West Riding of Yorkshire are appointed to send this petition, and are intended to Correspond with other County Committees in the same manner as those of the grand association."[40] Good *Private Eye* type humor two centuries ago.

V

Already in late January 1782 the scene had shifted to London. What is at first sight curious about the events of late January and early February 1782 is that the provincial press carried such poor accounts of the crucial meetings in London of delegates, committees, and M.P.s who gathered together when Parliament reassembled. Indeed, it is difficult to construct a coherent chronology of events from the Leeds, York and Norwich press and even more so from the West Country papers. The provincial newspapers had been important, especially in the manufacturing areas, in stating the facts that surrounded the controversy, and in initiating meetings to draw up resolutions and elect delegates. In the West Riding, the leading organizers of the manufacturers, John Hustler, a Bradford wool stapler, and Charles Clapham, a Leeds worsted manufacturer and merchant, had used the press to focus opinion and carry their case into the other manufacturing areas. When events moved to London this chain of information, never complete, split. Hustler, Clapham, and the other leaders had other things to do. There was a tight schedule of meetings, M.P.s were constantly sought out; petitions and handbills were printed, pamphlets organized. Communication between London and the provinces still took two or three days and the newspapers appeared only weekly. Although they wrote a stream of letters to their brethren at home they did not appear to have informed the printers of their actions. As is evident from looking through Sir Joseph Banks's manuscripts, events were much better covered in the London papers.[41] They were used to call committee meetings and to give accounts of delegates' meetings with the government. And the government itself put out reports of their views, and meetings between ministers and the leaders of both sides in the controversy. Since London was now largely the scene of action this extended coverage is not surprising. The provincial printers simply lifted those items from the London papers which they thought would interest their readers. They all carried accounts therefore of the representatives of the manufacturers' meeting with Lord North and the walkout by the Lincolnshire landowners from a joint meeting with the manufacturers on 2 February. But what they did not do was provide a consistent week-by-week narrative of events in London.

The delegates of both the manufacturers and growers met in London in late January. It was evident from the outset that the manufacturers were far better organized. They held a preliminary meeting of delegates at the Kings Arms Tavern on 28 January and, two days later, they went along to the long advertised meeting of the Lincolnshire growers at the St. Albans Tavern. As Sir Joseph Banks reported to Sir John Dalrymple, it was in many ways a fiasco for the Lincolnshire growers. They

> . . . stood alone no other county or Body of Men of any description . . . and they were represented by a small part indeed of the men of property in the county most of whom literally came up on Tuesday the day before and came into the meeting declaring beforehand that they came for information. The Manufacturers on the other hand attended in a well arrang'd body of members of the House of Commons headed by several good Businessmen who well know how to arrange the Ideas of the whole proceeding.[42]

They pressed the Lincolnshire 'Bablers' on their returns of wool and gave them an elementary lesson in gathering and presenting statistics. Banks concluded, very gloomily, with comments about the diligence and ability of the manufacturers and the 'Idleness and apathy' of the Lincolnshire gentry. It is an interesting letter which shows how in a Parliament composed principally of landowners, the commercial and industrial interests in England—this was a point made by many political economists in the eighteenth century—were able effectively to assert their policies. On Sunday, 2 February, a general meeting was held at the Thatched House Tavern under the chairmanship of Lord Brownlow. James Oakes, a Bury St. Edmunds yarn dealer and a delegate from Suffolk, recorded an outline of events in his diary.[43] About two hundred merchants and manufacturers attended, fifty of whom, according to Oakes, were Members of Parliament. After discussion a motion was proposed declaring the export of raw wool to be "prejudicial to the Commercial and Landed interests of the Kingdom," and the chairman and thirty or forty Lincolnshire gentlemen stormed out. The veteran Yorkshire M.P. Sir George Savile was elected to the chair and the controversial motion was carried unanimously.

Some of these exciting events appeared in the London papers, although none hinted at the hopelessness of the graziers' case. But the provincial press, except recording the walkout of the Lincolnshire landowners, provided no consistent reporting of events. And when items appeared it was often after a good deal of time had elapsed. Detailed reports of the late January–early February proceedings were not carried in the *Ipswich Journal* before 21 March. The Suffolk yarn makers must have had accounts from James Oakes, who returned straight to Bury after the meeting on 2 February. In the *Norwich Mercury* a brief report of the Thatched House Tavern session appeared in the issue of 9 February, although a more extended account of the meetings between 28 January and 6 February with the resolutions of the manufacturers were not printed until 23 February.

Subsequent events have to be pieced together from the books of papers and press cuttings that Sir Joseph Banks so industriously collected about his multifarious interests. In spite of his gloom about the Lincolnshire graziers' inability to collect the returns of unsold wool, and even more to present their case, the delegates decided, after their meetings in London with the manufacturers, that no arguments had been advanced to prevent them going ahead with their petition. They determined therefore to invite "by Public Advertisement" the other long wool-growing counties to join them in presenting it to Parliament. Opinion in each of these counties should be canvassed at the forthcoming Lent Assizes. A petition, printed on 12 February, called for relief for the growers of long wool by allowing the export of combing wool, a reasonable time after the clip, on the payment of a duty which Parliament would determine. Copies were dispatched to the high sheriffs of the combing wool counties and a general meeting called at Lincoln on 8 March. It was clear from the outset that little aid was forthcoming. Meetings of interested M.P.s on 26 and 28 February in London were poorly attended, and when one took place a month later, at which representatives from the other counties were to meet the Lincolnshire leaders, it was adjourned, on the grounds that the Lent Assizes were "not

The NORWICH MERCURY.

Printed by W. CHASE, in the COCKEY-LANE.

Price THREE-PENCE.] SATURDAY, December 6, 1777. [No. 1436.

Monday's Post.

HOUSE of LORDS.

HOUSE of COMMONS.

BANKRUPTS.

NORFOLK, SUFFOLK, &c.

LINCOLNSHIRE.

NORFOLK.

SWAFFHAM ASSOCIATION.

CREDITORS.

NORWICH, &c.

The NORWICH and NORFOLK COMPLETE MEMORANDUM-BOOK, For the YEAR 1778.

The *Norwich Mercury,* Saturday, 6 December 1777 (British Library Newspaper Library).

yet concluded," until 16 April.[44] Then on 16 February the meeting was postponed to "the first Tuesday after the next meeting of Parliament" because it was too late to proceed in "the advanced state of the present session of Parliament." Three days earlier Charles Chaplin, almost alone amongst the Lincolnshire landowners in his vigorous prosecution of the graziers' case, conceded defeat. He denounced Lord Rockingham's new ministry which had "long since declared against our Wool bill" and "the irresolute, pitiful and weak conduct of many of our Countrymen."[45]

Even the most ardent reader of the London press would have found it hard to follow the collapse of the graziers' campaign from its pages. This is not to conclude that the press closed up, as the campaign of both the manufacturers and graziers moved out of the assembly rooms of the more commodious inns in Leeds, Lincoln, and Westminster, into the book rooms of those M.P.s whose constituents were drawn from the wool-growing and manufacturing counties. But in the infancy of press reporting, there was clearly a breakdown in providing readers with a coherent and well-informed account of events.

The London printers were far better placed to provide coverage of the campaign once it moved to the capital, as Sir Joseph Banks's papers show. He found the *London Courant* "the best channel of information respecting the woollen business." Printers provided readers with three types of information. Firstly, they inserted the notices and resolutions of the public meetings held in the capital. Secondly, their papers carried miscellaneous material, correspondence, résumés of pamphlets, and what Banks called "squibbs and their Answers,"[46] i.e., snippets of information supplied about the case of either party, which forced leaders of the campaign to provide an answer or denial. Thirdly, the government and opposition parties supplied the printers with material about their views on the subject.[47] Then there were reports about the King's conversation with Sir John Dalrymple and a leading manufacturer, and Lord North's interview with the deputies from the different manufacturing counties. Perhaps most interesting was the *Morning Herald* of 9 February 1782 which gave readers an account of Burke's and Fox's views. Burke covered old ground. He saw the whole wool question simply as an adjunct of the American war. He had heard the views of West Riding merchants, expressed by Lord Rockingham, too often to conclude any differently than that peace "will make wool be forgotten." Fox believed that the wool business had "driven people to associate—to choose Committees—and to send delegates to a general meeting—This is a very good beginning" if it resulted in the overthrow of Lord North's ministry.

The London papers were the basis of a good deal of material about the export of wool which the provincial printers gathered. After the meetings of late January–early February 1782, it was evident to all but the graziers themselves that they had lost their case. Subsequently the subject was only briefly mentioned even in the West Riding newspapers. The best coverage was to be found in the *Cambridge Chronicle,* which carried a long series of letters, and the *Norwich Mercury* and *Norfolk Chronicle.* The latter gave events a good local twist which was unusual in this period. Not only was the big meeting in Norwich on 20 February to discuss "the progress of the opposition to the intended application of the Lincolnshire wool growers" fully reported, but also the meetings of the Corporation and the Independent Club which thanked the three Norwich delegates Jeremiah Ives, Robert Partridge, and John Gurney. The first, the doyen of Norwich manufacturers, had chaired the meetings of the manufacturers in London and led their delegation to Lord North. The two papers also covered the presentation of a portrait commissioned by the manufacturers—a rather grand gesture by the Norwich men in spite of all the gloom about the city's industry—of Sir Harbord Harbord, one of the Norfolk M.P.s and a proven friend of their cause.[48] Only the *Norfolk Chronicle* reported the end of the campaign when it succinctly informed its readers on 1 June, "The Lincolnshire gentlemen have withdrawn their intention of petitioning for an export of wool this year by a compromise with the Ministry that if the price sinks before the next meeting of Parliament to 7s. a todd, all the weight of Ministry shall then be exerted in favour of the measure."

The collapse of the Lincolnshire graziers' case in the early spring of 1782 owed nothing to the shortcomings of the provincial press in reporting events. In supplying information and opinion the printers of the West Riding, Norwich, Cambridge, and the London papers provided their readers with a better service than in any domestic economic controversy hitherto. The American war and the association movement ushered in new levels of press coverage in key events. There were still shortcomings, of course. Once the campaign was centered in London, the provincial printers had to rely largely on what they could glean from the London papers. And in any case, as they soon realized, the great excitement of October 1781—early February 1782 evaporated as quickly as it had formed. It was replaced by the affairs of the East India Company and above all by the demise of Lord North's infamous ministry. Everyone realized that the new one, formed by Lord Rockingham, was no friend to the graziers, for a good deal of his electoral base over the past thirty years in Yorkshire had depended upon his careful nurturing of the interests of the West Riding manufacturing and commercial classes.[49] Yet had there been no change of ministry the graziers' case would have fared no differently, for they prosecuted their case with an extraordinary feebleness. It led Sir John Dalrymple, Arthur Young, and Lord Sheffield all to bemoan the constant outmaneuvering of the landowners by the merchants in any contest between the two groups.[50] Benjamin Stephenson, Sir Joseph Banks's intelligent Lincolnshire steward, summed it up in simplest terms: "Merchants are artful as well as powerful, and have always seen when theirs and the landed Interest have stood in competition, they have got the better."[51] One of their more recent stratagems was an effective use of the provincial press.

VI

The resounding defeat of the Lincolnshire graziers was not the end of the wool affair. It came to the fore again in 1786, although in a different form. Issues were not as clear cut as in 1781–82 and the whole business became bogged down in the fearsome quagmire of the wool export laws. The use of the press to coordinate action and arouse opinion, however, was again extremely important. The economic background in 1786 was quite altered. Cloth exports recovered remarkably quickly at the conclusion of war in 1783 and trade with the new United States settled down to a decade of unparalleled progress. And wool prices advanced exactly as the manufacturers had predicted in 1781–82. From an account of "the Growers and one large buyer," amongst Sir Joseph Banks's papers, Lincolnshire long wool rose from 9/6*d.* per tod in 1782 to 17/3*d.* in 1787, regaining the levels of the 1767–76 period.[52] Indeed they advanced so sharply, especially those of short carding wools, that the manufacturers became alarmed. This was true in the West Country, and even more especially in Norwich and Colchester, but all three centers had never had much trade with America and they were in the 1780s unable to break into it, dominated as it was by pushing Yorkshire merchants and a few big manufacturers.[53] The other different factor in 1786–88 was the experience of "association." Once the delegates from the various manufacturing regions had been brought together in January–February 1782 their ties, long after the furore subsided in the summer, remained fastened. Therefore when Pitt's ministry introduced its resolutions abut Irish trade, and entered into negotiations about the commercial treaty with France, the wool cloth merchants and manufacturers automatically put their views together. They did not do so as forcibly as those from Manchester, Glasgow, and Birmingham who together formed a General Chamber of Manufacturers in 1785–87 to examine the Irish and French proposals and make recommendations to the government.[54] It is clear that the cotton manufacturers of Glasgow and Manchester had learnt a good deal about the use of delegates, procedures, and the press from the wool export debate of 1782 when they defeated Pitt's excise tax on fustians in 1784–85. And very similar procedures were used to coordinate the business of the General Chamber.

When Pitt proposed a new look at trade with Ireland the wool cloth merchants and clothiers again entered into correspondence.[55] There were fears not only about the growth of the textile industry in Ireland if Pitt's liberalizing measures were passed, but also more generally about the renewed competition from the cotton industry, and also a widespread belief that the easing of customs with France would allow a general export of wool. The leaders this time came from the West Country—the subsequent agitation was throughout orchestrated by a Gloucestershire clothier, John Anstie—and the movement only regained life in the late spring of 1786 when they produced a draft bill "For amending and reducing into one Act of Parliament the several laws now in being for preventing the Exportation of Live Sheep . . . Wool . . . Yarn . . . and for preventing Frauds and Deceits in the Winding of Wool." It was a draconian affair of almost fifty pages. Sir Joseph Banks scribbled across his copy, "This is the original bill attempted by the manufacturers in 1786 judged too bad for even an attempt at a second reading." Regulations about the clipping of sheep and the movement of fleeces were greatly tightened. The old idea, dropped in 1740, of a register of wool for all those who resided within fifteen miles of the sea was revived, and imprisonment was introduced as a penalty for offenders. Graphic figures about the level of smuggling to France and Holland were produced, and the old arguments about French worsteds being unable to be made without English combing wool, because theirs was too coarse and straight to produce a good warp yarn, were repeated. The common figure bandied about was that 13,000 packs were smuggled and that this, with 40,000 packs of French wool mixed with the imported wool, deprived the English manufacture of vast sums and rendered thousands unemployed.[56] The English clothiers drew the inevitable conclusion from these figures: widespread smuggling led to higher wool prices at home. The long wool producers were furious. Charles Chaplin thought "the whole plan . . . calculated to keep down the price of Wool . . . and should this Bill pass there wou'd be no end to Persecutions and Penalties."[57] The manufacturers' delegates met twice in London in April and again for three days at the Crown and Anchor Tavern in the Strand in May.[58] But it was far too late in the session for the Bill to make progress that year and in any case there was serious opposition to it within the manufacturers' ranks.

A meeting at Norwich in early October 1786 according to the *Norfolk Chronicle* disclosed no disharmony publicly.[59] The strength of that opposition was stated—overstated as events turned out—by Pemberton Milnes, the wealthy Wakefield merchant and Yorkshire and Lincolnshire landowner, in a letter about a meeting of merchants and manufacturers at Bradford on 4 January. A paragraph is worth quoting in full:

> This infamous Bill hath other Objects in View than to prevent Smuggling of Wool when the Secret come to be unravelled it will be found, that the principle and real cause is, to strike at the very existence and stab our Yorkshire and Lancashire Trade to the Heart at one Blow, by depriving us coming at the raw Materials in the way we do at present. The Trade in many of our Southern County's has for many years been much upon the decline, those of Yorkshire, Lancashire and other Northern ones much upon the increase, their decrease, and our increase, is the cause of the present Bill, which is meant to prevent us coming at the raw Articles for

> our Manufacturing in the way we do now, to Cloy the Growers of Wool sending it Coastways in the present way, my own Opinion is and I believe it [is of] almost every Merchant and Manufacturer in Yorkshire and Lancashire, that this Bill ought to be rejected in toto by the Meeting, its principles are founded in Iniquity, will tend to the Ruin of many Trading Towns and Manufactory's, will Harrass and plague the Growers of Wool and ought to be Burnt at the Market Cross in every Town in the Kingdom.[60]

Milnes chaired the Bradford meeting. Not quite the unanimity he had intimated prevailed. But what is fascinating is that a committee of twenty-five delegates, five each from the principal clothing towns in the West Riding, was formed, each one of whom had to be elected by the merchants and clothiers in the centers. All the resolutions and notices about the elections were printed in both the *Intelligencer* and the *Mercury*.[61] Three weeks later Milnes reported to Sir Joseph Banks that the committee of twenty-five "proceded in reading over the Bill clause by clause. At Ten O'clock at Night they had got to the eighth Page of that very columinous Bill."[62] It is a good example of grass-roots 'association' democracy at work. The committee by no means represented the views of Milnes and the West Riding merchants and landowners, even so they mauled Anstie's Bill so much that it made no further progress that year. A meeting of delegates in London in April was forced to concede that it should be dropped, "On account *Only* of the advanced and unexpected state of public business in the present session of Parliament." Anstie, worried about criticism and lack of progress, insisted that the papers both in London and the country should announce that application would be made to Parliament the first week of the next session and that the delegates were pledged to support the bill through Parliament. It was also stated in the *General Advertiser* that the most controversial clauses had been dropped and the Yorkshire delegates' demands met.[63]

It was fortunate for the wool growers that the progress of the bill was halted by the split in the manufacturers' ranks, for the opposition from the landowners was little more effective than in 1782. Again it centered upon Sir Joseph Banks. He drew in Arthur Young and Lord Sheffield. They wrote to each other, collected statistics, circulated pamphlets and newspapers, harangued every M.P. and landowner they met at their country assizes and race meetings. Young, in typical polemic style, ridiculed the manufacturers' case in the *Annals of Agriculture,* attacked their figures and accused the Norfolk and Suffolk yarnmakers of reducing spinning rates in the recession of 1787–88.[64] In the Norwich newspapers he instigated a long correspondence. One accused him, in his own language, of aiming "at the total extinction of the manufacture of these counties by recommending the exportation of wool and robbing the poor of the employment they at present enjoy . . . and reducing them to the experiment of *fattening upon hot potatoes,* which you lately made with so much success upon the squeaking quadrupeds of your own family."[65] Sir Joseph Banks and Lord Sheffield wielded less controversial quills, and all three were busy in organizing opposition to Anstie's bill in Lincolnshire, Sussex, and Suffolk. A meeting at Lincolnshire on 19 October 1787 resolved that changes in the law were unnecessary, that a committee of M.P.s and others should be formed and a subscription entered into. The resolutions were printed in two London papers, as well as the Lincoln, York, and Cambridge weeklies.

After a further five-day meeting of between thirty and forty delegates of manufacturers in London in February, prolonged largely to placate the aggreived Anstie, the bill, now much amended by the Yorkshire members, was rushed through the Commons in the summer of 1788.[66] The newspapers were particularly comprehensive in their coverage. Largely this was because the bill was examined in Committee by both Houses of Parliament. Therefore the press could comment at length on M.P.'s voting intentions and speeches, the evidence of Arthur Young, Sir Joseph Banks, Anstie, and the leading worsted manufacturers from Norwich and the West Riding.[67] In this sense, because issues were public the coverage was better than in 1782 when the Lincolnshire petition never reached Parliament. The newspapers also proved themselves again in the basic organization of the campaign: besides details of meetings and their resolutions, they provided information about where petitions might be signed and, by the publication of subscription lists, shamed laggards into action. When he called a meeting in Sussex Lord Sheffield took care to engage "all the considerable and opulent People from Arundel to Eastbourne . . . by Insertions in the County Newspapers the last two weeks. I thought it better to use vigorous Resolutions as I had no doubt of carrying them."[68]

But the wool business had dragged on too long; the compromises reached were too marked. It almost ceased to be a matter of interest, except with Anstie and the most zealous worsted manufacturers and merchants. The smuggling issue had been much exaggerated, although the landowners were careful not to decry it altogether. Moreover, other new items were more pressing on public notice—the saga of Lady Strathmore and Mr. Bowes, the impeachment of Sir Elijah Impey and Warren Hastings and, in the commercial world, the credit crisis in the cotton industry and the contraction of the worsted industry in East Anglia. In the Commons itself interest in Anstie's revised bill was minimal. It was a favourite ploy of the Lincolnshire M.P.'s to delay business by counting out the House of Commons. It succeeded on 24 April and only failed by a hair's breadth six days later. One M.P. stated, "he was ashamed to think that on a political question, brought forward the preceding day, 400 members attended; but, on a question which more nearly interested their constituents, they paid no attendance."[69] Yet when an attempt was made to postpone the bill for another session the proposition was lost by 47 to 112 votes. In spite of spirited opposition from Sir John Thorold, one of the Lincolnshire M.P.'s, arguing that the present legislation was sufficient, that smuggling was minimal, and that the principle of the bill originated "in the mean and rapacious spirit of avarice and monopoly," the bill passed its third reading on 19 May.[70] Although the landowners not unnaturally hoped for further delay in the House of Lords, it passed in late June after their Lordships had listened to a repetition of the evidence given before the Commons. As soon as the news reached Leeds, Norwich, and Bury St. Edmunds the bells were set ringing and the traditional processions organized.[71] Yet in many respects it was a hollow victory. Not only was there depression in East Anglia—James Oakes refused to allow his combers to join in the jollifications "on acct. of the melancholy and oppressed state of the trade at this time"—and credit in trade so shaken by events in South Lancashire, but also the Act (28 George III 638) was little more than a codification of past statutes, and few prosecutions were ever brought. Moreover, it did not mark a final victory for those who had attempted to stop the liberalization of the laws about the export of raw materials. Within forty years, in 1824, exports of wool were allowed, because imports of wool had grown so significantly after 1790 and English wool further increased in coarseness, as the feeding of sheep improved and breeding was concentrated on producing a bigger carcass.[72] Agricultural improvements and the growth of the industry in the end smashed the manufacturers' much prized monopoly of the British wool clip.

VII

In its coverage of the controversy about the export of wool in the 1780s, the press, both in London and the provinces, discussed issues in unprecedented detail. Hitherto there had been little comment about businessmen and economic affairs unless they had been closely linked with war or ministerial policy. Then the emphasis, as in the American war or over Walpole's controversial economic policies in the 1730s, had been different. Now a major issue materially affecting the landowners, farmers, and the country's biggest industry was analyzed directly for the ways it might harm these interests. Both sides of the case were discussed in the newspapers' coverage of meetings and in their correspondence. Both sides in the controversy for the first time realized that the newspapers were essential for circulating information and forming opinion. The traditional use of markets, meetings, and personal correspondence was no longer sufficient. The coverage in detail was far from perfect. Printers, especially in the provinces, were only as good as the material fed to them. But many were beginning to see the potential of economic issues and discussions about the interests of the business community beyond the space devoted to stolen horses, runaway apprentices, and lists of prices and bankrupts. At one level an issue like the export of wool controversy generated a great deal of extra business for them in the printing and circulation of handbills, petitions, pamphlets, bills and résumés of existing legislation. At another they realized the growing importance of industrial and commercial affairs and fed upon and encouraged the spirit that generated pride in England's economic ascendancy. In Norwich the newspapers often touched upon the city's great civic identity. In Birmingham and Leeds they dwelt upon the towns' bustle and emergence as two of the country's leading industrial centers. And in the discussion of the export of wool they stumbled on one of the great underlying issues of the eighteenth century—the precarious balance between the landowning and industrial interests and the way it was shifting, as Sir Joseph Banks, Lord Sheffield, and Arthur Young lamented, more and more in favor of the latter.

The earliest newspapers were primarily, advertisements apart, vehicles for political news and views. Then as their readership widened after the 1760s they expanded on a firmer, more closely defined regional base. Their printers, still limited in various ways, could cover a politico-business issue like the wool controversy quite easily. No longer did printers in York, Norwich, Leeds, and Stamford have to pillage news from the London press, but they could gingerly begin to include local industrial and commercial news which would go down well with their more broadly based readership. It was still not ready to digest extended industrial and agricultural coverage. It had a low margin of tolerance for the finer points of the wool export controversy. Nevertheless, those parties involved in this major economic issue realized how essential newspapers had become in formulating and forwarding views. Discussion was more extensive and on an improved information base. And once industrial items captured the nation's imagination around the 1790s the printers of the provincial press were ready to provide the kind of information that was central for an informed discussion of the role of industry, trade, and agriculture in creating Britain's new wealth and strength.

PART TWO
The Nineteenth Century

Introduction

Although the bulk of surviving copies of the eighteenth-century newspapers is prodigious, there is within them a certain uniformity in style and approach. It is possible to get one's bearings with reasonable ease. The publications of the nineteenth century are an altogether different matter and the sheer scale and range of material is alarming. To a great extent this is a reflection of the continuous involvement of newspapers and periodicals in the massive and accelerating changes taking place in English society. On the production side the interactions are often clear enough. Technological innovation, for example, impinged directly on the internal organization of the press as it underwent a protracted if erratic industrialization. The introduction of modified presses, the use of the burgeoning railway network in distribution and the application of the telegraph to news gathering, all stimulated and shaped the process of growth. In terms of content and readership, the links between the expanding press and developments in nineteenth-century society at large are much harder to define. Rapid population growth, widespread urbanization, the extension of literacy and educational opportunity, as well as the emergence of new forms of social and political organization, all had far-reaching implications for the English press which it is peculiarly difficult to isolate. Much more detailed work needs to be done before the answerable questions about the relationship between the press and society are resolved. The chapters in Part Two represent a further stage in the buildup of material which is the essential preliminary to the construction of a more comprehensive and integrated analysis.

In many studies of the nineteenth-century English press 1855 is taken as a break point. The repeal of the Stamp Tax in that year and the removal of the related imposts on advertising and paper at about the same time, as well as representing a triumph for radicialism, had a substantial practical impact on the structure of the press. Besides the overnight creation of the cheap newspaper, the 1855 repeal brought about a major shift in the balance of output from London to the provinces, broadened the range of news-carrying publications and substantially altered the character of political involvement with the press. None the less, it is possible to overstate the importance of repeal particularly in the context of a Westminster-centered study of party politics.[1] The long-established commercial constraints were given an even sharper significance by the removal of the "taxes on knowledge," and the general readjustment between sections of the press which took place during subsequent decades represented more an acceleration of developments already under way than a break with the past. None of the chapters that follow are concerned with party politics or specifically with the categories of publication in which political involvement was focused. By identifying content areas outside this framework the contributions give a greater emphasis to continuity and to a pattern of development in which repeal is a major but not necessarily the predominant element.

From the seventeenth century the newspaper had been adopted as a means of consolidating support and projecting opinion. However, its use in this way was limited very largely to the groups of political insiders whose parliamentary manoeuvers lay at the heart of their newspaper interests. From the late eighteenth century, as the vertical structures of a mainly rural society began to break down, the range and character of direct involvement with the press was considerably extended. Almost every group with a shared objective whose access to existing publications was limited or blocked altogether became directly involved in newspaper or periodical publication at either national or local level. Throughout the nineteenth century the organizations developed within the prolix religious groupings or based on the miscellaneous activities of the emergent working class were likely to be involved with the press. The unstamped and Chartist papers and the pre–socialist union publications, though with a very different class orientation, ran parallel to the religious output charted here by Louis Billington.[2] At the same time, while organizations across both these broad categories could be described as pressure groups, a further range of overlapping organizations set up to promote specific measures of reform became increasingly involved in the publication of periodicals. The temperance movement was only the largest and best organized of a range of such groups whose objectives included the abolition of slavery, smoking and vivisection, and the promotion of women's suffrage. In every case the press continued to fulfill the three major functions identified by Brian Harrison as inspirational, informative, and integrating.[3]

If commercial considerations were secondary to the sponsors of this sort of committed output, which remained predominantly inward-looking and didactic in tone, they were nonetheless helping during the 1820s and 1830s to open up new areas of readership with a rich potential for commercial publishers. Some of the most successful of these began their careers in association with papers catering for the religious, radical, or reformist groups, only later adopting a more directly commercial line. The apotheosis of this alternative approach appeared in the popular Sunday newspapers.[4] Directed from the first at a working-class readership, they brought together in a commercial setting the traditions of radical journalism and popular street literature. The formula, involving a good deal of readership participation, criticism of the establishment, and a substantial amount of police news, sensation, and scandal, proved immensely popular; even by the 1840s the Sundays had prefigured many of the developments which were to spread through the press later in the century.

The contrast between the interest-group publications and the popular Sundays brings into focus the tension which lay at the heart of the development of the press in the later nineteenth century. On one hand, the newspapers and periodicals were seen primarily as vehicles of opinion and instruction, the position they held within the framework of the traditional 'liberal' ideology; on the other they appeared as predominantly commercial enterprises with market forces providing the main guide to their conduct. The commercial preoccupations were given a sharp boost in midcentury as the build-up in competition and the opportunities of an expanding market were emphasized by the series of tax repeals. From the 1850s the search for readers took on an increasing urgency not only in the newspaper and periodical press, but also in the area of general publishing where the mushroom growth of output contributed to a further blurring of frontiers between overlapping forms of publication. Though it is difficult to generalize when faced with the extravagant range of material produced during the later nineteenth century, modifications in the content of the periodicals and newspapers were broadly characterized by the interconnected processes of "specialization" and "diversification". Each reflected the shifting relationship between press and readers as commercial pressure hastened the move away from the provision of precept and instruction toward the gratification of a range of established tastes. Specialization by audience targeting was a long-standing process within the commercial periodicals. The eighteenth-century monthlies, for example, identified and catered for a broad range of social and interest groups within the middle ranks.[5] However, from the midnineteenth century a notable expansion took place in this form of publication with the existing categories of readers increasingly subdivided by age, sex and interest as well as by class. The acceleration of specialist publishing was focused in the London-based weeklies and was evident across both commercial and committed publications. As Alan Lee has pointed out,

> There were literary, religious and academic papers, papers for gardeners, for soldiers and sailors, for lawyers, doctors and chemists, for bakers, tailors and pawnbrokers, for speculators and promoters, for women, for musicians and music lovers, for the volunteers, for architects, for foreigners, for everybody. Papers also of all kinds, from the serious to the comic, from the drab to the illustrated.[6]

The growth of the specialist press was a striking testimony to the involvement of the periodical in the life of the community at a variety of social levels, and according to one contemporary estimate the number of such weeklies rose from 53 in 1851 to 794 in 1880.[7]

While specialization characterized sections of the periodical press, so diversification was the distinctive feature of the newspapers which were facing a continuous buildup in commercial pressure. Running a newspaper was becoming an increasingly expensive business as the cost of plant and staff continued to rise. In order to enter or succeed in the market publishers were obliged to look for an expanding readership which could not only provide an effective level of sales income but also, and perhaps more importantly, attract the advertisers, whose contribution to newspaper finance was crucial. One response to the problem was the linking of newspapers in ownership chains, a system which in the end dominated the provincial and suburban press. Another and not necessarily unrelated reaction lay in broadening the appeal of the content to attract an ever-widening range of readers. Expansion of this sort was inevitably made toward the lower end of the social scale where the popular Sundays remained the dominant interest and it was their example which was often most evident in the subsequent redeployment of material and the modification of approach. The impetus to move in this direction was experienced not only within the commercial publications but also in the major religious and pressure-group papers, which with rather more mixed motives, sought to widen their audiences through the inclusion of news, advertising, and other miscellaneous material.

The elements of what is loosely described here as 'diversification' were scattered through both the upper and lower levels of the newspaper press. The expansion of miscellaneous features, which gave the newspaper a flavor of the magazine, was accompanied by some general readjustment in the balance of material offered. This can perhaps be most clearly seen in the relationship between sport, which was expanding in volume and becoming increasingly pervasive, and coverage of politics, particularly parliamentary affairs, which were undergoing a protracted decline. Together with a general lightening in tone, which involved publication of some serialized fiction, the newspapers also underwent a slow modification in layout. Since the seventeenth century they had appeared in small type laid out remorselessly in multiple columns. Illustration represented one way of alleviating the growing monotony as page sizes increased and the typeface lost much of its early character. However, in spite of some occasional use of illustration, usually in the form of maps and diagrams, and the successful development of a branch of pictorial journalism in such weeklies as the *Illustrated London News*, even the popular Sundays were slow to employ the device as a regular feature.[8] None the less, the old stereotyped style of presentation was beginning to come under pressure from within as well as without. From the 1870s the demands of advertising, the most potent commercial force at work on the press, involved the introduction of an increasing amount of pictorial material as well as the breakup of the inflexible columns in ways which were soon reflected in other areas of content. Taken together these developments made up what was ironically described from the 1880s as "the new journalism," and it was the comprehensive application of the whole range of reader-centered approaches that underlay the success of the *Daily Mail* and the other cheap London papers published in the following decade. Using cross-column headlines, illustrations of all kinds, and a deliberately simplified style, they set out to offer the general public what it was thought they wanted.[9]

At the end of the nineteenth century the shifts in the character of the press, which led to some polarization of the newspapers and periodicals, was still not complete. The London newspapers in particular were not yet established as "national" publications and the formation of a "mass" readership was not to be achieved until the 1920s. Direct evidence for both the extent and character of the readership during the second half of the century, when, for example, the newspaper stamp figures are no longer available, is both limited and impressionistic.[10] None the less, the specialization and diversification within the output of the press were in themselves manifestations of the way in which newspapers and periodicals were gradually permeating society from top to bottom. This almost inescapable pervasiveness is emphasized by Joanne Shattock and Michael Wolff who point out that "The Press, in all its manifestations became during the Victorian period the context within which people lived and worked and thought, and from which they derived their (in most cases quite new) sense of the outside world."[11] As the major vehicle for the transmission of ideas and information the press reflected and reinforced developments taking place across society, and if its role as teacher and guide was subordinated to that of informant and entertainer, its liberating influence was as powerful as that of the other great social force of the period—the railway. Taken as a package of news, comment, and advertising the output of the English press provided readers, particularly at the lower levels of society, with the opportunity to participate in new patterns of social activity. Hire purchase and seaside holidays, for example, those two most characteristic elements of life in late Victorian England, owed their development directly to the newspapers and periodicals.[12]

The chapters in Part Two pick up some of the content-oriented themes suggested in outline here. In a pioneering overview of religion in the press Louis Billington follows up Thomas O'Malley's more tightly focused study with an investigation of its treatment in the later periodicals. By charting the full range of output he is able to bring together the broad developments taking place in the press and shifts in both the character of, and attitudes towards, organised religion. Diana Dixon, on the other hand, surveys the broad spectrum of periodicals directed at readers under twenty which was produced during the second half of the nineteenth century. By investigating the involvement of organizations both commercial and committed in this output and surveying the full range of its content she produces a rare view of the complex interaction between the specialist periodical and its readership. Advertising was the area of newspaper content which formed the closest link between the internal and external relations of the press. Terry Nevett provides an analysis both of the changes in the character of advertising material and of the ways in which it underpinned the expansion of the press during the nineteenth century. In particular he assesses the extent to which advertising directly influenced newspaper content through the potentially difficult relationship between the agencies and the editors and proprietors. Tony Mason, through an examination of sport as a theme of specialist publications as well as an element in the content of the generalist newspapers, links the output of the press to a range of social issues. He indicates the way in which increased leisure and prosperity and the development of new forms of organized sport interacted with the press to create a major branch of popular journalism. Catherine Hughes contributes a detailed investigation of one element of the 'new journalism' represented by the cartoon material published in the *Daily Mail.* Through an analysis of this form of content she is able to show how its use reflected the modified relationship between the newspaper and its readers and in particular how the issue of imperialism was handled in the emotive context of the Boer War. In the final essay of this collection Virginia Berridge comes to grips with the central problem of the historian attempting to place the newspaper in a realistic social context. By providing a review of the development and potential use of content analysis she brings into focus a method of research which will have to be applied much more widely before the history of the British press can be fully understood.

5
The Religious Periodical and Newspaper Press, 1770–1870

Louis Billington

INTRODUCTION

In the 1770s there were only a handful of religious magazines of limited range and price. A century later, periodicals and newspapers with a religious purpose could be numbered in hundreds. They were issued in bewildering profusion by individuals, sects, denominations, religious societies and pressure groups, and commercial publishers. They varied greatly in their frequency of appearance, format, content, price, and prospective audience, with a growing volume of publications for both general markets and special interests. Besides providing spiritual guidance, education, and religious news, the Christian press had become much concerned with the marketing of religious entertainment, although what constituted the 'Christian's Amusement' had changed considerably since the appearance of the pioneer serial of that title in 1741. These changes took place in the context of, and partly as responses to, other religious, social, and economic changes. Firstly, the religious press must be related to the general patterns of religious change, such movements, for example, as the growth of Evangelicalism and the rise of new sects having a major impact on the shaping of the press. Secondly, the churches utilized the press to defend their political rights, claim or restrict freedoms, and challenge social injustice or public disorder in a century of rapid industrialization. Finally, the religious press was responsive to technical changes in printing, binding and distribution, legal reforms, and the competition of commercial publishers.

The religious magazines produced by the early Evangelical revival were markedly different from the news-sheets and anti-Catholic publications of earlier decades. The first of these magazines appeared in September 1741, the *Christian's Amusement* commencing a series that, with some interruptions and title changes, ran until June 1748.[1] The series was designed to promote a religious awakening, strengthen converts, and bind together George Whitefield's followers. The magazine reflected the pattern of the revival, appearing as a penny weekly during months of greatest activity. Of course,

Whitefield and his preachers made great use of the spoken word and religious tracts, but it was felt appropriate that Christians should have their own periodical:

> Shall the polite world have their Spectators, Tatlers, Guardians and comedies? Shall the curious have his daily and weekly news, his Advertiser, Gazeteer, Miscellany? and shall the children of God also have their weekly amusement, their Divine Miscellany and historical account of the progress of their Lord's Kingdom?[2]

The *Christian's Amusement* and associated periodicals were issued by John Lewis, who like many later promoters of religious magazines, was a printer and bookseller. He had the backing of a wealthy sponsor, and a ready-made distribution system through the itinerant preachers whose work he publicized. The magazine legitimized the revival by providing historical and doctrinal justifications and fueled it by printing letters reporting new awakenings. Reports of mob violence and persecutions demonstrated the suffering of the 'saints' and a friendly rivalry grew up with friends in Scotland and America in the promotion of the Lord's work. Similar magazines appeared in those countries and in turn were heavily drawn upon by Lewis. There were also advertisements from "brothers and sisters" of the artisan classes seeking employment.[3] Many of these features characterized the later religious press.

Other early religious magazines were speculative ventures by eccentric, even unsavory, characters who mixed religious instructions with the hope of financial gain. As in the political and literary press, the dialogue was a popular device in these magazines. John Allen's *Royal Spiritual Magazine* was a high Calvinist spiritual dialogue written by a Baptist minister and linen draper, who was later acquitted of forgery and emigrated to New England.[4] A more notorious figure was Dr. William Dodd, an Anglican clergyman who used his popularity as a preacher at the Magadalene Hospital to launch the *Christian Magazine* as a source of income and a vehicle for his own writings. Dodd was bitterly opposed to Wesley, and his attacks won the support of Augustus Toplady and respectable Calvinists, who tried to keep the "Macaroni Preacher" on a steady course, but forgery led Dodd to the gallows.[5] An honest but equally controversial author, Anne Dutton, used magazines as well as books and pamphlets to publicize her distinct version of Calvinism.[6] By the 1760s, better-known Calvinist leaders were developing magazines of which the most important were the *Gospel Magazine* and Toplady's successor publication of similar title. These magazines contained very little religious news and information compared with the *Christian's Amusement* and *Weekly History*, though Toplady's monthly did have a short chronicle of general news, ecclesiastical preferments, and births, marriages, and deaths. The *Gospel Magazine's* staple was polemical theology and sermons with hymns, poetry, and other inspirational pieces. Opposition to Wesley increased over the years until it became quite hysterical. Circulation of these magazines, which cost sixpence or a shilling, is difficult to assess, though the later *Gospel Magazine* claimed "extensive" sales among Anglicans and Dissenters.[7] Liberal Christians were also active in the field, but Joseph Priestley's *Theological Repository* was essentially a series of learned articles by Priestley and his friends published three or four times a year in part form. The cost varied from sixpence to one-and-sixpence, according to the size of issue, and the short-lived venture was clearly aimed at a quite different audience from the readers of the *Christian's Amusement*.[8]

THE DENOMINATIONAL AND SECTARIAN PRESS, 1770–1820

Of the early religious periodicals only the first serials published by Whitefield's followers acted as the voice of a dynamic evangelistic movement, but with the appearance of Wesley's *Arminian Magazine* in 1778 the old tone was recaptured.[9] The fifty years after 1770 witnessed the revitalization of the Baptists and Congregationalists, the appearance of a coherent and articulate group of Anglican Evangelicals, and the growth of a huge interlocking network of missionary, Sunday school, and similar societies. Early attempts at interdenominational cooperation gradually weakened, and Wesley's movement, while growing rapidly, also suffered major schisms.[10] As a religious publisher, Wesley established a model which was to be widely used by all branches of Methodism. In 1778 his followers numbered many thousands, but even excellent organization and constant traveling could not completely overcome the dangers of fragmentation. Wesley already owned a printing press and Book Room, or publishing department, which issued a wide range of literature, and he felt the need for a periodical to unite his scattered followers, provide them with models of behavior, stimulate them to greater effort, and defend them against embittered Calvinists.

After Wesley's death the press and Book Room passed into the hands of the Conference, which appointed an editor and book steward or business manager.[11] These became part of a tightly knit secretariat which increasingly dominated Wesleyan Methodism. By the 1820s editor and book steward received salaries around £260 per annum, much larger than those of ordinary ministers, but perhaps not excessive considering the weight of their responsibilities.[12] The editor and book steward with a Conference-appointed Book Room Committee scrutinized the publication of every item including the contents of the magazine. The books, pamphlets, and articles of unfavored ministers and laymen were rejected,and even if they found alternative publishers, they were not allowed to advertise on the covers of the official magazine. Control of advertising often seemed almost as important to the editor and book steward as control of publication.[13] For many years the editors, including Wesley, wrote a substantial part of the magazine and received unpaid contributions and denominational news reports, biographical sketches and obituaries from the itinerant ministers. An assistant editor was soon necessary and young ministers were somemtimes seconded to the Book Room on a temporary basis. The printing and other manual staff increased with the size of the operation, and a professional book-keeper also became necessary.[14]

The contents of the *Arminian Magazine* remained very similar for many decades. Key features were polemical and doctrinal articles, sermons, biographies, obituaries, revival news, and poetry. Engravings of prominent ministers were another popular item which remained for over a hundred years. There was no secular news, 'snippets' or short pieces, or book reviews, which Wesley lacked the time to undertake.[15] After Wesley's death, some of the contents were gradually modified. His liking for reports of strange and providential happenings was not shared by his successors, who also toned down reports of sensational revivals and excluded news of women preachers, whom Wesley had favored.[16] Book reviews became important, and there was an increasingly conscious imitating of the standards of the Nonconformist religious press.[17] Many of Wesley's editorial successors were scholars, who tried to improve the literary quality of the magazine. In 1811 the number of pages was doubled and an abridged edition introduced: the large magazine remained a shilling and the abridgment was sixpence. Methodist ministers were obliged to sell the magazine with other official literature and alllowed a discount on the proceeds.[18] As part of the profits of the Book Room went into a retirement fund, ministers had an additional motive to promote sales. Exaggerated circulation figures for the magazine have sometimes been claimed, but 17–18,000 copies of the large edition and the abridged version were printed by the 1820s. The profits of the magazine were rarely calculated separately from the book and tract business, but between 1793 and 1806 total profits of £23,000 were claimed, and returns of that order continued for many years.[19] Unfortunately, the Conference got into the habit of relying on Book Room profits for pensions and the deficits of poorer circuits, and the Book Room often had to borrow to obtain ready cash. By the early 1820s annual interest charges as high as £1,900 were being paid. Bad debts also remained a problem with a core of ministers unable or unwilling to return payment for the books which they had received for distribution.[20]

The Methodist New Connexion, Primitive Methodists, Bible Christians, and the other schismatic Methodist groups of this period all struggled to establish their own periodical press.[21] The New Connexion's founder employed a magazine in his initial battle with the Wesleyan leadership, and his followers quickly established a Book Room and commenced a Connexional magazine. However, they did not acquire a press and relied on a succession of members who were printers and booksellers.[22] The Primitive Methodists did the same for their earliest magazines, but soon acquired their own printing and publishing business, although ownership was not vested in the Conference for some years.[23] The Bible Christians followed a similar pattern with a prominent member being both the official publisher and a commercial printer and publisher.[24] Given the smaller numbers and generally poorer memberhip of the majority of these sects, their magazines were usually smaller and cheaper than those of the Wesleyans. With the exception of the New Connexion's magazine, the contents of these periodicals was simpler and more sensational, with a heavy emphasis on extracts from preachers' journals and revival news. Wesley's liking for providential happenings remained firmly enshrined here, and ghosts and apparitions stalked the early volumes.[25] There was, however, much informative material on the history of the different sects, and a sustained effort was made to weld revival movements into churches.[26] The smallest and most radical groups, which rejected a paid ministry and central control, had the greatest difficulty in sustaining a periodical, and intermittent publications rested heavily on the shoulders and purses of one or two members. The content of such journals was very similar to that of the *Primitive Methodist Magazine*.[27] Of course, a wealthy man could easily bring about a small local schism, and finance his own magazine, but these were generally ephemeral.[28] By the 1820s the Methodist schisms had a collective membership of thirty to forty thousand and some were growing rapidly. Control of the Book Room was more informal than with the Wesleyans and often rested with the founders of the sect. There is little evidence of profits at this time, although the usual practice of distribution by the preachers was adopted. Circulation of the magazines varied from a few hundred to four thousand copies, though in this milieu, even more than among the Wesleyans, copies were widely exchanged, read aloud in meetings, and borrowed from Sunday school and chapel libraries.[29]

By the 1790s enterprising Evangelicals were adopting a more moderate theology, and were less concerned with speculative controversy than positive evangelism. They still nurtured hopes of cooperation across denominational boundaries, at least among those who saw themselves as Calvinists. Many looked back to Whitefield and the spectacular awakenings which had been reported so fully in the *Christian's Amusement* and the American and Scottish religious press. It was the minister of Whitefield's former London church, Matthew Wilks, aided by well-known Congregationalists and some Anglicans, who founded the *Evangelical Magazine* in 1793. It aimed at being an interdenominational journal providing for Calvinists what the *Arminian Magazine* did for Wesley's people, but the tone of the *Evangelical Magazine* was much less acrimonious than that of the *Gosepel Magazine* in its discussion of disputed questions.[30] The control of the new magazine was in the hands of twenty-four directors—prominent ministers—who were also contributors and subeditors. A commerical firm handled the printing and publishing. The first editor was an Anglican, the second, George Burder, was a Congregationalist who was also secretary of the London Missionary Society, which the magazine helped to promote.[31] Priced sixpence, the format and key features of the magazine were similar to those of its Wesleyan rival, but with a moderate Calvinist emphasis. American religious news was well covered and there were book reviews from the beginning. It was perhaps more of a minister's magazine than the cheap journals of the 1740s, but it carried reports of a wide range of evangelistic enterprises and awakenings. Advertisements on the covers were controlled, not to regulate opinion, but to exclude the 'indelicate or immoral.'[32] Although lacking the official distribution system of the Wesleyans, the *Evangelical Magazine* was strongly recommended by ministers and quickly gained support, despite short-lived rivals of similar theological orientation.[33] The absence of a regular denominational press before 1800 favoured the *Evangelical Magazine* and estimates of a circulation of about 18,000 would seem reasonable. Profits, which were managed by trustees, went to the widows of Evangelical ministers of many denominations and missionary enterprises. Between 1793 and 1826 profits of nearly £20,000 were distributed in this way.[34]

Moderate Calvinist and Methodist magazines did not represent the distinctive views of high Calvinists, Arminian Baptists, Universalists, Unitarians, Swedenborgians, and other groups which struggled to establish their own press. High or hyper-Calvinists reviewed the *Gospel Magazine,* which kept up a bitter attack not only on the Wesleyans but on the promoters of the *Evangelical Magazine,* which was described as "this repository of unevangelical trash".[35] Hyper-Calvinists were a moderately large group, but many smaller religious movements lacked the resources to maintain a regular magazine, or made many false starts before such an enterprise was accomplished. Many magazines were the creations of single individuals, often printers or booksellers. These men were sect founders and often combined publishing with the work of the ministry. Robert Hindmarsh, for example, the Swedenborgian pioneer, persisted with many magazines and could afford to spend nearly one hundred guineas advertising his first magazine in the "town and country" press.[36] The Scotch Baptist leader, William Jones, showed equal persistence in magazine publishing.[37] The small Catholic community suffered from civil disabilities and was divided as to how best to overcome them. Clerical leadership was weak, and many of the early sixpenny magazines perished after a few issues. William E. Andrews was the most successful of the Catholic journalists and printers, grasping the need for a cheap press and making a brave but premature venture into newspaper publishing.[38]

After 1800 support for the *Evangelical Magazine* gradually weakened as Evangelical Anglicans, Baptists and others created journals with more positive denominational or party identity. This process mirrored what was happening in other fields, although much Evangelical cooperation continued. The publishing arrangements and editorial policies of many of these new journals followed the pattern of the *Evangelical Magazine,* with the editor and his associates writing much of the copy and profits going to approved causes. Local ministers provided denominational news, obituaries, and reports of evangelistic work, while close links were maintained with missionary societies and coreligionists in the United States and elsewhere. Though the denominational or party emphasis was clear, the range of features in these magazines was often similar to those in the *Evangelical Magazine* or *Methodist Magazine.* The most popular price was sixpence per monthly issue, but the Anglican *Christian Observer* started at a shilling. The *Christian Observer* was established by the closely knit members of the 'Clapham Sect' and the story of its founding has often been told. Finance, editorial staff, and contributors were all drawn from the same group, who aimed to promote sound Evangelical doctrine.[39] The *Christian Observer* was wary of "extravagance and enthusiasm", and kept up a running fight with Methodists and Dissenters when they endorsed more sensational types of revivalism.[40] The *Christian Observer* also combated the literary quarterlies and High Church magazines like the *British Critic,* and had an extensive review section with a separate index.[41] It was a much more polished product than the later Nonconformist denominational magazines, with the exception of the Unitarian *Monthly Repository* and the *Eclectic Review,* which was developed to give Evangelical Dissenters their own literary and intellectual quarterly, but never enjoyed extensive support.[42] Many Evangelical Anglicans and some Unitarians also favored more prosaic journals like the *Christian Guardian* and the *Christian Reformer.*[43]

The *Baptist Annual Register* had done much to foster a Baptist sense of identity, but it was too infrequent and too concerned with history and the detailed listing of Baptist churches to act as a regular denominational monthly.[44] That role was fulfilled by the *Baptist Magazine* started under the auspices of the Western Baptist Association in 1809, and then taken up by the newly formed Baptist Union. The initial circulation was four thousand but in the first fifteen years profits were sufficient to distribute £2,500 among the "necessitous widows of deceased ministers."[45] Nearly ten years later the Congregationalists, who had seen the *Evangelical Magazine* become identified with their church, also felt the need for a more distinctly denominational journal. After much conflict because of the threat it was thought to pose to the *Evangelical Magazine,* the *London Christian Instructor* was established, which soon became the *Congregational Magazine.* Even the Countess of Huntingdon's Connexion, tiny as it was, followed suit a few years after.[46]

GROWTH OF SPECIALIZED RELIGIOUS MAGAZINES, 1790–1840

Among the earliest of the specialized religious journals were those devoted to the promotion of foreign missions. These publications consisted of suitably edited reports from missionaries, obituaries, accounts of indigenous cultures from a Christian viewpoint, lists of subscribers, and news of home-based fund-raising efforts. Many missionary reports were incorporated into the general religious press or appeared as supplements, but many appeared between separate covers.[47] Circulations of twenty thousand or more were claimed, and the covers provided a useful advertising medium. Magazines focusing on one region or type of mission were a refinement of this type of journalism, and illustrated juvenile missionary magazines were another early development.[48] Home missionary societies produced a similar literature aimed at financial supporters. These magazines contained letters and intelligences from home mission stations, lists of contributors, and accounts of the predominantly rural lower classes, whose fairs, revels, sports, and open hostility to missionary enterprise were described in the same terms as the alien cultures encountered by overseas missionaries. Occasionally, reports of this type were tempered by more perceptive comments on lower-class economic and social conditions.[49] The supporters of these movements also backed the new city missions of the 1830s, which produced their own monthly press, concentrating on slum missionaries' journals and the problems of poverty, prostitution, and Sabbath breaking.[50] Home and city missionary magazines were supplemented by other publications which called for the adoption of more dynamic American techniques of revivalism or were much more sympathetic toward the new temperance movement than the bulk of the religious press.[51]

Evangelists required cheap literature, and tracts had long been used, but by the 1820s more and more periodicals entered the field. Many were little more than monthly penny tracts of a narrowly pious and improving kind, and were distributed free through Sunday schools and house-to-house visitation. The *Cottager Magazine* and Carus Wilson's *Friendly Visitor* were among Evangelical Anglican pioneers, and although conversions were attributed to their distribution, the clumsy moralizing and crude attempts at social control must have alienated most lower-class readers, if they were read much at all by the classes for whom they were designed. Later High Anglican and Methodist examples of the genre were better illustrated and contained useful information on health, agriculture, and natural history. By the 1830s numerous organizations and individuals were producing these journals, which were never able to compete in popularity with either sensational working-class literature or the new illustrated penny weeklies.[52]

The 1820s also saw the rapid growth of children's magazines. Early publications like the *Youth's Magazine* and the Wesleyan *Youth's Instructor* cost between threepence and sixpence and were aimed more at the children of ministers and the pious laity than the masses. They contained useful information, history, and biography as well as pious material, though the juvenile obituaries in the Wesleyan magazine were a sobering reminder of eternity.[53] Circulation of this type of magazine never compared with that of the later penny children's monthlies which were popularized by the Religious Tract Society with the *Child's Companion* in 1824. The Wesleyans competed with their *Child's Magazine*, which quickly claimed a circulation of more than 42,000.[54] The other Methodist bodies quickly followed, as did Anglicans and Nonconformists, their children's periodicals having a circulation from a few hundred to some thousands, many being given away as gifts and Sunday school rewards. High Anglicans and hyper-Calvinists added to this plethora of penny children's journals down to the 1850s and beyond.[55] These magazines were usually small (5½ × 3½ inches) and contained short items and simple illustrations. While moral tales and simple Christian instruction remained and thrift, industry, and cleanliness were regularly inculcated, these periodicals increasingly contained simple science and technology, nature study, travel, and biblical history. Many contained a mixture of cultural chauvinism, racial stereotyping, and serious attempts at explaining other cultures to children.[56] Some, like Carus Wilson's *Children's Friend*, were morbidly pious with regular "lines on an infant who died at daybreak" and similar tombstone pieces, but gradually even the more sectarian children's serials came to include much popular information, with nature study the most common subject.[57] Other groups, such as Sunday school teachers and lay preachers, also became the focus of special literature designed to aid them in their work. Some of these journals were ephemeral, but others had long and profitable careers.[58]

RELIGIOUS NEWSPAPERS

Publication of a successful weekly religious newspaper assumed the existence of sufficient members of a denomination or party able to afford the usual price of sixpence or sevenpence per copy. The struggle for Catholic emancipation and the defense of Nonconformist rights by the Protestant Society for the Protection of Religious Liberty produced early weeklies, but many of the pioneering efforts in this field were stillborn or collapsed after a few issues.[59]

At least one early editor was grateful for the "very fine turkey" and "excellent sparerib of pork" which he received to aid him in his work, and efforts by comparatively small sects to maintain weekly newspapers were usually failures.[60] From the late 1820s, however, with the appearance of the Evangelical Anglican *Record*, successful papers increased rapidly. None were official enterprises though some, like the Wesleyan *Watchman*, became closely identified with the views of a ruling clique.[61] Some, like the Unitarian *Inquirer*, were individually owned, but many, especially of the Nonconformist enterprises, were vested in a small group of laymen and ministers who acted as trustees and distributed any profits to approved causes.[62] Initial capital was often small and editorial arrangements makeshift, with commercial publishers and printers handling the production side of the business. Some early ventures, like the Catholic *Tablet,* ran into difficulties when commercial partners went bankrupt in separate ventures or tried to start rival papers.[63] Editors often had other political, journalistic, clerical, or business commitments. With much news taken from the daily and foreign press, and a network of religious contacts providing reports of denominational affairs, local events, reviews and other features, the life of an editor was not too hard, though on occasion they were known to write much of the copy.[64]

Initial circulations were often small, and many religious weeklies averaged around 2,500 copies for long periods. The *Nonconformist,* which claimed to be the most popular dissenting weekly in the 1850s, had only a circulation of 3,200 in 1853, while the Anglican *Record* averaged about 4,000 copies by that date.[65] Many denominations resisted the publication of weeklies, fearing harm to the existing monthly press.[66] Probably the majority of churchgoers did not subscribe to a weekly, through lack of interest, or money, or because they were offended by editorial policy. This was certainly true among the Wesleyans, when after the demise of the controversial *Christian Advocate,* several ephemeral newspapers culminating in the *Wesleyan Times* headed a liberal movement resulting in the great Methodist disruption of the 1850s.[67] The *Wesleyan Times* was not only politically liberal but favored temperance and popular revivalism, movements viewed with disfavor by the Wesleyan establishment. The ephemeral *Bible Christian* and Primitive Methodist weeklies were much more radical but lacked an adequate constituency to survive.[68]

By the 1840s Evangelical Dissenters had a choice between the old established and moderate *Patriot* and the better known and more radical *Nonconformist* with its support of the Complete Suffrage Union, Anti-Corn Law League, and disestablishment. The Unitarian *Inquirer* like the *Patriot* aimed at a "liberal political position, without party prejudice or violence."[69] All three of these papers maintained strong links with American Christians and took a close interest in the development of the antislavery movement in the United States.[70] Anglicans had a variety of papers reflecting the different parties within the church, while Catholics enjoyed a choice between the increasingly pro-Irish *Tablet* and the *Weekly Register* or the *Catholic Standard.*[71]

Many of the papers had a similar format with a leader and news reports under such headings as "Parliament," "Foreign," "Agriculture," "Markets," and other standard topics. The material here was taken from other domestic and foreign papers. There was also much denominational and general religious news with extensive reports of the meetings of churches and great religious societies. The more radical papers also provided extensive coverage of political reform movements and of temperance, peace, antislavery, and allied campaigns, Anglicans, of course, took a much greater interest in preferments and university news and in the doings of the hierarchy and the national religous societies. There were also extensive reviews, sketches, correspondence, poetry, and similar features. While stressing the need for papers which would exclude everything injurious to religion and morality, many of the religious weeklies reported sensational crimes, devoting three columns or more to a sensational poisoning or a good abduction.[72] In the weeklies, the bulk of the advertisements were for religious societies and meetings, books, consumer goods, employment, schools, births, marriages, and deaths. Theological loyalties extended to employment, with "Wesleyan preferred" or "of decidedly evangelical sentiments" and similar descriptions appearing in many of the advertisements. With the growth of the total abstinence movement, papers like the *Watchman* faced bitter opposition from Methodist temperance workers when they continued to advertise alcoholic liquors.

A curious and long-lived publication was the *Ecclesiastical Gazette*, an Anglican trade paper, which was distributed free to all beneficed clergy of the Church of England and sold to the public for sixpence. The *Gazette* reported parliamentary debates and the law courts, especially as they related to the Church, and covered university news and the work of the great religious societies, but the bulk of its contents consisted of advertisements for livings and clerical employment. The tone was quite different from similar advertisements in the *Record* or *Guardian* which emphasized piety and principles. Here income, houses, and personal convenience were the predominant themes, with the quality of the hunting and fishing as important as more obviously clerical matters. While the rich and well connected sought livings worth from £1,000 to £2,000 per annum, college fellows pursued "temporary duty during the Long Vacation," and poor curates and schoolmasters competed for employment at £40 to £100.[73]

NEW MAGAZINES OF CHURCH AND SECT, 1830–1860

Many religious serials which appeared in this period can only be touched on here. Cheaper printing costs and the growth of church membership facilitated the appearance of local and regional journals often designed to unite Nonconformist congregations or promote Evangelism. Catholic emancipation, the Oxford movement, and the reestablishment of the Catholic hierarchy stimulated a great wave of militantly anti-Catholic magazines ranging from comparatively scholarly journals edited by college principals to scurrilous penny magazines, which although appearing under clerical auspices came close to pornography with their stories of such "fruits of nunneries" as transvestism and infanticide.[74] Of course, Catholics defended themselves against such ridiculous charges, and in this period had more success in establishing a regular periodical press. William Ar
and his family published a succession of cheap weekly, fortnight

monthly magazines bearing the word *Orthodox* in their titles which ran until 1849. Each number contained domestic and foreign Catholic news including Ireland, articles defending the Catholic tradition, reports on the work of Catholic schools, tract societies and similar agencies, and items of general Catholic interest. In later years, a correspondence column, book reviews, and a weekly diary of festivals were popular features.[75] Competition came from a succession of more expensive and scholarly Catholic magazines published in Edinburgh, London, and other cities. Usually priced sixpence, they adhered to a monthly schedule and in the hands of Charles Dolman became literary magazines.[76] Wealthy and well-educated Catholics also founded a high quality literary and intellectual press, which has already attracted much scholarly attention. Similar developments also occurred in the Nonconformist and Methodist press.[77]

Established groups like the Quakers did not begin a regular religious press until this period, while smaller bodies which had failed in the past were now able to acquire regular monthlies. A few, like the Moravians, still found the going tough because of the smallness of their communions or disagreements about the format and contents of their magazines.[78] The continuing conflict and schisms among the Wesleyan Methodists also produced a large periodical literature of roughly two types. There were ephemeral and irregular sheets put out by the Wesleyan leadership and their opponents. These were fiercely polemical and abusive, and disappeared as conflict ended in schism. New sects and Book Rooms were organized and new magazines appeared still modeled on the Wesleyan magazine.[79] The great Methodist disruption of midcentury produced a flood of magazines which mirrored discontent at many levels, and the Wesleyan Book Room tried to combat this literature. In time the anti-Wesleyan magazines disappeared or were replaced by the publications of the new United Methodist Free Church which absorbed most of the schismatics. Like the newspapers of this movement, the magazines were more sympathetic toward temperance, revivalism, disestablishment, and radical politics, though many of the well-established features of Methodist magazine journalism were also retained.[80] Other branches of Methodism also had their malcontents, with Joseph Barker, the ex–New Connexion preacher, making the most vigorous use of the cheap magazine to chart his move toward radical free thought.[81]

By the 1830s the majority of Particular Baptists supported the liberal Baptist Union, but many congregations resisted this trend, restricting communion to believers who had undergone baptism by immersion, and emphasizing a rigid Calvinism in which Christ's atonement was for a particular and predestined group chosen before the foundation of the world. Hyper-Calvinist views were already expressed through the *Gospel Magazine,* the *Spiritual Magazine* and other monthlies, but these did not speak exclusively for Baptists.[82] There were probably three or four hundred rigidly sectarian Baptist churches, a few of them large, but the majority having no more than thirty or forty members, who were largely shopkeepers, artisans, and their families. Some congregations were prosperous with well-educated ministers including converts from the Church of England, but the majority struggled along without full-time pastors.[83] Although some of these congregations did support local and regional associations, their principal method of communication was through cheap magazines whose editors were sect leaders. Such men as Samuel Collins, William and John Gadsby, J. C. Philpot, James Wells, and Charles Banks were spiritual giants in their milieu. To outsiders, their magazines, the *Gospel Herald,* the *Gospel Standard,* the *Gospel Ambassador,* and the *Earthen Vessel,* seemed very similar, with a heavy emphasis on Puritan divinity, sermons and controversial articles stressing sound doctrine, the dying words of "saints," preaching appointments, and poetry. Some journals were less rigid than others in their contents, but they shared a curiously old-fashioned and verbose language with much emphasis on "poor worms and sinners," "sovereign grace," and "separation from worldly professors."[84] They were recommended from the pulpit, and sold in vestries as well as by booksellers and rarely cost more than twopence.[85] Much of the energy of these congregations was consumed not in conflict with liberal Baptists but with each other, in obscure but passionately conducted debates about the "Sonship of the Lord Jesus Christ" and similar questions. Some conservative Baptists tried to occupy a middle ground between the Baptist Union and the hyper-Calvinists developing a periodical literature which was more open to new ideas and supported the major Evangelical societies. Towards the end of this period Spurgeon rallied Baptists of this type and as a great popular preacher issued his own magazines.[86] Baptist magazines in this tradition drew heavily on the Calvinist periodicals of the eighteenth century and advertisements reflected the narrow world of the chapel, where ironmongers offered goods to fellow believers in "free grace" and offered apprentices homes where "truth was taught."[87]

Periodicals also occupied an important but varying place in the development of new sects in this period. With their tight discipline and organization, the Mormons relied heavily on a single publication which expounded the new revelation, charted the history of the movement, fought its battles, and bound together the converts for the journey to America.[88] Also American influenced, the Churches of Christ were a much looser confederation without paid ministers, and early controversies found expression in conflicting magazines, until a powerful leader established a firm grip on the sect and its literature. Millenarianism was a powerful force in both movements, but some adventist sects like Millerites scarcely existed long enough to organize a separate press.[89] Although sects of this type possessed prosperous members, the majority were artisans and laborers similar to those who attended, for example, Primitive Methodist chapels, where the new sects tried to recruit. The style and intellectual level of sect periodicals reflect this situation and an awareness that most members were not going to purchase much literature beyond the magazines themselves. Other new sects with millenarian preoccupations recruited more business and professional men, and could support a much more extensive literature of which periodicals were only a small part. Pamphlets and books, for example, featured largely in the early history and controversies of the Irvingites and the Brethren, although magazines played a part, and it was not until the Brethren divided in the 1840s that the Open Brethren commenced magazine publishing on an extensive scale, aiming as much at evangelism as the edification of existing members.[90]

THE IMPACT OF THE CHEAP PRESS, 1830–1870

By the 1830s new technology made possible cheap illustrated magazines in great quantities. Although the churches constantly expressed alarm about the "pernicious trash" which circulated among the lower classes, it was the better quality cheap magazines that offered direct competition to religious publishers. Both the *Penny Magazine* and *Chambers's Edinburgh Magazine* which sold for three-halfpence were too factual and abstruse for many, but they appealed to churchgoing skilled artisans and shopkeepers and their families. The solid information, larger pages, and numerous illustrations in the new journals set high standards for religious publishers who aimed at more than sectarian audiences.[91] In addition, commercial publishers soon devised new types of penny weeklies like the *Family Herald* which also enjoyed favor with the petty bourgeoisie and labor aristocracy. Each sixteen-page issue contained an instalment of a serial, a short piece of fiction, answers to correspondents, informative articles on history and biography, and one or more pieces on contemporary problems. There was no theology and the editor came from a radical Universalist background.[92] As with the *Penny Magazine,* the *Herald* and its imitators offered much more of a threat to the circulation of religious literature than the more sensational weeklies or secularist magazines.

> Many a domestic circle that would justly repel the organ of atheistic secularism, or the grossly immoral trash of the Reynolds' school, because their irreligion is too palpable, admit the *Herald* for its "recreation and harmless pastimes" whilst receiving along with it (knowingly or unknowingly) the teachings of an infidel theology.[93]

By 1850 Unitarian home missionaries in Leicester were reporting that merely religious literature had little circulation but that weeklies like the *Family Herald* sold almost as many copies as periodicals which specialized in stories of the "Newgate Calendar class."[94] The demand was more and more heard within the churches for cheap magazines of useful information and amusement which were in harmony with sound religious principles.[95]

The *Penny Magazine* quickly faced competition from journals of popular education issued by the large religious publishing organizations. The SPCK published the *Saturday Magazine,* an eight-page weekly priced at one penny. It had a large format, vivid illustrations, and lively articles on such subjects as science, biography, and travel written from a Christian perspective.[96] The Religious Tract Society's *Weekly Visitor* was an even cheaper version of the same genre.[97] Both these magazines appealed to a similar audience as the *Penny Magazine* and *Chambers's.* But the great majority of cheap religious periodicals which flooded the market in the 1830s and early 1840s remained narrowly pious and often denominational. Many were little more than better illustrated and updated versions of the "Cottagers" type of monthly, designed for free distribution to the poor, while numerous others were essentially simplified versions of the sixpenny and shilling denominational press aimed at poorer members, young people, and children. There were a bewildering range of titles and only a few examples can be cited here. Many sold only a few hundred or a few thousand copies, while claims of huge circulations can often be explained by the discovery of charitable organizations designed to promote free distribution.[98]

Catholics ventured as readily into this field as Protestants, though Catholic penny weeklies and fortnightlies had a high death rate. Nonconformists largely restricted their activity to penny and twopenny monthly magazines reporting denominational affairs, Sunday school news, evangelistic work and sometimes politics.[99] Hyper-Calvinist publications like *Zion's Trumpet* or the *Penny Spiritual Magazine* sold only a few thousand copies among the true believers. On the other hand, the long-running *Church of England Magazine,* a weekly selling for three-halfpence, aimed at a broad cross section of Anglican families, with religious biography, history, sermons, essays, and religious news. It avoided a dogmatic party line, but probably had little appeal outside the churchgoing middle classes.[100] The Wesleyans' *Cottager's Friend* always contained simple articles on science and popular education and when transformed into the *Christian Miscellany* became a twopenny monthly aimed at the younger and poorer sections of the denomination. It remained an uneasy mixture of piety and popular education, but easily outsold the regular denominational magazines.[101]

Difficulties associated with publishing a growing range of serials, competition from nonreligious publishers, and attempts at countering that competition, all produced problems for religious publishers and especially for the Methodist Book Rooms. Wesleyans and Primitive Methodists were forced to abandon their own presses in favor of more competitive contract printers, and most Methodist publishing operations were centralized in London. More staff were recruited and larger premises engaged, and although most contributors remained unpaid, some copy was purchased.

The format and content of the different Methodist magazines were revised on a number of occasions, but although some success was achieved, sales of sixpenny and shilling denominational journals did not keep pace with the growth of membership.[102] This was also true of many of the older non-Methodist monthlies which generally survived but with little liveliness or growth.

Among the Congregationalists, the cheap magazines aggressively edited by John Campbell helped to kill the old *Congregational Magazine*. Campbell's *Christian Witness* became the official organ of the Congregational Union until his liking for violent controversy resulted in the withdrawal of official favor in the late 1850s. The *Witness* barely covered costs from subscriptions, and profits, which went to retired ministers, came almost entirely from advertisements.[103] The *Baptist Magazine* also faced competition from cheap local and regional journals, with Benjamin Evans as perhaps the best known of the popular ministerial journalists.[104] By midcentury certain commercial publishers and printers like Nisbet had come to occupy an important position in the religious publishing field, while smaller houses catered to the needs of more specialist markets with, for example, Houlston and Stone, and Gadsby publishing much conservative Baptist material, while Wilks fulfilled a similar role among the General Baptists. Large interdenominational agencies like the SPCK, the Religious Tract Society, and the Sunday School Union were also a major force in religious publishing, especially in the area of popular education and entertainment, where the pioneering penny magazines of the 1830s were replaced by new and glossier weeklies.[105]

The Religious Tract Society's *Weekly Visitor* had become a monthly after a few years but maintained a high standard of articles on natural history, astronomy, travel, and other useful subjects.[106] In 1858 the *Visitor* was absorbed in the new *Leisure Hour,* a penny weekly which quickly won widespread church support. It was not strictly a religious publication but a magazine of popular entertainment with articles on travel, science, manufacturing, and similar informative topics. Some features were clearly carried over from the earlier magazine. The purpose was to produce a popular journal written from a decidedly Christian viewpoint. A companion magazine, *Sunday at Home,* had a similar format but more obviously religious content. They were both designed for family reading.[107] From the midfifties more and more publishers entered this field, with some commercial firms like Cassell drawing upon their success in general magazine publishing. These new journals of instruction, entertainment, and religion appeared both weekly and monthly, and were welcomed by many churches as superior to literature of the *Family Herald* type.[108] Magazines such as *Good Words,* the *Quiver,* the *Hive, Our Own Fireside* and many others were often edited by popular ministers and clergymen, and contained well-written articles by public figures and writers. Fiction became an increasingly important feature, and illustrations were numerous and lavish.[109] Some magazines which competed in this market like the *Sunday Magazine,* the *Christian Treasury,* and the *Churchman's Family Magazine* were more distinctly religious or denominational, but their format and contents were influenced by the new penny magazines, which represented a transformation of popular religious journalism.[110] In a modest way the Catholic press also reflected the change, with the *Lamp* struggling on for many years as a distinctly Catholic penny magazine devoted to literature, science, and general instruction.[111]

Many of the new magazines of religious entertainment sold in weekly or monthly parts, and as volumes, thus maximizing circulation, while their advertising covers focused on food, clothing, and furniture with advertisements for branded goods taking up increasing space. Most liberal denominations welcomed these developments though they often had to alter their own publications, increasing page sizes, improving illustrations, paying contributors, and gradually including fiction.[112] Conservative Evangelicals, however, bitterly opposed the trend, the *Record* publishing a fierce attack on *Good Words* for its "unorthodox" contributors and its high proportion of secular material which might be read on the Sabbath. Other new popular magazines faced similar battles, the so-called "Second Evangelical Awakening" stimulating a wave of conservative activity.[113]

"The Awakening" produced renewed interest in revivalism, perfectionism, and millenarianism, and strengthened opposition to liberal theology, scientific thought, and the secularization of society. The conservatives were not united, but a large group expressed their interest in popular evangelism through the *Revival* (later the *Christian*), which first appeared as a halfpenny weekly in July 1859. It aimed to report and promote the current revival and became a rallying point for many Evangelical Anglicans, conservative Nonconformists, and Brethren in their support for the later campaigns of Moody and Sankey, the Keswick Convention, and what was to become Fundamentalism. The publisher of the *Christian,* R. C. Morgan, was to become a partner in the premier firm in this field, but he had many rivals.[114] Conservative Methodists also supported their own press with a succession of cheap magazines like the *Revival Advocate,* the *Messenger of Life,* and the *Revivalist,* which fulfilled similar functions to the *Revival,* but lacked its permanence. These magazines were often the voice of a particular British or American revivalist, just as William Booth acquired his own magazine to promote the East London Mission, later the Salvation Army.[115] Open Brethren both supported Morgan and had their own publishing houses, while Michael Baxter's *Signs of the Times* and *Christian Herald* catered to the interest in millenarianism. Theologically and often socially conservative, all these magazines reported revival campaigns, Bible conventions, and holiness meetings and included much devotional and inspirational writing. Fiction and light entertainment were generally excluded and illustrations remained sparse.[116] The conservatives also supported a huge number of specialist agencies which built on the foundations of the home and city missionary societies, the Sunday schools and similar organizations developed early in the century. Magazines appeared which focused on ragged children, cabmen, navvies, soldiers, sailors, and many other groups. Evangelicals were not alone in undertaking this work, but they were its main supporters. The magazines were aimed at both financial supporters and 'victims,' and in the case of the latter type of journal they were often distributed free. This remained true of much of the conservative religious press with, for example, thousands of magazines being given away to promote revival campaigns.[117]

CHEAP RELIGIOUS NEWSPAPERS AFTER 1850

The abolition of the Advertisement Tax in 1853, of the Newspaper Stamp Duty in 1855, and of the Paper Duty in 1861, were crucial in the development of cheap religious newspapers. Earlier efforts to establish cheap newspapers had been made, especially by John Campbell, who persuaded the proprietors of the sevenpenny *Patriot* to back him in issuing a cheap Congregationalist weekly. Campbell used the *British Banner* to ride his hobbyhorses, and by 1856 his violent and dogmatic views, especially on theology, led to the withdrawal of official Congregationalist support and the paper's demise. The ebullient Campbell started other papers, but by then competition in the field was increasing, and he relied heavily on subsidies from backers who took up to five thousand copies each for free distribution.[118] With the abolition of the Stamp Duty, the Baptists quickly started their own weekly paper, but this was little different from exisiting religious newspapers, which were themselves reducing their prices. The *Freeman* aimed to provide a complete family newspaper from a Baptist and liberal perspective, and offered the usual range of foreign and domestic news plus denominational reports, reviews, and entertainment. A circulation of about two thousand placed it firmly in the older tradition of religious newspaper journalism.[119]

From the late 1850s there emerged a new type of penny religious newspaper which attracted a much wider audience. A pioneer in this field was the Nonconformist *Christian World,* founded in 1857 and soon acquired by James Clarke, perhaps the ablest journalist in the field. Clarke enlisted gifted writers from among Nonconformists, and adopted a liberal policy on theology and politics. He was quick to include fiction and much travel writing by well-known ministers, and tried to appeal to the widest audience. Clarke also recognized other markets, issuing the more sober fourpenny *English Independent* as a rival to the *Nonconformist,* and publishing magazines in many other religious fields.[120] The 1860s saw a spate of short-lived Nonconformist penny weekly newspapers reflecting personal ambitions and political differences. Samuel Morley and other wealthy businessmen underwrote many of these enterprises which grew upon the journalistic skills of men like David Thomas and J. B. Paton, who had already written at length for the press.[121] Some penny weeklies came close to being popular magazines rather than newspapers, with a few secular items, limited religious news, and much space devoted to sermons, anecdotes, poetry, hints on health and behavior, and fiction. At the end of this period the American-influenced *Christian Age* commenced a long history as a weekly of this latter type.[122]

The more distinctly denominational penny weeklies were more like genuine newspapers than the *Christian Age,* though they lacked the coverage of the older and more expensive papers. As with Campbell's *British Banner* and James Clarke's enterprises, both types of newspapers were often issued by the same company. As early as 1859 the Wesleyan Book Room was urged to publish a penny religious newspaper but declined to undertake the project, fearing conflict with the *Watchman* and political controversy.[123] A group of younger ministers persisted, however, and in April 1861 the *Methodist Recorder* appeared. Ownership soon passed to the Wesleyan Methodist Newspaper Company controlled by wealthy laymen and ministers, who also owned the *Watchman.*[124] Like many papers of this type, the *Methodist Recorder* had an average of a dozen pages of which three or four were devoted to advertisements, largely for books and consumer goods, with some half and whole-page displays of branded goods. Secular news occupied only three or four columns and the bulk of the paper covered denominational reports, general church news, reviews, correspondence, and short items. Fiction began to appear by the 1870s and the political tone was liberal compared with the *Watchman.*[125]

The Primitive Methodists entered the field a few years later with the privately owned *Primitive Methodist,* which gradually won official approval. Format and contents were broadly similar to those of the *Recorder* but the politics were more firmly identified with the Liberal party.[126] Catholic ventures into cheap weekly journalism included the *Universe* and a succession of papers which became the popular Liverpool-based *Catholic Times.* Both papers had a long struggle before achieving success, as did the moderately High Anglican *Church Times* which first appeared as an eight-page weekly in 1863. Ultra-Evangelical Anglicans had the *Rock,* whose militant anti-Catholicism began to make the older *Record* seem moderate.[127] By the early 1870s, with the appearance of the *Baptist Times* edited by G. A. Hutchinson, who later moved on to the *Boy's Own Paper,* most influential religious groups had acquired a penny weekly press.[128]

CONCLUSION

By 1870 old denominational monthlies like the *Wesleyan Methodist Magazine* had lost ground. They were bought more from loyalty than preference, and their declining circulation reflected discontent with their form and contents and the availability of more attractive alternatives. The early magazines had tried to cater to a broad audience, but the growth of specialist publications for children, young people, ministers, and other groups had eaten into their market. Popular religious newspapers replaced magazines as the principal voice of the church, and although they commented on the public issues of the day, their inclusion of nonreligious material also reflected congregations which had grown comfortable and were expanding more by natural increase and social convention than by vigorous Evangelism. Even the flood of Evangelistic literature promoted by conservative Christians was probably more important in uniting the promoters than reaching the unchurched masses, who remained largely indifferent to the free literature pushed in their direction. Sects like the Primitive Methodists, which had once possessed techniques to reach the lower classes, had become churches of the lower middle classes, whose literature reflected the distance that they had moved from their origins. Cheap publishing costs allowed sectarian magazines to flourish, but most of them remained unknown beyond very narrow circles. It is difficult to escape the conclusion that by 1870 the massively expanded religious press was closer to its secular counterpart in tone and business methods than it had been at the beginning of the century. This conclusion is reinforced when one turns to the religious literature of popular instruction and entertainment created by commercial publishers and large religious agencies after 1850. These journals reflected a new level of professionalism in both contributors and publishers, but they blurred distinctions between the secular and the religious, and offered a reassuring but undemanding faith.

6
Children and the Press, 1866–1914

Diana Dixon

Between 1866 and 1914 there were over five hundred periodicals for children and young people in existence. Although some only survived for a few weeks, the large number of titles indicates a recognition by publishers that the juvenile market was ripe for exploitation. Periodicals for children certainly existed before 1866, but with a very few exceptions they were religious and decidely serious in their tone. The year 1866 marked a watershed because three very different, but important, periodicals were started:*Aunt Judy's Magazine* (1866–85); *Boys of England* (1866–99) and *Chatterbox* (1866–1948). Their significance was that they all had the avowed intention of amusing as well as instructing their readers. They were presented much more attractively and they appealed to their young readers much more than the austere and dull formats of periodicals like the *Children's Companion* (1824–1932) and the *Little Gleaner* (1854–ca.1946).

Juvenile periodicals fall into several distinct groups. Some were directed at a particular age group or sex. Others were intended for members of a particular religious denomination, but many were general in character and intended for young people between the ages of about ten and twenty. Most did not restrict themselves to a particular social class; for instance, the Religious Tract Society insisted the *Childs' Companion* was as suitable for "children in the gentleman's lodge as the cottage home."[1] Likewise, the *Girl's Own Paper* (1880–1956) reminded a correspondent, "Our girls are of all classes in life and we are anxious to be a real friend to all of them."[2]

Over a third of all titles were intended specifically for boys, and the majority of these were weeklies selling at 1d. a copy or less. The boys' penny weekly has attracted the most attention from critics, both at the time and since.[3] Even this group can be divided into those that were considered respectable and those that were not. It is the more lurid and sensational ones, direct successors to the penny dreadfuls of the 1840s and 1850s, that evoked the wrath of contemporary critics. Many of these periodicals, of which Brett's *Boys of England,* is the best known, emanated from a small band of publishers and were noteworthy for their shoddy appearance, their shallow and sensational fiction, and their transience. The critics sug-

BOYS OF ENGLAND

A Young Gentleman's Journal
OF SPORT, SENSATION, FUN AND INSTRUCTION.

Vol. II.—No. 35.] Conducted by Edwin J. Brett. [Price One Penny

"HANDS OFF, SCOUNDREL!"

THE CAPTAIN OF THE SCHOOL.

By the Author of "Giles Evergreen."

CHAPTER I.

THE CRICKET-MATCH.

THE EIGHTEENTH OF JUNE.

ODAY famous in the annals of the world, and ever to be remembered for having brought face to face two of the bravest and pluckiest armies in the world, was likewise one of great excitement and expectation in the town and adjacent neighbourhood of Riverdale.

It had been long looked forward to with feelings of great enthusiasm by all classes—the high born and the low caste, the merchant and the mechanic, the peer and the plebian, the countess and the cottager, alike partook in the excitement of the day, and at the earliest dawn were making preparations for the great event.

The lofty chimnies of the huge factories emitted no smoke, the thousand looms that went up and down with an almost ceaseless din and clang were silent; the ledger and the cash-book were permitted to slumber, the shops were closed, the taverns were unfrequented, spirited visitors they had none; there was no customer to give a cordial welcome to, and to a stranger it might have appeared that the Angel of Death and Desolation had marked the town for its own, save that though

Saturday, July 20, 1867.

***Boys of England* 35, Saturday, 20 July 1867 (British Library).**

gested they were vicious and depraved and claimed they caused impressionable youths to become criminals.[4] It is difficult to find evidence to support these assertions, and although the contents may have been feeble, superficial, and stereotyped, they were not intrisically evil. Certainly their editors did not see them in this light at all. An air of pompous complacency and moral rectitude exuded from the editorials of even the most ephemeral titles. The first number of the *Bad Boys' Paper* (1889) claimed "to provide a healthy and entertaining paper," yet this very paper was singled out as "dangerous, foolish and vicious" in the *Quarterly Review*.[5]

Who were these periodicals intended for? Between 1870 and 1885 the number of children receiving an elementary education trebled and publishers were quick to realize that this represented a vast, hitherto untapped potential market. It was recognized that literacy standards were low and that the fare provided had to be simple. It seems likely that many of these boys' weeklies were directed at the urban school leavers working in offices, shops, and factories. The absence of references to periodicals in memoirs of rural life suggests that they probably were considered an expensive luxury. Joseph Ashby of Tysoe[6] recalled how the *Boy's Own Paper* (1879–1967) circulated among all the children in the village. On the other hand, the urban working lad could probably afford to part with 1*d*. a week and publishers exercised their ingenuity to ensure loyalty to a particular title.

Competition between titles was fierce and the transient lives of many indicates that the market was fickle. It is hard to define the ingredient of success. Brett's *Boys of England* survived for thirty-three years, and it is claimed that it enjoyed remarkably large circulation figures in its early years. By its eighteenth number in 1866 it boasted a circulation of 150,000 weekly. Yet, in appearance and substance it was not very different from its less successful rivals. All provided fiction designed to transport their readers into a glamorous fantasy world of heroes in bizarre situations of mistaken identity, historical epics, and highly improbable adventures in darkest Africa or Greenland. Even the settings of public school stories were as alien to their readers as those of tiger hunts in Asia. For a penny a week, a dimension of glamour and excitement was added to a life that was at best unexciting. Many urban school-leavers lived in dark, insanitary, and overcrowded tenements and frequently worked long hours. Their lives were often mundane, dreary and hard.

What is interesting about the large number of sensational boys' weeklies in the period 1866–95 is that they were produced by a remarkably small band of publishers. Best known are Brett, Emmett, Fox, Rayner, Rollington, Shurey and Stevens. Apart from the well-documented rivalry between Brett and Emmett,[7] Rollington suggests that most were the greatest of friends, and the keen rivalry displayed in the editorials did not extend into their private lives.[8] Penny pinching was certainly a characteristic of their operations. Reputable boys' authors never contributed to these magazines. Contributors seemed to write exclusively for the sensational weeklies, and apart from stories by the creator of Jack Harkaway, Bracebridge Hemyng, they never featured elsewhere. Impecunious proprietors could affect a certain versatility by presenting anonymous stories or by using pseudonyms. In a single issue of *Young Briton's Journal*[9] in 1888 the unsuccessful but resourceful Guy Rayner (S. Dacre Clark) tried to give his readers the impression of a thriving team of authors by adopting three different pseudonyms. A regular contributor to many of these weeklies, Alf Burrage, had a string of pseudonyms including Cyril Hathaway, Alf Sherrington, Philander Jackson, and H.U.A. (Hard Up Author). Because so many journals were short-lived it was possible to use the same material over and over again. Rayner's material appeared in his own journals, and also in some of Rollington's before being reprinted by Shurey and Fox.

The 1890s saw the demise of these papers. Although this can partly be attributed to the success of the *Boy's Own Paper,* it is more likely because Harmsworth, Pearson, Newnes, and the Aldine Company were able to present similar material at half the price. Their secret was that they catered for all sections of the reading public rather than concentrating exclusively on boys' publications, and the scale of their operations meant that they were able to take advantage of improved production methods to produce magazines at ½*d.* a copy. The older proprietors simply could not afford to invest in new machinery and so were effectively undercut and were forced out of business.

By the first decade of the twentieth century, Harmsworth, Pearson, Newnes, and the Aldine Publishing Company had successfully captured the market of the cheap, popular boys' weekly. Articles in the *Publishers' Circular*[10] demonstrated their success, and it was claimed that Harmsworth's most successful titles sold over a million copies a week. Despite a vigorous campaign by Harmsworth to demonstrate the superiority of his product, in content and style it was very little different from its predecessors. The truth was that he was quite content to employ some of those authors he so sanctimoniously denounced as "drunken, sodden, creatures, whose lives have been one unbroken story of failure."[11] In addition he had a particular flair for picking authors whose characters became enduring household favorites. Sexton Blake made his first appearance in the *Halfpenny Marvel* (1893–1922), and later featured regularly in the *Union Jack* (1895–1932) and *Pluck* (1895–1916); and Billy Bunter made his debut in the *Magnet* (1908–29). Interestingly enough, however, few of Harmsworth's boys' authors ventured outside his publications.

None of the popular boys' weeklies saw themselves as appealing to one class of boy. The number of queries concerning professional training and career prospects in many of the more sensational weeklies does suggest they hoped to appeal to an upwardly mobile class. Louis James[12] gives us evidence to support this assertion. The spate of critical condemnations that appeared in the periodical press from 1870 onward attempted to influence middle-class parents against allowing children to read such trash. Boys may have derived considerable pleasure from surreptitious glances at those periodicals they were denied access to. That this was the case seems to be borne out by an editorial in *Every Boy's Journal*[13] (1884), "We do not want readers of this journal to hide it away or to read it in secret as if it were something to be ashamed of." Unfortunately, references in memoirs to such periodicals are extremely rare. An exception is George Sturt,[14] a newsagent's son, who recalls, "I liked to look at the *Young Men of Great Britain,* for the sake of its pictures of red Indians—a journal for some reason frowned upon by the seniors, but to my taste, far more attractive than the *Boys of England* substituted for it. These two journals could sometimes be found by rummaging in the piles stacked away in the dark under the shop window." similarly F. Gordon Roe[15] suggests, "Some productions, some far more reputable than others, were eagerly seized upon by boys in general, and not least by boys whose home-reading had been too strictly supervised. The contrast between Dean Farrar's mawkish school story *Eric, or, Little by Little* . . . and the dashing adventures of Jack Harkaway in the *Boys of England* was too strong for resistance. Old men, my father among them, were to cherish the liveliest boyhood memories of Jack's unbelievable exploits."

The success of the *Boy's Own Paper* was that it appealed to the boys as well as to their parents, and it satisfied a very real need. It was "founded with the express purpose of counteracting, nay of destroying and throwing out in the field, those publications which have a very large circulation, and which are of the most pernicious kind, and obtained eagerly by boys and girls of our streets."[16] A periodical that attracted the very best authors and illustrators of the day which inculcated the virtues of manliness and honesty, and hailed from the eminently respectable stable of the Religious Tract Society was applauded. Its formula was simple: stories by established and popular authors like Henty, Ballantyne, and Kingston, quality illustrations sometimes in color, and a substantial diet of information on practical matters and sport. In short, a periodical produced with the boy in mind. It is frequently singled out in memoirs with nostalgic affection. J. W. Robertson Scott remembers, "I read the *Boy's Own Paper* . . . relishing the *Fifth Form at St Dominics* and could not understand how some of my schoolfellows delighted in a blood-and-thundery rival called *Union Jack*."[17] The practical emphasis was recalled by John Middleton Murry, "Then at about fourteen, with one or two cronies, I would spend hours talking of a marvellous boat we were to build. What tiny fragment of substance this dream of ours possessed was derived from the *Boy's Own Paper* which had a series of articles telling you 'How to build sailing ships.' "[18]

Other periodicals tried to emulate the *Boy's Own Paper* but none was as successful. Griffith and Farran introduced *Union Jack* (1880–83) with W. H.

G. Kingston at the helm. It differed very little in content, appearance, and style from the *Boy's Own Paper* but it was never so successful. On assuming the editorial chair on the death of Kingston, Henty implored readers to find extra subscribers.[19] In 1892 Cassell's introduced *Chums* (1892–1934) but this, like Newnes's *Captain* (1899–1924), was clearly directed to middle-class boys. Both periodicals were designed to be read by public-school boys and to this end the *Captain* published photographs of the captains of the leading public schools. Both periodicals attracted leading authors, many of whom also contributed to the *Boy's Own Paper.* "There are, too, nowadays, many excellent journals published for boys," wrote Charles Russell in 1905, "The best of these is the *Captain,* a monthly journal, and *Chums,* which is published weekly. Either of these publications may be placed with confidence in the hands of any lad. There was a controversy in a London daily paper some time ago as to what girls read, and a number of fair correspondents declared that they preferred the *Captain* to the *Girl's Own Paper.*"[20]

In contrast to the lavish provision of titles of all sorts for boys, their sisters were not nearly so well provided for. Between 1870 and 1910 under 10 percent of all juvenile periodicals were intended for girls. They too benefited from the various Education Acts, but publishers never really regarded them as a market ripe for exploitation. The absence of a clearly defined periodical press for girls probably reflects their role in life. Even if she was literate, the female school-leaver probably did not have the reading time available to her that her brothers did. If she was in service, a girl was likely to work between fourteen and sixteen hours a day with very little time for relaxation. Even if she worked in an office, shop, or factory and lived at home she would be expected to take her share of housework and minding the younger children. Assuming she read at all, the materials at her disposal were likely to be religious periodicals or the penny novelettes. E. Salmon is particularly critical of the injurious effects of such literature:[6] . . . "there is hardly a magazine read by working class girls which it would not be a moral benefit to have swept off the face of the earth."[21]

Girls at this period could not retain their youthfulness like their brothers, and where girls' periodicals existed there was always a firm emphasis on homemaking.

Periodicals for girls always seemed a little uncertain of the age of their readers. A glance at the ages of winners of the prize competitions in the *Girl's Own Paper* reveals that in July 1887 they ranged from twelve to twenty-six years old. In *Atalanta* (1887–98) in November of the same year they were eighteen and nineteen years old, but readers were informed that the competitions were open to all under the age of twenty-five. It seems that they were intended for young women rather than girls. The *Girl's Own Paper* advertised itself in the *Newspaper Press Directory* as "a paper for young women and their mothers," and added the subtitle "And Women's Magazine" in 1908 in an attempt to extend its readership and clarify the ambiguity. Several girls' papers made it rather clear that they were not really intended for the lower orders. Neither *Atalanta* nor the *Girl's Realm* (1898–1915) contained material that would interest girls working in nonprofessional occupations. Indeed, the *Girl's Realm* explicitly stated that it catered for the better-class women and described itself as a high-class monthly. The *Girl's Own Paper* tried to be more democratic but more space was devoted to the problems of management of a home than to those of serving in it. Considerable space was devoted to the accomplishments of dressmaking, embroidery, and menu planning and most of the fashion plates depicted garments far beyond the reach of the factory girl or servant. What places the girls' magazine most firmly in its middle-class context is its price. Because they were more lavishly illustrated, with garlands of flowers as mastheads and pretty covers, they were more expensive to produce than those for boys, and many, like *Atalanta,* retailed at 6*d.* monthly. The emphasis seems to have been on quality, and reputable and famous authors like Mrs Molesworth and L. T. Meade featured in all the leading girls' periodicals, as did famous illustrators like Walter Crane, who illustrated *Atalanta,* and Kate Greenaway, the *Girl's Own Paper.*

There was no equivalent for girls of the sensational boys' weekly. Harmsworth produced a few girls' titles but many were of the caliber of the *Girl's Best Friend* (1898–1931) and contained "powerful dramatic love stories," that would have been considered suitable only for the servants' hall. On the whole, girls' periodicals were not as successful as those for their brothers, as is demonstrated by the short lives of many.

Many girls clearly enjoyed reading their brothers' magazines. Alice Pollock recalls her preference for boys' periodicals in *Portrait of my Victorian Youth.*[22] Correspondence columns in many boys' periodicals indicate girls were regular readers. In November 1894 the *Boy's Own paper* reassured a young lady, "You do not need to apologise for liking the B.O.P. Thousands of girls take it."[23] Pressure from girl readers, led the *Boy Amateur* to change its title to the *British Amateur* in December 1882.

One reason for the paucity of titles for girls, especially before 1880, may have been because girls were expected to enjoy some of the excellent general periodicals intended for middle-class children of both sexes. Examples of these are *Aunt Judy's Magazine, Good Words for the Young* (1868–77), *Merry and Wise* (1865–87) and *Kind Words for Boys and Girls* (1866–80). Despite the originality of the fiction and the excellence of the illustrations—*Aunt Judy's Magazine* attracted contributions from Lewis Carroll, Mrs. Molesworth, and Hans Christian Andersen, and W. H. G. Kingston and Ballantyne wrote for *Merry and Wise*—with the exception of *Kind Words,* which was produced by the Sunday School Union, few of these high-quality periodicals were economically viable. Even a famous author in the editorial chair did not guarantee success as is demonstrated by the short lives of *Aunt Judy's Magazine* under Mrs Ewing, *Union Jack* under Henty, and the girls' periodical *Atalanta* under L. T. Meade. Although several memoirs remember these magazines with affection, there is no doubt that the fact that they retailed at 6*d.* monthly made them less attractive to children and their parents.

The success of Cassell's *Little Folks* (1872–1933) was that it was aimed at a wider market than many of its rivals, and Simon Nowell-Smith suggests it owed its success to the fact it was "less didactic, less obtrusively pious, less 'goody-goody'" than its rivals.[24] Certainly the importance of reader participation was recognized in its correspondence columns and competitions. The wide age appeal is seen in the list of prize winners for December 1879, ranging from six to fifteen-and-a-half. Various writers recall their delight in receiving it. Mary Hughes notes, "After a while we were in sufficient funds to take in some magazines, *Sunshine* and *Little Folks* for the younger ones."[25]

Although *Little Folks* was intended for a wide age group, Cassell's later produced a magazine for the very young. Some nursery periodicals like *Bo-Peep* (1882–1962), *Our Little Dots* (1887–1940) and *Tiny Tots* (1899–1940) enjoyed long lives. Nonetheless, magazines for the young accounted for less than 8 percent of the total up to 1914.[26] Most of the major publishing houses, religious and commercial, aimed at least one title at the nursery. A number of these had suitably appealing titles like *Bright Eyes* (1893–1900) *Toddles* (1900), and *Tiny Trots* (1894) and were presented attractively, with an abundance of colored plates. Youthful readers were attracted by the large print and simplified spelling, but because they cost more to produce many were very short-lived.

Chatterbox was not envisaged as a nursery periodical by its founder, J. Erskine Clarke, but the slightness of its contents meant that it gained a loyal readership in the nursery. It had been intended as a wholesome, instructive, and amusing alternative to penny dreadfuls for children of the lower classes. Part of its appeal was its price: it retailed at ½*d.* a copy. Children enjoyed it, and Alison Uttley is only one of many who remembered with enthusiasm "my yearly *Chatterbox,* which I knew from cover to cover so I could repeat long portions of the stories."[27]

All the periodicals considered so far aimed at entertaining their young readers as well as instructing them. In sharp contrast to these were a large number of periodicals which existed for the sole purpose of providing moral edification. Many were expressly designed for reading on Sunday. In *Our Mothers,*[28] we are reminded that "Sundays were a day of torment for the young." Toys and playing games were forbidden and suitably selected devotional reading was all that was allowed between visits to church and Sunday school. There is no doubt that religion played an important part in the lives of many Victorian and Edwardian children. Over a third of all children's periodicals produced during this period were religious in character and many had an avowed crusading mission. Throughout the period religious periodicals could retail at consistently lower prices than their secular rivals. Many sold at ½*d.* a copy and thus could rival those from Harmsworth and Newnes in cheapness. The reason was that many were subsidized by their parent body and did not expect to make a profit. Production costs were minimal as contributors rarely expected payment, and illustrations, if they existed, were sparse. It is also probably reasonably safe to assume that circulations were assured, because readers were committed to the issuing body through membership of Sunday school or Church. Many titles became standard Sunday school prizes, as is revealed by plates in copies that have survived. It was probably no coincidence that the *Children's Prize* (1863–1931) was thus named.

The major religious publishing houses, the Religious Tract Society, Sunday School Union, and the SPCK all produced a number of successful titles. There was very little to choose between the best of their publications and those from their commercial rivals. Certainly the *Boy's Own Paper* and the *Girl's Own Paper* from the RTS were undisputed leaders in the field. The most successful title from the SSU was *Kind Words,* which became *Young England* in 1880. Less prominent were publications from the SPCK, but *Golden Sunbeams* (1896–1916) was an attractively presented periodical.

If the major religious publishing houses were not responsible for the spate of unedifying dreary magazines for the young, who was? Most churches, religious groups, boys' brigades, and Bands of Hope produced a periodical for their followers, either at national or local level. The titles alone do not suggest that readers could look forward to being amused or entertained by many of them: the *Jewish Advocate for the Young* (1846–), the *Juvenile Missionary Magazine* (1844–1946), and *South American Missionary Society's Juvenile Gift* (1872–9).

There were a number of publishers who specialized in low-cost, often low-quality, devotional reading. Some, like Wells, Gardner and Darton specialized in attractive annuals and gift books as well as periodicals, of which *Chatterbox* is the best known. Others penny-pinched to produce material as economically as possible. Juvenile periodicals from publishing houses like Nisbet, S. W. Partridge, G. Stoneman, F. E. Longley and Houlston are memorable for the dreariness of their presentation. Houlston's *Little Gleaner* is a particularly uninspiring example of its kind. Illustrations, in the 1892 volume, covered such miserable titles as "The tomb of a noted unbeliever," "Tell me why you took that orange?" and "A lie will burn in the memory"—all in black and white. The stories often contained a strong moral message in accordance with the expressed intention of "containing moral and religious readings". Readers of these dreary little magazines were not cocooned from harsh reality, as is demonstrated in an editorial in the *Child's Friend* (1865–1916) for 1872:

> This New Year will be the last some of you will spend on earth. Yes, it may be that even before the birds begin to sing their sweet spring songs, or

> the star-like primroses cover the mossy banks that you may be called to lie below a little grassy hillock. Dear young friend, if it should be your lot are you ready to die?[29]

It must be remembered that many of these periodicals enjoyed a long life and clearly achieved reasonable circulations. It is very difficult to trace circulation figures for this period, as figures are often extravagant claims intended to boost confidence in flagging ventures, or are nonexistent. However, in 1870 the *Newspaper Press Directory* carried an advertisement claiming a circulation of 64,000 for the *Juvenile Instructor*. This is modest in comparison with the 150,000 claimed by Brett for his *Boys of England*, but the readership was more loyal and less susceptible to enticements of rival publications. Even so, the religious press needed to encourage new subscribers in order to remain solvent, and like their less respectable rivals, were not above bribing their readers to recruit new readers. In 1913 the *Catholic Junior* was offering 5*s.* to the reader attracting the most new subscriptions.[30] It was interesting that contributors were frequently clergymen, who must have regarded their gratis literary contributions as a convenient extension of their pastoral duties. Wells, Gardner and Darton employed the Rev. J. Erskine Clarke to edit their juvenile periodicals, and Stoneman employed the Rev. W. M. Whittemore to edit *Little Star* (1886–89) and *Golden Hours* (1896–1916) among others. A particularly dreary little magazine, the *Children's Sunbeam* (1880–84) was edited by the Rev. W. Newton for F. E. Longley and featured stories with titles like "The Dangers of Temptation." Besides the clergy, there was a band of regular contributors whose writings rarely appeared outside the devotional press. Emily Searchfield, Edith Cuthell, and M. I. Hurrell were examples of writers who provided moral and edifying prose and poetry.

The juvenile religious press flourished because it catered for a captive audience, and because the cheapness of the magazines meant that even the lower classes could afford to buy them. It was frequently claimed that these periodicals countered the depraving effects of the penny dreadfuls and deterred their young readers from lives of crime. A variety of organizations were started with the intention of guiding the young into healthy and worthwhile lives, to protect them from lives of crime and depravity in the cities. Thus, the Band of Hope, Girls' Friendly Societies, and Boys' Brigades soon gained large followings and, of course, produced magazines.

In urban areas, particularly, young people were encouraged to join temperance movements. The Band of Hope movement began in Leeds in 1847, not only to combat the evils of drink but also "to inculcate a new sense of identity in their young members." The *Band of Hope Review* (1851–1937), retailing at ½*d.* a month, was assured a wide readership, as by the end of the century the Band of Hope was claiming a membership of over three million.[31] Many Band of Hope Unions produced their own journals, as for example, the Manchester and Cheshire Unions' *Onward* (1865–1909). Other temperance bodies issued their own periodicals; the Order of the Sons of the Temperance Friendly Society produced the *Cadet's Own* (1894–ca. 1917) which aimed to give temperance teaching and juvenile instruction.

Similar in their intention morally to uplift the lives of the young were the Boys' Brigade and the Girls' Friendly Society. The former was founded in 1883 and was responsible for at least three journals; the *Boys' Brigade Gazette* (1895–1900) was the official voice of the organization, but in 1900 it was amalgamated with the Sunday School Union's successful *Young England*. The Girls' Friendly Society was firmly lower class in its membership, as it was founded in 1857 with the intention of providing social amenities and good advice for serving girls. It was extremely successful and by 1874 had attracted one hundred thousand members, at least half of whom were servants. Inevitably a number of journals were started, of which the most attractive and enduring was *Friendly Leaves* (1876–1917).

A number of Christian organizations directed their attention to young office workers and message boys and inevitably they led to a number of journals, of which the *Boy Messenger* (1910–15) is typical. Toward the end of the period the Boy Scout movement was launched and by the end of 1908 the membership had already reached one hundred thousand. Within a few years no less than three scouting periodicals were in existence, but only the *Scout* (1908–66) was destined for a long and successful life.

The success of many of the organizations directed to instilling discipline and character in the young reveals a willingness among them to have their leisure time constructively organized. Although many of these movements were really intended for lower-class youths, the proprietors of many magazines wished to inculcate a charitable awareness among middle-class children. Readers of the religious press were, of course, constantly reminded of the plight of the poor and needy, and the virtues of charity were extolled. In some cases charitable organizations started junior branches and in many cases members were expected to subscribe to periodicals. Representative of this type of publication is the *Children's League of Pity Paper* (1893–1916) and the joint venture of the RSPCA and the Band of Mercy entitled the *Band of Mercy Advocate* (1879–1934).

Editors of children's periodicals soon realized that it was easy to manipulate their readers into supporting charitable causes. Beds in hospitals, homes for orphans, convalescent homes, and clothing for the needy were all means by which a periodical could associate itself with charity at the reader's expense. Various devices were employed. Some made a straightforward appeal for funds to support a particular cause. For example, *Little Wideawake*[32] supported a cot in Sydenham Hospital for Children, and *Aunt Judy's Magazine*[33] issued regular statements on the health of the occupants of their cots at the Great Ormond Street Hospital. To encourage funds the magazines issued regular statements naming subscribers. Although it tended to be the more respectable journals that were prominent in founding charitable ventures, even the less reputable ones, like Brett's *Boys of England* supported a lifeboat. Children were not reluctant to contribute: the *Girl's Own Paper* raised £260 0*s.* 5½*d.* for its convalescent home appeal within nine months in 1888.[34] Clearly the charity was carefully chosen to appeal to the readers of the journal: thus in 1892 *Young Man* promoted a collection to provide Christmas dinners for poor and hungry children.[35] Not all periodicals openly solicited financial contributions. Competitions were run for girls to make items of clothing for the needy. *Playtime* ran such a competition in 1901, and *Aunt Judy's Magazine* encouraged readers to provide clothing for children's hospitals in London in January 1882.

By the last decade of the nineteenth century a number of emotive issues like vegetarianism, pacificism, theosophy, and anti–cigarette smoking, were seeking juvenile support. Although in contrast to the numbers of adult periodicals those for juveniles were few, nonetheless several existed. The Anti-Cigarette League issued the *Boy's Outlook* (1907–8) and no less than three vegetarian periodicals existed for the young, of which the *Children's Garden* (1890–1905) enjoyed a fairly healthy existence. Other organizations that issued children's papers included the Peace Society, *Olive Leaf* (1903–15), and the League of Empire, *All Red Mail* (1907–18). There was also a theosophist *Lotus Journal* (1903–12).

It is a feature of children's periodical publishing in this period that it tended to be general in character and was largely exempt from the spate of numerous specialist periodicals that characterized adult journals. Nonetheless there were a few specialist titles, but under twenty such titles have been traced in all. Examples are the *Junior Photographer* (1894–1900), and the *Young Naturalist* (1879–1900). It has to be remembered that there was considerable space devoted to such matters in papers like the *Boy's Own Paper* and that the true specialist would soon turn to the titles intended for adults.

Many children probably did not see children's periodicals at all, but relied on the numerous family magazines that were intended for reading aloud. Into this category came titles like *Cassell's Family Magazine, Good Words, Leisure Hour,* and *Sunday at Home.* Mary Hughes singled out *Cassell's Family Magazine* as a particular favourite: it "provided stronger meat, far more substantial than we get in the average magazine today. It had to last a month and I think every word found some reader in the family."[36] F. Gordon Roe reminds us that although they were not really intended for children, periodicals like *Punch, Fun,* and the forerunners of the modern children's comic, *Ally Sloper's Half Holiday, Comic Cuts,* and *Chips* were eagerly devoured by young readers.[37] This is confirmed by Lady Bell, writing about the reading habits of youths in Middlesbrough: "The boys read papers that make them laugh, *Comic Cuts* and the like."[38]

It is reasonably safe to assume that many of the long-running nonsectarian papers reflected the interests of their readers. Many successful papers like the *Boy's Own Paper* and *Little Folks* devoted considerable space to practical matters. Besides regular columns on stamp collecting and photography, they even covered taxidermy and construction of intricate models. These ranged from rabbit hutches to complex lanterns and those in the *Boy's Own Paper* were beautifully illustrated, if requiring a fair amount of constructional competence. Girls' magazines stressed the practical aspects of homemaking and were full of recipes, instructions for lace making, embroidery, and crochet. Some, like *Little Girl's Treasure* (1875), gave away paper dress patterns. Fashion was an important element of standard quality girls' journals and the quality of the illustrations in *Girl's Own Paper* and *Atalanta* was excellent. Natural history was well represented and free colored plates of birds' eggs, butterflies and the like were a regular feature. Sport was extremely popular in boys' periodicals and it became fashionable to employ leading sports personalities to write for them. The *Boy's Own Paper* achieved a coup with W. G. Grace, and the *Captain* later emulated this with C. B. Fry. It should not be assumed that sport only appealed to public-school boys, for leading sportsmen were also idolized by youths from more humble origins. Among the farmhands and laboring boys of rural Derbyshire in the 1890s, C. B. Fry was a particular favourite. "C. B. Fry was their hero. They saved up their pocket money to buy his magazine, the *Captain*."[39]

The correspondence columns reveal much about the hopes and interests of young people of the period. Most boys' popular weeklies contained a weekly correspondence column, and there is remarkably little difference between those in the titles condemned by the critics and their more respectable counterparts. Career prospects occupied considerable space in both boys' and girls' papers and revealed the desire of many to elevate their status by careers in the professions and the army and navy. Pet care was another major preoccupation. It is clear that many children owned pets and were concerned for their welfare, and besides answering queries concerning health the periodicals carried regular features on pets.

Questions concerning physical appearance featured prominently. Some titles like the *Boy's Own Paper* and *Girl's Own Paper* ran regular articles by Medicus—Dr Gordon Stables—and all answered questions concerning stature, pimples, protruding teeth, and ears. Most were dismissed brusquely: "You can no more stop the growing of your nose than you can your hair. Let it alone."[40] Some matters were taboo: sexual matters were never discussed, and on the whole a no-nonsense attitude prevailed. A cold bath was the cure for most ills.

The editors of correspondence columns rarely spared the feelings of their contributors, and replies were often caustic. Many children were concerned with calligraphic and literary skills and obviously sent samples of their work for comment. Flattery was not the order of the day, and replies like "We fear from the specimen before us that your talent for story writing is very small. The plot is old and worn out, the language crude and the handwriting in places is almost illegible"[41] were not uncommon. It should be remembered that the preoccupation with literary skills was probably prompted by the many essay and poetry competitions offering attractive prizes that so many juvenile magazines promoted. Even the more devotional ones were not exempt, although they tended to be less generous, with prizes of 5*s.* or 6*s.*, whereas the *Boy's Own Paper* offered 20*s.*, 15*s.*, and 10*s.* for competitions requiring literary skill.

It was a feature of the more sensational titles to offer extremely generous prizes devised to appeal to the acquisitive dreams of many a youth. Harmsworth and Newnes were not innovators in offering enormous prizes, the stage having been set by E. J. Brett in his *Boys of England*[42] in 1866 when the impressive list included two Shetland ponies and six Newfoundland dogs. Even the most short-lived titles boasted long lists of prizes, many of which were beyond the wildest dreams of many a boy. Model locomotives and yachts, boxing gloves, sets of paints, pen-knives, watches, and magic lanterns were eagerly sought after by boys of the period. History does not relate whether the more ephemeral titles ever awarded the prizes, since as unlike their more reputable rivals they did not publish lists of prize winners.

The fictional content of magazines was a direct result of the editorial policy of the magazine and did not necessarily reflect the tastes of the readers. Nonetheless longevity of a title suggests that the content of the periodical was acceptable to its readers, even if much has occasioned the derision of later critics. Those periodicals that were particularly praised for their fiction both at the time and since—*Aunt Judy's Magazine, Atalanta,* and Henty's *Union Jack*—were short-lived, yet the *Little Gleaner* survived for ninety-two years. There are remarkable similarities between the contents of *Atalanta* and the *Girl's Own Paper* and between *Union Jack* and the *Boy's Own Paper,* and many of the same contributors wrote for both. This seems to suggest that quality was not the deciding factor in purchasing a particular periodical.

What does seem to be an interesting indication of the interests of the young, especially of boys, can be gleaned from an examination of the advertisements found on the wrappers of weeklies, and in the preliminary pages of some annuals. Advertisements were aimed at those likely to purchase products, and those in the nursery periodicals were directed at the mothers, not the child. For this reason baby foods, coffee, cocoa, and Stork waterproof pants featured prominently in titles like *Our Little Dots* and the *Child's Companion.* The hazy definition of what was the intended age of readers of girls' periodicals is clearly revealed by the advertisements. The October 1900 issue of the *Girl's Own Paper* carried advertisements for Bird's Custard, cocoa, soaps, infant foods, marking ink, Reckitt's Blue, and an impressive array of patent medicines, of which Cheltine Anaemic Food and Carter's Little Liver Pills were probably bought for girls. Nothing here is directed to the interests of young girls and the emphasis is clearly on the clean and healthy home.

In contrast, advertisements in boys' periodicals were firmly directed at the reader. Stamps, sports equipment, bicycles, and cocoa featured prominently. An issue of *Chums* in 1910 contained Fry's cocoa, O'Brien cycles, scouts' tools, stamps, silkworms, and Gamages. This differed very little from the very first *Boy's Own Paper* which listed internal telephones, stamps, magic lantern slides, jack-knives and sports equipment. On the whole the boy reader was immune from the barrage of patent medicine advertisements that prevailed in those for the young, but those from the less reputable publishers certainly admitted a few. Hair restorers and mustache encouragers were favored in the *Boy's World* and *Boy's Standard*. There is no doubt that the rather dubious products that claimed to enhance powers of memory, mesmerism, and thought reading which so frequently appeared in the pages of the boys' popular weeklies of the Brett variety, and later among Harmsworth's advertisements, showed less concern for the welfare of the boy than for the revenue offered by the advertiser. The Sunday School Union was sufficiently concerned with the effect of advertising to forbid it in all periodicals for the young. Advertisements like that in *Little Wideawake* for 1889, "Do not let your child die—Fennings Children's Powders," could clearly be harmful, and for this reason the *Friendly Companion* did not allow advertisements for patent medicines.

A change in attitude to children can be detected in the editorials of periodicals during this period. In the 1860s and 1870s the tone was always authoritarian and patronizing, but toward the end of the period editors relaxed and many adopted a chummy attitude. While in 1874 it was quite in order for the editor of the *Lads of the Village* (1874–5) to state "it is intended to be not only amusing but instructive and that without the meretricious aids of robbers, pirates, and highwaymen,"[43] readers thirty years later would have found it difficult to swallow. In 1910 the editor of *Boy's World* (1905–7) was writing, "Then if you're a healthy chap you wants lots of adventure. You shall have it. If our pages don't drip with the blood of villains and resound with the victorious cry of the virtuous hero you can call round my office with a club."[44] A similar friendly tone crept into correspondence columns, and readers were treated much more sympathetically than in the early years. The changing attitudes of editors toward their readers undoubtedly reflects the change in society's view of children in this period. Children were no longer kept at a distance. This is aptly demonstrated in an editorial in *Bull's Eye*[45] in 1898: "When you have known me a little, you shall regard me not merely as a cold, austere, anonymous individual but a warm close personal friend."

The juvenile periodical press of the period 1866–1914 gives a very valuable insight into the lives of young people at the time. The correspondence columns and features reveal the interests and aspirations of the young. Illustrations and fiction were designed to entertain, but many of the periodicals did not spare their readers from reminders of the more serious side of life. The wide circulation of religious periodicals for the young with their emphasis on death and the evil consequences of sin indicates that life was a solemn business for many. At the same time many periodicals did provide amusement and entertainment and were extremely popular. What is interesting is the way in which class barriers were broken by many juvenile periodicals. Those that tried too consciously to appeal to middle-class readers, like *Aunt Judy's Magazine* and *Atalanta,* failed because they were not financially viable. The appeal of successful titles like the *Boy's Own Paper* was that they did not restrict themselves to too narrow a social stratum. Juvenile periodicals should not be overlooked as a vital source of social history.

7
Advertising and Editorial Integrity in the Nineteenth Century

Terry Nevett

We are concerned here with the growth of advertising in the nineteenth century, and in particular with the efforts of advertisers to obtain favorable editorial treatment for themselves and their products, notably in the form of "puffs" disguised as items of news.

Until 1853 newspaper advertisements were subject to a flat rate duty, the amount payable in respect of each issue of a paper being calculated by the clerks in the Stamp Office, and returns compiled from their figures subsequently published in the House of Commons Accounts and Papers.[1] If the number of advertisements appearing each year is multiplied by the average cost per insertion, it is possible to estimate approximately the level of national expenditure on newspaper advertising, which rose from about £160,000 in 1800 to some £500,000 by 1848.[2]

Since the duty only applied to advertisements in those publications obliged to pay the newspaper stamp, there was a natural tendency on the part of advertisers to avoid paying it by using other media. According to "R. K. D." in his *Letter to Viscount Lord Althorp:*

> As one channel narrows, so other channels become proportionately enlarged. The advertisement duty merely swells the number of placards and circulars, and compels the shopkeeper to have recourse to round-

---

Newspaper circulation figures quoted in this chapter are taken from A. P. Wadsworth, 'Newspaper circulations, 1800–1954,' *Transactions of the Manchester Statistical Society* 4 (1955), and figures for the expenditure of individual advertisers from T. R. Nevett, 'The development of commercial advertising, 1800–1914' (Ph.D. thesis, University of London, 1979). Other works to which the author is indebted include A. Aspinall, 'The social status of journalists at the beginning of the nineteenth century,' *Review of English Studies* 21 (July 1945); I. Asquith, 'Advertising and the press in the late eighteenth and early nineteenth centuries,' *Historical Journal* 18 (1975); and V. S. Berridge, 'Popular journalism and working class attitudes, 1854–86, (Ph.D. thesis, University of London 1976).

The author would also like publicly to express his thanks to James Derriman of Charles Barker ABH International, Gordon Phillips of *The Times,* and the Newspaper Society for permission to work on records in their keeping.

> about and less efficient methods of setting forth the merits and cheapness of his wares, instead of courting the attention of customers in the pages of a public journal.[3]

The impression conveyed by the very considerable expenditure on posters, handbills, advertising carts, illuminated displays, sandwich men, criers, and a variety of other methods, not to mention unstamped publications, is that it could easily have been equal to that in stamped newspapers. This would mean a total national expenditure by midcentury of around £1 million.

After the abolition of the duty in 1853, there is no reliable source on which estimates can be based. By the early years of the present century, the level of expenditure on advertising had become a matter of general interest, but the figures quoted by contemporaries are little more than wild guesses. The advertisement manager of the *Financial Times* writing in 1910 estimated national expenditure as £10 million per annum, *The Times* two years later put it at £100 million, and Sir William Crawford (born 1878), a highly respected advertising agent, wrote in 1931 that spending in 1913 had totaled £25 million. Dunbar presents a more acceptable estimate, based on the returns made by the printing and allied trades for the Census of Production, together with the indices of advertising space volume produced by *Advertising World* magazine.[4] He calculates that expenditure for 1912 probably totaled some £15 million, with £13 million of that being spent in the press and the remainder on posters and transport advertising.

Throughout the nineteenth century new advertisers were constantly being tempted into the field, and individual advertising budgets were growing ever larger. In the earlier decades, leading newspapers included auctioneers, publishers, retailers, and medical quacks, though legal and public notices, situations vacant, and property sales also figure prominently. From the seventies onwards, consumer choice began to expand for the working class, and this began to be reflected in the type of advertisements carried in mass-circulation newspapers. First came utilitarian products concerned with washing, cleaning, and livening up food—sauces, relishes, meat extracts and the like. These were followed by sets of furniture, ready-to-wear suits for men, and sewing machines and paper patterns for women. By the early years of the present century popular dailies were also carrying advertising for confectionery, cigarettes, and large-scale retailers—notably the growing number of department stores.

The Times observed in 1909 that advertising had been used to introduce a number of inventions to the public during the previous quarter of a century, including "type-writers, fountain-pens, calculating machines, piano-players, phonographs, cameras, safety razors, patent book-cases and motor cars." The paper also pointed out that "A variety of staple products are now chiefly or largely sold through advertising of specific brands"—an important factor in the growth of expenditure, though it should be remembered that a number of branded products were already being advertised widely in the first decades of the nineteenth century.

Although it was in the area of consumer goods that advertising showed the most rapid growth, it should not be overlooked that there were also considerable developments in other fields. Applications were invited for shares in newly floated companies, charities appealed for funds and election candidates for support, while coach, wagon, railway, and steamship companies competed for the change to transport the public and their chattels. To a large extent the specialist advertising content of a particular newspaper was determined by the area in which it circulated and the class of people who read it. During the Napoleonic Wars, sales of French and American ships seized as prizes were advertised in *Felix Farley's Bristol Journal,* and country estates in the *Stamford Mercury.* Notices about enclosures, turnpikes, and stolen sheep appear in the country papers, inns and shops for sale in the *Morning Advertiser,* fashionable entertainments in the *Morning Chronicle* and *The Times,* and cures for venereal disease practically everywhere.

An increasing range of goods and services were being advertised because advertising itself was becoming regarded as a normal part of business practice. Carlyle might complain in *Past and Present* (1843) that "There is not a man or hat-maker born into the world but feels, or has felt, that he is degrading himself if he speaks of his excellences or prowesses, and supremacy in his craft," but in fact ever more tradesmen were doing so. Four decades later in Gilbert and Sullivan's *Ruddigore* (1887) Robin Oakapple could proclaim:

If you wish in the world to advance,
Your merits you're bound to enhance,
You must stir it and stump it
And blow your own trumpet
Or, trust me, you haven't a chance!

A similar sentiment is to be found in H. G. Wells's *Tono-Bungay* (1909):

"Some businesses are straight and quiet, anyhow; supply a sound article that is really needed, don't shout advertisements."
"No, George. There you're behind the times. The last of that sort was sold up 'bout five years ago."

As the number of advertisers increased, so did the amounts they were spending. Thomas Holloway, whose expenditure on promoting his medicines was estimated at £5,000 in 1842, raised this to £30,000 in 1855, £40,000, in 1864 and £50,000 in 1883, the year of his death. Thomas Beecham increased his advertising expenditure from £22,000 in 1884 to £120,000 in 1891. Leading retailers were also among the heaviest spenders, the *Quarterly Review* estimating in 1855 that Moses and Son's advertising budget was some £10,000 per annum, Heal and Son's £6,000, and Nichol's £4,500. By 1910 it was said that a retailer could make 'a reasonable showing' with £10,000 to £15,000, though Selfridge spent an estimated £36,000 on advertising his Oxford Street store even before it had opened. By this time, manufacturers of branded soap products had also joined the ranks of leading advertisers, with Pears said in 1905 to be spending £126,000 annually and Lever credited with an expenditure of some £2 million in twenty years.

The growth of advertising was closely linked with the expansion of the press, mass circulation newspapers providing the advertiser with an effective means of bringing nationally distributed products to the notice of a mass consumer market. In 1801 *The Times* had a daily sale of between 2,500 and 3,000 copies. Twenty years later with the aid of its new steam presses it was selling 7,000, and by 1858 had reached 60,000, while none of its rivals even approached 10,000. By 1880 the *Daily Telegraph* was selling 300,000 and before the end of the century both *Lloyd's Weekly* and the *Daily Mail* claimed to have passed one million.

There was also a dramatic increase in the number of titles published, particularly after the abolition of the stamp duty. In 1854 only five dailies were published outside London. Ten years later the figure had risen to 51 and by 1889 it was 155. The five years following repeal also saw 120 papers established in 102 towns where none had previously existed.

To a large extent it was advertising which made possible an expansion on this scale. Firstly, advertisements attracted readers. According to Daniel Stuart, "Numerous and various advertisements attract numerous and various readers, looking out for employment, servants, sales, and purchases, &c &c. Advertisements act and react. They attract readers, promote circulation, and circulation attracts advertisements."[5] Secondly, newspapers needed the income which their advertising columns provided. Charles Knight estimated in 1836 that a daily paper with a circulation of 12,000 would only cover its expenses with revenue from the sale of copies, any profit coming from its advertisements.[6] McCulloch, too, observed in his *Dictionary of Commerce* that "advertisements form a considerable source of profit to newspapers; and without this source, some of the most widely-circulated of them could not support their great expenditure."[7]

Since the success of a newspaper depended on its ability to attract advertising, it is important to understand something of the process by which advertisers or their agents decided which papers were to carry their announcements. Before the advent of national circulations, the area in which a paper was sold was a major consideration since manufacturers naturally wanted their announcements to appear in towns where their products were on sale. At the same time, the promise of promotional support was used to induce the retailer to stock a particular product, advertisements carrying his name being placed in the paper of his choice at the manufacturer's expense in proportion to the size of his order.

The political views expressed by a newspaper were also an important criterion, especially in the first half of the century. The various guides for advertisers generally carry this information, though Charles Mitchell in the first edition of his *Newspaper Press Directory* (1846) warned his readers that "Advertising is of no party. The advertiser looks for notoriety—for publicity—for benefits—from the expense he goes to in advertising. He should, therefore, not confine his advertisements to those journals which may advocate the same principles as he himself professes, but look to that most likely to promote his interests. . . ."[8]

Cost does not seem to have been a crucial factor until the later decades of the century. Initially there seems to have been two bands of roughly similar rates, one operating in respect of London papers and the other for their country counterparts. The only factor affecting the cost of an advertisement was therefore its length, calculated in terms of the number of lines, and the standard rates were so well known that the newspaper guides published for the use of adevertisers do not usually bother to include them. The situation changed, however, as the press expanded. Bigger circulations meant a correspondingly greater difference between the sales of various newspapers—a matter of a few hundred in the early years of the century but of many hundreds of thousands by the end. Advertisers accordingly began to think in terms other than the length of their advertisements when considering costs, but after the abolition of the stamp duty in 1853 there were no reliable figures for newspaper circulations. Some publications, including *The Times,* even claimed to be withholding information in the interests of advertisers, arguing that they would not be able to understand it and would therefore be misled. In other cases publishers quoted the number of copies printed as distinct from sold, or simply invented figures to suit the occasion. In spite of heavy pressure from leading advertisers, it was not until the early years of the present century that a few papers began to guarantee circulation statements or to issue audited sales figures. The result was a tendency to treat cost as the only variable, and to buy whatever was offered at the cheapest rate.

A further factor affecting the advertiser's choice was the degree of cooperation offered by particular newspapers. The expansion of the press meant that, in addition to larger individual circulations, there were hundreds more titles competing for the advertiser's patronage, and it was inevitable that in their desire to attract revenue they would yield to commercial pressures. Gradually publishers were forced to allow advertisements which were several columns in width, breaking through the column rules which had traditionally contained them, and to permit the use of bold display types and eventually of illustrations. Yet although this had a profound effect on the appearance of newspapers, there were potentially more far-reaching and more sinister implications in the efforts made by advertisers to secure favorable editorial coverage of their products.

The low reputation of the profession of journalist and editor persisted well into the nineteenth century, the Benchers of Lincoln's Inn making a rule in 1807 that no one who had written for a newspaper could be called to the bar, and as late as 1846 Charles Mitchell could observe in his *Newspaper Press Directory* that "English editors, unlike those of their class in France, hold, at best, but a dubious position in Society." It should therefore come as no surprise that advertisers expected to see favorable mentions of themselves and their products in the editorial columns, and that publishers, in need of advertising revenue, frequently acceded to their wishes.

In the first quarter of the century, puffs were a clearly accepted part of the relationship between advertisers and newspapers. According to James Savage writing about 1812, "Any man, for half a guinea, may puff his own writings, inventions, and fame, in a paragraph in any of the papers."[9] Even the most reputable of publishers seem to have regarded puffing as normal practice and a necessary source of revenue. Cobbett wrote in the *Political Register,* "But for the gain upon the advertisements, and for certain paragraphs, the insertion of which is paid for, a daily paper could never stand."[10] The highly respected James Perry of the *Morning Chronicle,* who was known not to accept hush money, quoted rates for paragraphs in the editorial columns which were considerably higher than the paper's normal advertising rates, an editorial puff on the front page for example costing 10*s.* 6*d.* compared with 6*s.* for a small front page advertisement.[11]

The paid paragraph posed a difficult problem for the Stamp Office, which until 1853 was responsible for collecting the duty levied on newspaper advertisements. The official view seems to have been that if an editorial item had been paid for, then it was a *de facto* advertisement and as such was liable to duty. The clerks in the Stamp Office then had the task of deciding which items in the editorial columns constituted genuine news and which were really puffs. Sometimes a publisher might include an indication such as "Advt." in small letters at the end of the paragraph, but this was not popular with advertisers and was frequently omitted. The clerks then had to rely on their own judgment, apparently with somewhat erratic results. According to Thomas Gwynne, Solicitor of Legacy in the Stamp Office:

> The clerks in the newpaper office are not men of sufficient intelligence, and do not possess, in my opinion the necessary information to enable them to determine whether a paragraph in a newspaper is in the nature of an advertisement or not; an advertisement is a word of very difficult and very doubtful determination, and to bring it within the terms in which duty is claimed on an advertisement requires some skill and some knowledge; I do not think the officers in that department possess that knowledge . . . I believe there are many paragraphs in the nature of puffs which pass without observation.[12]

Gwynne estimated that such inefficiencies in collection were costing £20,000 a year in lost revenue. On the other hand, there are many complaints about the criteria which the clerks employed, notably their assumption that any review notice couched in favorable terms could only be the result of some financial benefit accruing to the reviewer. The net was in fact cast so wide that it even caught the following innocuous paragraph in the *Newcastle Chronicle:*

> A sermon will be preached in Saint Andrew's Church in this town, on the forenoon of Sunday the 10th instant, by the Rev. James Birkett, jun., A.M. after which a collection will be made towards defraying the expenses to be incurred by the construction of an Hospital, in Newcastle upon Tyne, for the reception of poor married women, lying-in.[13]

The puff inserted for money may perhaps be seen as a development which rationalized and brought some degree of respectability to the earlier system of subsidy and bribery. In that it formed part of an openly conducted commercial transaction, it represented far less of a threat to editorial objectivity than did the puff which an advertiser managed to have inserted without payment, either because of its supposed news value or because pressure could be brought to bear on the publisher.

Considerable ingenuity was exercised in the effort to obtain free puffs. A writer in 1868 described how an event such as a wedding might be exploited, the report being written by a "liner" or special correspondent who would work in puffs for the carriage, trousseau, cake, photographer, and so on. These mentions would probably appear in print because the subeditors would not feel it to be worth striking them out. The writer commented, "It not only puts other and more modest tradesmen to a disadvantage, but it imposes upon the general public who do not see that this advertisement is an advertisement and nothing more."[14]

Sometimes a more direct approach was employed, making contact directly with the editor. H. J. Palmer of the *Yorkshire Post* estimated in 1895 that half the letters he received each day were requesting some kind of editorial mention. In his view, "It is not so much that there is a shabby desire to shirk the mere money cost of advertising. The great idea is to secure the advertisement without appearing to have had any hand in it."[15] A correspondent writing in the same year to the Newspaper Society *Circular* complained that he had received twelve puffs in six days. By way of variation, women were sometimes used to call on editors to persuade them—by what means is not clear—to insert puffs for a particular manufacturer.

The increasing popularity of branded food products offered further possibilities for free publicity. The Grape Nuts Company, for example, sent out to newpapers a series of recipes for publication on the women's page. The service was free, the main ingredient in each case being of course Grape Nuts. Along similar lines, the syndicated newsletters which developed in the second half of the century were also exploited in the interests of advertisers, sometimes to the point where they were in effect just a series of puffs strung together. Judging from comments in the Provincial Newspaper Society's *Circular,* a Mrs. Lankester who wrote a syndicated fashion column under the name "Penelope" enjoyed a particularly dubious reputation in this respect.[16]

From infiltration of the editorial columns by stealth, it was perhaps a short step to the falsification of news in the interests of advertisers. According to the *Circular,* this was happening to a considerable extent in the reporting of fires, suicides, and similar events, and had prompted *The Times* and the Press Association to bring an action against two reporters involved in such practices, one of whom was sentenced to six months' imprisonment.[17]

Certain types of business were notorious for the use they made of editorial puffs in promoting their interests. In the first half of the century, the book trade indulged in puffing on a massive scale. An anonymous writer in 1812 complained of the activities of the book-selling auctioneer that "As he pays the newpaper well for every lie they tell for him, they put it into as many shapes as he chooses to hire them for."[18] *Ainsworth's Magazine* published a "Paper on puffing," setting out the different approaches which could be used to stimulate public interest in a particular work.[19] Probably the most celebrated attack, however, came from Macaulay writing in the *Edinburgh Review* in 1830:

> Men of letters . . . have begun to court the public. They formerly used flattery. They now use puffing. . . . The puffing of books is now so shamefully and so successfully practised, that it is the duty of all who are anxious for the purity of national taste, or the honour of the literary character, to join in discountenancing it. . . . We expect some reserve, some decent pride, in our hatter and bootmaker. But no artifice by which notoriety can be obtained is thought too abject for a man of letters.[20]

A further attack on the puffing of books was launched in 1833 by John Livesey writing in the *Moral Reformer,* a journal which he conducted himself:

> In the first place you must advertise it in the papers, and unite with it a paragraph commencing, "It is with great pleasure that we direct our readers to the valuable work advertised in our columns." The editors . . . are sure, *if you pay them,* to praise your book. In the next place, get the interest of the "reviewers," those who presume to direct the judgments of the literati of the country, and for a guinea you will get your work praised by these men, even though they will never have taken time to read it.[21]

If a seller or publisher of books was also involved in the publication of a periodical, he enjoyed the advantage of being able to puff his own books to whatever extent he wished. One of the best-known exponents of this technique was Henry Colburn, proprietor of several journals and joint owner of the *Literary Gazette,* which on one occasion was said to have carried some twenty-one columns of editorial devoted to works published by Colburn, compared with one-eighth of a column concerned with those of his rival John Murray. In the words of Macaulay, "The publisher is often the publisher of some periodical work. In this periodical work the first flourish of the trumpets is sounded. The peal is then echoed and re-echoed by all the other periodical works over which the publisher or the author, or the author's coterie, may have any influence."

By the third quarter of the century, it was noted that the volume of government advertising was being reduced, while at the same time increased use was being made of "news" paragraphs which were expected to be inserted free of charge. In 1873, for example, the Census Office sent out details and prices of the 1871 Census volumes for publication as a news item, while four years later a memorandum on the new Births and Deaths Registration Act was reckoned to take up three-quarters of a column of editorial space. Considerable resentment was occasioned in newpaper circles by such practices, though it arose from consternation at the loss of advertising revenue rather than worries about possible government influence on the conduct of newspapers.

Quack doctors and patent medicine vendors were also noted for their use of the puff. Thomas Holloway, famed for his pills and ointments, seems to have dealt particularly roughly with newspaper publishers, regarding the editorial columns as available to the advertiser and open to negotiation as part of a deal for the purchase of advertising space. In 1878 he wrote to a provincial newspaper offering £4 for the insertion of an advertisement every week for a year, demanding as a condition that the paper insert without charge a weekly news paragraph about Holloway's products and a monthly editorial article of at least forty lines. He was also to be supplied with a free copy of every issue.[22]

A similar approach—possibly by Holloway himself—is reported in the *Language of the Walls* (1855). 'The advertisement is enclosed and the manager is requested to insert it for twenty-one weeks for £10; along with it there are also twenty-one puffs to be inserted as news, in order to draw attention to the advertisement during the above time.'[23]

Toward the end of the century, company promoters were also making considerable use of the editorial columns. They were prepared to pay higher rates for an announcement which did not have the appearance of an advertisement, was preferably set in the paper's editorial typeface, and which appeared among items of bona fide financial news. According to H. J. Palmer, this practice—which he describes as "bribery by advertisement"—did not extend to the leading morning papers.

In the first decade of the present century, puffing was brought under public scrutiny as a result of the activities of the automobile industry. On 31 December 1907 *The Times* devoted some one and a third columns to what it

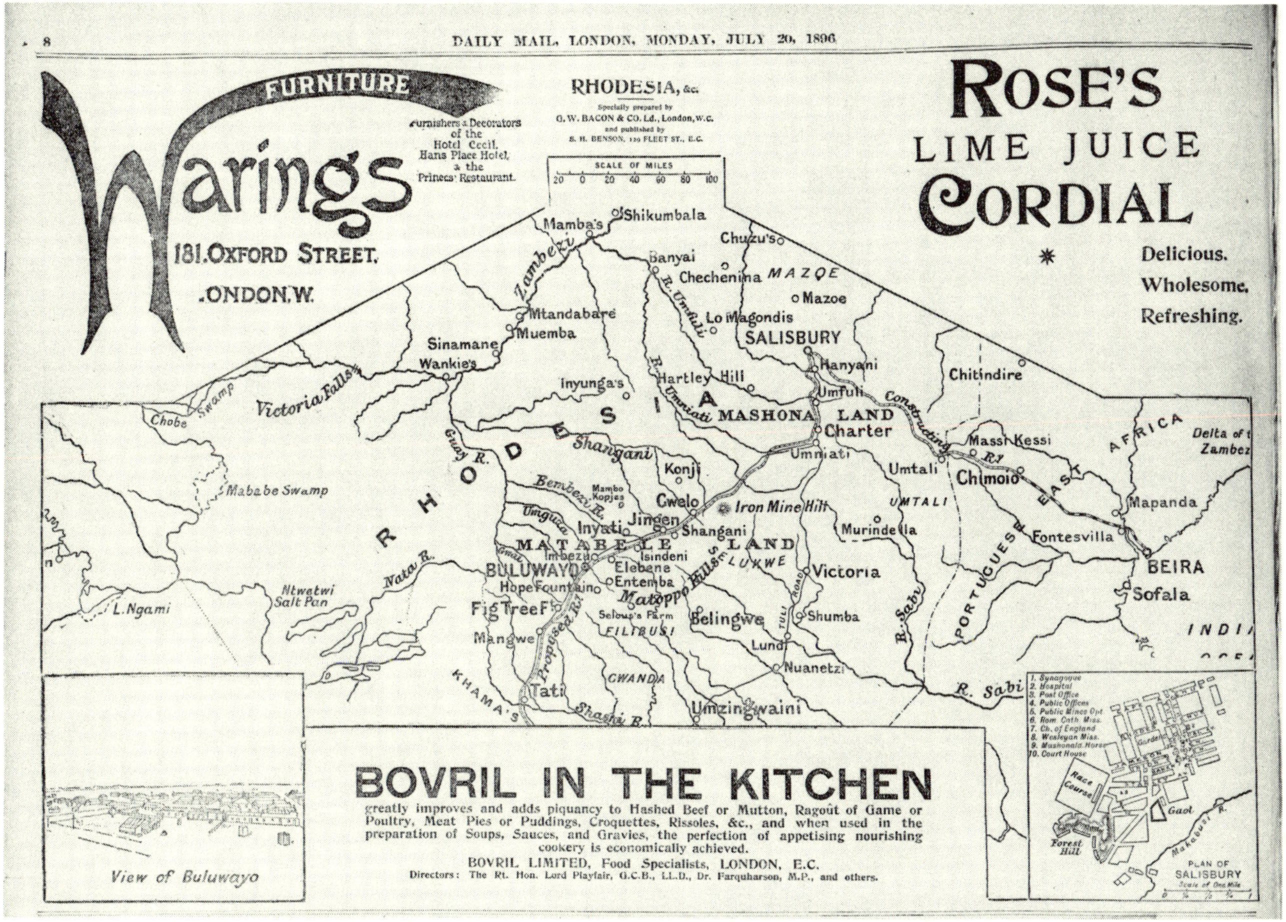

8 DAILY MAIL, LONDON, MONDAY, JULY 20, 1896

FURNITURE
Warings
181, OXFORD STREET,
LONDON, W.
Furnishers & Decorators of the Hotel Cecil, Hans Place Hotel, & the Princes' Restaurant.

RHODESIA, &c.
Specially prepared by G. W. BACON & CO. Ld., London, W.C. and published by S. H. BENSON, 110 FLEET ST., E.C.

ROSE'S
LIME JUICE
CORDIAL
Delicious.
Wholesome.
Refreshing.

BOVRIL IN THE KITCHEN
greatly improves and adds piquancy to Hashed Beef or Mutton, Ragoût of Game or Poultry, Meat Pies or Puddings, Croquettes, Rissoles, &c., and when used in the preparation of Soups, Sauces, and Gravies, the perfection of appetising nourishing cookery is economically achieved.
BOVRIL LIMITED, Food Specialists, LONDON, E.C.
Directors: The Rt. Hon. Lord Playfair, G.C.B., LL.D., Dr. Farquharson, M.P., and others.

News and advertising from the *Daily Mail*, Monday, 20 July 1896 (British Library Newspaper Library).

condemned as the corrupt practice of obtaining puffs in return for booking advertising space, declaring:

> It is certain now that in a great number, the majority, in fact, of London's morning newspapers of reputation, the criticisms and reports printed about cars and things connected with them are not, as in the public interest they most unquestionably ought to be, wholly and absolutely independent of advertisements "given" or "refused."

On 4 January 1908 the paper published a letter from 'A Motor Manufacturer' fully supporting its allegations:

> I can confirm the statements of your correspondent that certain daily papers do permit manufacturers who advertise in their columns to write editorial matter concerning their goods, and that certain motor papers practically ignore in their editorial columns the performances and claims of cars which are not advertised.

Three days later came a letter from the editor of the *Automobile and Carriage Builder's Journal,* denying that advertising had any effect on whether a product was praised or otherwise, but admitting somewhat equivocally, "If we have two cars, or parts of cars, before us which are of equal merit and one is advertised whilst the other is not, we naturally, and (as I think very properly), give preference to the advertised article." *The Times*'s view, however, received further backing on 14 January in the form of a congratulatory letter from the Society of Motor Manufacturers and Traders.

Two months later the controversy broadened into a general attack on the whole practice of puffing. A correspondent on 4 March noted that a London morning paper had published an article three columns in length concerning an exhibition at Olympia. The article in question was divided into ten sections, each of which was headed by the name of an exhibitor and took the form of a eulogistic puff. The article was surrounded by ten advertisements which, it was noted, were for the firms mentioned. In the opinion of the correspondent, "The boasted independence of the British Press is rapidly becoming a tradition of the past."

On 7 March a Mr. E. P. Mathers, describing himself as a newspaper owner, came to the defense of puffing, arguing that its practice was simply a way by which advertisers and newspapers helped each other and that nobody was deceived by it. Maintaining that the puff was "merely a gratuitous description which the reader is glad to get," he dismissed criticisms as "so much cant and humbug." Three days later another correspondent expressed the hope that Mathers was not typical of publishers, pointing out acidly that in any case he was only concerned with producing a weekly journal dealing with commercial affairs in South Africa.

Attention so far has been focused on the activities of advertisers. Equally central to the question of editorial manipulation, however, is the role of advertising agents. William Tayler, the earliest of whom any record remains, was in business in London in 1786, and the profession soon became of crucial importance to the provincial press. During the eighteenth century, London businessmen wishing to advertise in the provinces could hand in their copy at one of the many coffeehouses which accepted advertisements on behalf of the country newspapers. The advertising agent, however, acted for the advertiser. He was accepted in trade practice—though not in law—as a principal in his dealings with newspapers, which meant in effect that he guaranteed payment for any advertisement he booked for his clients. In return the papers granted agents a commission, normally 10 percent in the case of successful publications but rising to 30 percent or more in the instance of struggling titles desperate to attract advertising revenue. Agents also enjoyed extended credit, normally hoping to collect payment from their clients before their accounts with newspapers became due.

Advertisers stood to benefit in several ways if they dealt with advertising agents instead of directly with publishers. Before the advent of the mass circulation daily press, the agent had information on the hundreds of local papers from which a selection had to be made to obtain anything approaching coordinated coverage of a particular area of the country. He simplified the administration of an advertising campaign by presenting his client with a single consolidated account, thus saving him the trouble and expense of dealing with each paper individually. And the agent was able to strike better deals with publishers, both because of the volume of expenditure he controlled and because he could negotiate long-term contracts for special positions at exceedingly favorable rates.

From the outset, the two activities of advertising and the supply of news were closely interrelated. William Tayler not only acted as an advertising agent, but supplied country papers with accounts of parliamentary proceedings, proclamations, royal speeches, and current prices. The Lawson and Barker Agency (later known as Charles Barker), which was founded in 1812, enjoyed a close relationship with *The Times*. William Lawson was the paper's printer, the agency's office at 12 Birchin Lane was used by Alsager, *The Times*'s city correspondent, and Barker could refer to the address as "a branch of *The Times* where various articles are written."[24] Lawson and Barker seems originally to have been a press agency, sending parliamentary and financial newsletters to the country papers, and receiving reports from them on behalf of *The Times*. Gradually, however, their network of contacts became used for the placing of advertisements, and under Barker's control this became the firm's sole activity.

James White, another well-known agent who set up in business about 1800, also had close connections with the press. As well as being married to a prosperous bookseller's daughter, he was a close friend of Charles Lamb who wrote for leading newspapers and was a frequent guest at the celebrated "Lamb suppers," which were attended by many of the leading figures of the newspaper world. White also has the distinction of having employed Lamb to write puffs.

The control which agents exercised over the disposition of advertising campaigns meant that the fate of a large part of the British press was effectively in their hands. It was therefore essential for newspapers to seek and retain their favor. Accordingly, when pressure was applied to induce a paper to print an editorial commendation of a product being advertised in its columns, and when the advertising of that product was controlled by an agent whose expenditure on behalf of all his clients might be crucial to that paper's existence, it is hardly surprising that the reaction was frequently one of compliance. This power which the agents commanded was wielded to such effect that arranging the publication of puffs became an integral part of the service they offered. By 1888 the Provincial Newspaper Society's *Circular* was complaining:

> The scarcely veiled demands of advertising agents for the insertion of what they please to term "news paragraphs", show a tendency to increase. It is, indeed, almost a necessary qualification for any agent who hopes to be a success, that he should, in the opinion of his clients, the advertisers, be in a position to control the Press to the extent of occasionally securing for them the circulation of judiciously worded "news paragraphs".[25]

When Edmund Street, a leading agent, addressed the Royal Society of Arts in 1913, he staunchly maintained, "If an article is worth spending thousands of pounds upon in advertising, it should be deserving of a notice."[26] Street's agency, however, had been attracting unfavorable comments from publishers for many years for its attempts to secure puffs for its clients, Edmund's elder brother George having been castigated by the Provincial Newspaper Society in 1878.

Such was the power wielded by the biggest agents, that they were even able to lay down conditions as to how their puffs should be presented. Henry Sell, for example, stipulated that the word *Advertisement* was not to be used, that the item should be set in the same type as the editorial matter, and that any column in which one of his puffs appeared should otherwise be devoted entirely to editorial.[27]

By the early years of the present century the planting of puffs had developed into such a specialized activity that a new type of agent had emerged, dealing exclusively with what were euphemistically called "reading-notices." This new breed seems to have operated successfully without recourse to inducement by advertising, though a court case in 1904 gives some idea of the kind of methods they employed. In the case in question, in which a firm of turf accountants were charged with fraudulently obtaining money by means of a sweepstake, an agent named Henry Ereckson stated that he received typewritten information from the defendant and took it to a member of the newspaper's staff who wrote up a notice. For this the bookmaker paid £20, of which £10 went to the newspaper and £10 was kept by Ereckson himself. Such happenings, he said, were not unusual.[28] Thomas Russell, formerly advertising manager of *The Times,* noted at the end of the First World War, "There is an organized system of insinuating into the Press articles believed to serve the purpose of Advertising, without being printed and paid for as advertisements, and the calling of 'Press agent' is recognized by some directories."[29]

An agent's opportunities for editorial manipulation were increased immesurably if he had some financial interest in a particular publication. The Walter Judd Agency in its booklet *Financial Advertising,* published about 1912, boasted proudly that

> They also have certain exceptional facilities both for obtaining early information and for securing wide publicity in the chief Trade and Illustrated Journals, as their Principal is the chief proprietor in eight of the leading trade papers, besides being a director of two of the leading weekly illustrated Papers. They were the pioneers of the Illustrated Articles appearing in the Illustrated Papers descriptive of the great Industrial Concerns of the world, and to this day WALTER JUDD Ltd, make a special feature of these articles preliminary to public issue. They undertake also the preparation of special articles to draw attention to Companies whos shares are standing at a figure below their proper value.

Clearly there was no awareness of any possible ethical objection, either to a situation in which an agent had a financial stake in a publication which was expressing a supposedly objective view about a client's business, or to offering the manipulation of share values as a commercial service.

A further threat to editorial independence came with attempts by advertising agents to supply "free" news in exchange for the free publication of advertisements. In 1875 the Provincial Newspaper Society warned its members against an agent who was offering a free weekly leading article together with a modest cash payment, in exchange for a weekly column of advertising space.[30] It was toward the end of the century, however, that matters came to a head in the so-called *per contra* controversy. Again it was the Newspaper Society (as it was now known) which sounded a warning to its members:

> At the present time strenuous efforts are being made to combine in one operation the business of supplying newspapers with news, and that of acting as their agent with the advertising world. The plan is to offer a service of news at a fixed rate per annum, or shorter period maybe, and at the same time to guarantee to send the newspaper a sufficient quantity of advertisements to balance the cost of the news during the stipulated period.

Any paper refusing to take the news would receive no advertising. The Society's reaction to such a proposition was predictable:

> Its extension . . . must in time have the effect of sapping the independence of the provincial press generally, reducing many now influential local journals to the position of mere agents of the metropolitan wire-pullers.[31]

A special meeting called in January 1897, chaired by H. J. Palmer of the *Yorkshire Post,* condemned such practices outright, and claimed to have received many letters of support from those unable to attend. There followed a joint meeting between the Newspaper Society and representatives of the advertising agents under the chairmanship of W. R. Horncastle, a leading agency proprietor. Once again the outcome was total condemnation. Strong backing also came in the form of two articles which appeared in the *Star* on 20 and 22 January, attacking the practice and claiming that it was employed particularly by agencies advertising company flotations as a means of avoiding loss should a company fail to form.

After having been brought into the open, these attempts to supply editorial matter on an organized and regular basis in exchange for advertisements seem to have been abandoned in Britain, though in some countries of the world it is not unusual even today to find the business of an advertising agency combined with that of supplying news, or even of publishing a newspaper.

By the early years of the present century, it is not clear which sections of the press would accept puffs and which would not. According to no less a source than the *Encyclopaedia Britannica* in 1910, leading newspapers declined to publish them, while H. J. Palmer, himself an editor, stated that they were refused by the top twenty or thirty morning papers. Thomas Russell went even further in 1919, declaring: "If, through some accident, an advertised product enters into the news, the papers will go ever so far round to avoid naming it. . . . If an advertiser really wants to obtain entrance into the news columns, he must either commit bigamy or have his factory burned down."[32] Some years later, however, Russell was painting a somewhat different picture which rings truer for newspapers as a whole: "Editors are often capricious in their attitude to advertising; some of them going out of their way to avoid mentioning an advertiser by name, while others undervalue their independence and give transparent puffs under the pressure of their colleagues on the business side of the paper."[33]

There can be no doubt that reputable national papers would no longer accept an obvious puff. *The Times* in particular, in spite of its financial difficulties, maintained an absolutely uncompromising attitude on the matter. When in 1902 the Apollinaris Company wrote asking for the insertion of a paragraph in news type, free or at nominal cost, the pained reply from

Moberly Bell, the paper's manager, was, "We could not possibly insert the enclosed paragraph as a news paragraph and we are surprised that a company of your standing should make such a suggestion."[34] Northcliffe, too, was violently opposed to the appearance of puffs in the pages of his publications, and was greatly upset when a patent medicine was praised by the *Daily Mail.* Advertising for the product in question was handled by the St. James Agency, a director of which was Percy Burton, Northcliffe's brother-in-law. In spite of this family connection, a quarrel ensued which led to Northcliffe's refusal to meet Burton, and the exclusion from the *Daily Mail* of any advertising for his clients.

The dilemma confronting publishers with regard to puffing is well illustrated by a memorandum written in 1907 by Moberly Bell.[35] He maintained that the ideal newspaper would confine itself to news and comment, and in order to preserve its impartiality would derive the whole of its income from the sale of copies. This being impossible in practice, papers are obliged to accept advertisements, many of which by their very nature deal with matters of public interest, particularly in the commercial field. In Bell's view, "The better class of newspapers no doubt seek to draw a marked distinction between advertisements and news but the distinction is becoming less and less and it is not unusual to find advertisers quoting their own advertisements as the opinion of the paper in which they paid to have it inserted."

Even this public deception he believed to be of small importance compared with the overall influence which the advertising business was able to exercise over the way a paper was run. "So long as a newspaper exists solely by the money which it receives from advertisers it cannot be expected to criticize impartially the projects of those advertisers. It has even been maintained that it is dishonourable on the part of a newspaper to take money for advertising an undertaking unless it is prepared either to support, or at least to treat with silence, that undertaking."

In an appendix to his memorandum, Bell gives examples of attempts to influence the editorial policy of *The Times.* A weekly column of advertisements from photographers was offered on condition that the paper would run a weekly column of photographic news. A full-page advertisement was offered provided that the paper undertook to say nothing hurtful about the company concerned. Nobel's offered a full-page advertisement every week for a year on condition that they could see and control all articles on explosives. The Great Western Railway Company withdrew all its advertising from the paper following adverse editorial comment on a railway accident. Unfavorable theatrical reviews frequently caused advertisements to be reduced, and sometimes to be stopped completely. The Gramophone Company withdrew all advertising when *The Times* failed to send a reporter to cover the laying of a foundation stone by Dame Nellie Melba, and gave the "event" only a short paragraph by way of mention. And after the appearance of an article on a new American sporting gun, an English gunmaker withdrew his advertising on the grounds that it was the duty of the paper to support the British trade. Bell also quotes examples of companies omitting *The Times* from their advertising schedules because its editorial coverage was so good that they felt able to confine their expenditure to other papers known to be inadequate in that department.

Thomas Russell confirmed that when he worked at *The Times* he was constantly receiving approaches from advertisers. His view of a paper's responsibilities, however, was very similar to that of Moberly Bell: "It should print nothing about any commodity, merchandise, or utility from any other motive than the desire or belief that the public needs, or its readers desire, information on the subject."[36]

Bell himself furnishes an interesting contrast in attitudes between his paper and another leading daily. "The *Daily Telegraph* refused to publish a letter from us answering a letter which had appeared from a publisher attacking us. On my remonstrating with Lawson he replied in a perfectly friendly letter that he 'ventured to doubt whether it was in the interest either of *The Times* or the *Daily Telegraph* to offend a large body of advertisers like the publishers.'"[37]

The celebrated incorruptibility of *The Times* made its imprimatur the most sought-after prize in advertising, though one which was destined to remain outside the advertiser's grasp.

The advertising fraternity seems to have been guilty of a certain lack of logic on the question of puffing. They went to enormous lengths to engineer the publication of puffs, but at the same time constantly denied any intention to mislead the public. If their intentions were strictly honorable, it is strange that they tried wherever possible to have omitted any designation that the item in question was an advertisement, or at least to show it in such form that it was by no means apparent to the reader what was meant. For example, three or four figures were sometimes included at the end of a paragraph, these being intended to signify to the reader that it was a puff. Such practices, the result of publishers trying to salve their consciences without upsetting their advertisers, achieved little, being described by H. J. Palmer as "feeble and ineffectual."

While it is easy to condemn the attitudes of advertisers and agents, there is one possible explanation for their desire to obtain favorable editorial mentions which would leave their honor reasonably intact. Columns full of advertising were probably read less thoroughly as the size of the paper and the number of advertisements increased. Since it was only toward the end of the century that papers began to allow advertisements to run across more than one column, and there were therefore few opportunities for visual devices to catch the eye, it may well have been thought—probably with justification—that an announcement in the editorial columns would simply be seen by many more readers.

Agents, as might be expected, defended the use of the puff. Charles Mitchell, a well-known proprietor, drew the following comparison between English and French techniques:

> In France, the art of advertisement-writing is carried to a much higher state of perfection than with us. Our ingenious neighbour, in the *indirect* announcements, which would be called with us familiarly "puffs"—far excel us, more sober islanders, in delicacy of insinuation, and in concealing the objects of the paragraph till the writer [reader] is too far advanced to throw it aside.[38]

Mitchell's attitude is not surprising since he himself was involved in securing favorable reviews from newspapers on behalf of his clients. There can be little doubt what lay behind his claim that he offered "a systematic arrangement by which BOOKS, PRINTS, and MUSIC are forwarded for Review, as well as ADVERTISEMENTS of the same . . ." particularly bearing in mind Moberly Bell's point about advertisements being cut back or withdrawn in the absence of good notices.

The editorial columns of newspapers were quite clearly influenced by the activities of advertisers and their agents during the nineteenth century. The question remaining to be answered is how far the public were deceived as a result?

Edmund Street, referring to what he called "the editorial advertisement"—that is to say the paid puff—declared that "the custom is now so largely practised that I very much doubt whether the public are for one moment misled."[39] It is certainly true that even if a puff were not designated as such, there were still clues for the reader as to its true identity. They were normally written in the same eulogistic terms as an advertisement, and contained references to companies and products which were frequently not permitted in normal editorial. In addition, many of the papers which allowed puffs seem to have grouped them at the bottom of columns. The combination of distinctive style, content, and position must therefore have made it possible for many readers to distinguish a puff from genuine editorial.

The absence of any kind of designation may well have meant that the public would not realize the true identity of a puff until after having read it. According to Clarence Moran, a barrister, writing at the beginning of the present century, this was frequently the case:

> The disguised puff is, indeed, one of the most prominent features of newspaper advertising at the present day. In some cases the disguise is more or less of a joke. The reader is beguiled into perusing what appears to be a piece of news, and finds that he is artfully led into a laudation of somebody's pills or soap.[40]

It does not seem to have occurred to any of the parties concerned that such tactics could lead to public anger being directed against the product, or against the newspaper which allowed such deceptions to be practiced in its columns, or both. The outcome in such a case could well be a decision not to purchase either product or paper again.

Puffs planted on the financial pages could do rather more damage. Editorial comment here would often relate to named companies, and would consider such matters as their performance, potential, and value as investments. A carefully planted puff would therefore be far less easy to detect. The bartering of news for advertising space, the regulation of advertising expenditures to secure favorable editorial comments, and the exploitation of financial interests in relevant publications were methods commonly used, though it is impossible to estimate the extent to which the unwary were duped into lavishing money on overvalued or worthless investments as a result of editorial impropriety.

The situation with regard to puffing in general was not thought serious enough to warrant any kind of official action. It is worth noting, however, that in a case at the Central Criminal Court in 1897 the Common Serjeant declared that the publication of undesignated puffs was reprehensible and ought to be abolished.[41]

Financial manipulation apart, it must be concluded that the influence of advertisers on the editorial content of newspapers did not constitute a serious threat to the public interest. The activities of advertisers were peripheral to those of gathering and presenting news. They concerned themselves with bringing their products to the notice of the public in the most favorable manner possible, or with the exclusion of items showing them in a bad light. As such, it was a long way from the old system of bribery and subsidy. Then the object had usually been to secure the presentation of political news in a form acceptable to the controller of the purse strings. Advertisers, however, were concerned only with that which related directly to them. If newspapers deviated somewhat from complete editorial objectivity with respect to advertised products, the result paradoxically was to ensure their freedom in the reporting and discussion of those events which were of truly national importance.

8
Sporting News, 1860–1914

Tony Mason

> I remember how a London curate who was the son of an eminent Conservative statesman, observing the rush for *Evening Standards* in a working men's club, rejoiced over this indubitable evidence of the existence of the Tory working man, but had his joy darkened by the discovery that the reason was that more late sporting news was attainable in that organ than in any other.[1]

If Horsley's curate had been more sophisticated he would have been less anxious. Sport was a safe enough pastime for the masses. Nonetheless, the sporting press was blamed for encouraging the social evil of gambling and the corruption of sport that, it was thought, inevitably accompanied it. It pandered to the worst manifestation of win-at-any-price professionalism, and far from encouraging participation in sport and therefore the attendant physical and moral benefits, was a prime factor in producing a race of narrow-chested, foul-mouthed spectators. There were dark hints about empires in decline. Meanwhile intellectual commentators on the press were equally hostile to this new development or, like H. R. Fox-Bourne, merely puzzled by it, and their anxieties were shared by the leaders of Nonconformity.[2]

When writing about sporting news in this period the historian faces two particular difficulties. The first in the nature and bulk of the material. These decades witnessed not only the expansion of organized sport but a corresponding growth of newspaper coverage of it. Not only did the specialist sporting press grow; by 1914 few local or national newspapers were without their sports columns. Very little of this material was in any sense reflective. It makes it very difficult to know how and where to begin, especially when there is no historiography to joust with or feed off. The second difficulty is the absence of those detailed printers' and publishers' records which could illuminate not only the day-to-day running and organization of a paper but the relationship between the paper and its readers. Of three of the four specialist sporting dailies which existed together for a short period in the 1880s, *Bell's Life* was taken over by the *Sporting Life* in 1886; that paper was bought by Odham's Press in 1920; the company captured the *Sportsman* four years later. The records of Odhams were destroyed during the war. Moreover the daily and weekly newspapers which devoted an increasing amount of their space to sporting news have not kept the records that would explain in detail how and why they did it.

By 1885 there were four major sporting daily newspapers, although one of them, *Bell's Life in London,* did not have a very long life in front of it. However, at the start of our period *Bell's* was something of a national institution, the premier, indeed unique, sporting paper, without which a gentleman's Sunday was incomplete. As it was not only the forerunner but in part the model for those which came later it might be useful to sketch the profile of a paper which Grant estimated brought in profits of £10,000 a year through the 1850s and into the 1860s.[3] *Bell's* first appeared in January 1822, the property of a London printer and newsvendor, Robert Bell. It set out to show life in London "as it really was."[4] It did not print only sporting news. In fact, in the first issue, the police intelligence had slightly more space than the sporting news which consisted largely of prizefighting, the latest betting on the horses entered for the forthcoming classics, and a report on a great footrace in Yorkshire.[5] It was only after it had been bought by the proprietor of the *Observer,* William Clement, in 1824, that it concentrated increasingly on sporting news. Even then it continued to publish a considerable amount of other forms of material until the 1860s.[6]

Clement, who had published Cobbett's *Register* and who owned the *Morning Chronicle* for twelve years, remained the owner of *Bell's* until his death in 1852 and allegedly raised the circulation from three to thirty thousand.[7] His major contribution to this success was probably the journalist whom he took from the *Observer* to become editor of his new paper, Vincent Dowling. Dowling held the post for twenty-eight years. He made *Bell's* both reliable and respectable by putting into operation Nimrod's famous dictum that although he had started with "the belief that to write for a sporting paper was no job for a gentleman, (it) was not long before he contended that no one but a gentleman was qualified for the position."[8] *Bell's* could be trusted, so much so that the paper was often the stakeholder for prize fights and for bets. It was estimated that between £8,000 and £10,000 a year passed through the paper's hands in this way by the 1850s.[9] Reliability, expert comment, and good writing made *Bell's* the sort of paper which could be taken into some of the best houses, particularly as its leaders were renowned for taking the British line on every subject.[10]

Bell's came out every Sunday until the 1860s and for several years in the fifties and sixties was published in three editions, town, country, and latest. The price of the paper fell from sevenpence to sixpence stamped, and it would occasionally issue free supplements, like the two pages which accompanied the eight-page proper on Sunday, 11 March 1860, containing items on racing in the West Indies and the U.S.A., an article on the origins of degeneracy in horses, one on the latest Enfield rifle, and some extra material under the usual headings. In the late 1860s the paper began to come out twice a week, an eight-page, forty-eight column paper on Saturdays for threepence with a stamp and twopence without, and a penny four-page number on Wednesdays. This change was almost certainly a reaction to the competition of the *Sporting Life* and the *Sportsman.*

The new format did not last long because by March 1872 *Bell's* had reverted to a weekly, coming out on a Saturday for fivepence, for which the reader got twelve pages. The space devoted to particular items had not altered much. In the issue of 16 March 1872, advertisements, largely dealing with livestock transactions, filled up the front page. Page two consisted of advertisements for various public amusements, details of pigeon shoots, and a chronological list of all the fights held in the previous year under the laconic heading of "The Ring." Otherwise horse racing and hunting occupied the most space, but most sports received some notice.

The fiftieth anniversary editorial was optimistic.

> It is our hope and belief that we have kept pace with the times, and that in suppressing or modifying sports that twenty years back would have been published as a matter of course an honest and prudent step has been adopted . . . every effort has been made to give prominence to some of the national amusements that formerly had but scant justice done them by the Newspaper press, for example, Coursing, The Chase, Aquatics. Year by year increased space has been devoted to cricket and that game and football in their season occupy as many columns as would hold the entire contents of the first *Bell's Life.*

Amateur athletics and pedestrianism were reported each week 'elaborately' and sports news from abroad had become an established feature.[11]

In fact, the paper had only fourteen more years of independent life. The difficulties began with the publication of a rival, the *Penny Bell's Life and Sporting News,* on 24 March 1859. Not only was this paper to be issued on Wednesday and Saturday, it was to cost one penny instead of fivepence; it even appeared to be poaching the old name to deceive the unwary reader. Clearly the owners of *Bell's* could not allow that, and they obtained an injunction in the court of chancery forbidding the new journal to use the old name. With the issue of 30 April 1859 the rival became known as the *Sporting Life,* dealing mainly with the sport of kings, which it was determined to clean up, but also offering other sports news which until that time *Bell's Life* had largely monopolized. By the end of April the new paper was trumpeting a sale of 150,000 copies per week, which, if true, left *Bell's* way behind. The new paper claimed to be the first in England "which attempted and successfully carried out, an effort to procure, *within twelve hours,* a detailed account of the contest for a Championship, three days before *Bell's.*"[12] In spite of soothing words about competition being beneficial to old and new alike, the intention of the upstart was made clear in the issue of 14 May 1850 when it exultantly proclaimed that the celebrated "Sentinel," late of *Bell's Life,* would in future write exclusively for the *Sporting Life.* Every trainer of horses in the United Kingdom was sent a copy of the new paper twice a week affording "an excellent medium for the advertisements of Race Programmes which will be placed in a conspicuous position on the first page and inserted at the reduced charge of sixpence a line."[13] The new paper also carried more and wider-ranging advertising than the old, from Blair's Gout and Rheumatic Pills to a book entitled *Duties of the butler,* price one and sixpence, a companion to J. Williams, *Footman's guide to his duties.*[14] In June 1859 the young pennyworth moved into bigger offices in Fleet Street.[15] Moreover, from 1865, another penny sporting paper, the *Sportsman,* joined the fray, and Hulton and Bleackley published their *Sporting Chronicle* from Manchester for the first time in 1871.

The Clement brothers, who had owned *Bell's* since their father had died in 1852, stuck it out until 1883. By then, unable to move with the times and "reduced to abject poverty," according to one observer, they sold the paper to a couple of racing reporters.[16] They attempted to meet the competition by publishiing twice a week and reducing the paper's price from sixpence to a penny.[17] They also claimed that in future, all sports would be dealt with in a popular and readable style, "with an absence of that verbiage which too often destroys the interest of the narrative" and that "a place will also be found for those causeries and trifles which go far to lighten the columns of a newspaper." The paper was to offer four pages on Wednesdays and eight on Saturdays. It was not enough.[18]

By 1885 *Bell's* had changed hands once again, purchased by Hulton and Bleackley, owners of the *Sporting Chronicle* and other northern papers, who tried to restore its fortunes by turning it into a daily. Largely increased staff and machinery capable of printing forty thousand copies an hour were of no avail.[19] Four daily sporting papers, each publishing a similar class of material on identical lines was at least one too many, and in May 1886 the name was sold to the *Sporting Life* with the proviso that Hulton and Bleackley should not publish a sporting paper in London.[20] Perhaps *Bell's* coverage and treatment had been too traditional. Perhaps the price of the journal should have been lowered earlier, particularly as the *Field* was also offering weekly competition at the expensive end of the market. Perhaps it should have entered the daily stakes earlier. Clearly once *Bell's* monopoly as suppliers of sporting news to their readers and other London papers was broken the paper's connections were going to have to rethink their strategy. Too little change too late would seem a not unsympathetic epitaph.

The three sporting dailies whose competition did so much to kill off old *Bell's* had three main characteristics in common. From their inception they had been really sporting papers. Save for the occasional article on the stage, nonsporting news was never included, although both the *Sporting Chronicle* and the *Sportsman* were not averse to the odd anti-Puritan editorial. Indeed, the *Sportsman* played a prominent role in the establishment of the Sporting

League, aimed specifically at combatting organizations like the Anti-Gambling League. The Sporting League interfered in elections and confronted hostile individuals like John Burns. In many respects all three papers represented the Tory individualism of the Liberty and Property Defence League, although they preferred not to harp on it.[21]

The second common characteristic was that they all concentrated heavily on horse racing. As the first editorial of the *Sportsman* said in 1865 "racing has always formed, and must continue to form, the most prominent feature in an English sporting newspaper."[22] All the papers paraded their inside knowledge from the training stables, all offered opinions about which horses would win and all offered the latest betting intelligence. It was the growth of horse racing that eventually prompted all three papers to publish daily.[23] By the 1880s there were few days in the year, weather permitting, when racing was not taking place somewhere in the United Kingdom. But in this period these papers never became simply racing sheets, although some midweek editions were monopolized by the horses: in fact all of them provided space for the popular team games of football and cricket, and especially the activities of the professional élite, but also the expanding though less numerically popular sports and pastimes like quoits, golf, and tennis.

Finally, all three papers followed *Bell's* in promoting and sponsoring sport. They did not reflect its growth merely, but encouraged it by holding stakes, providing judges with referees, and presenting trophies. This was particularly true for those activities which could not command the greatest spectator interest, like swimming, billiards, bagatelle, and amateur boxing. Moreover, all the papers published sporting annuals and guides and other sporting accessories from the cricket score sheets offered at a penny each or ninepence per dozen by the *Sporting Life* in 1874 to the *Sportsman*'s *Monthly Guide to the Turf,* which appeared regularly from 1884 to 1919.[24] All were national papers, even the Manchester-based *Sporting Chronicle,* although it did give some preference to local sporting activities, and all, as penny papers, were aimed at the masses as well as the middle classes.

By the time the three major sporting dailies were thriving in the mid-1880s, there was also a flourishing weekly sporting press with at least two outstandingly successful if very different exemplars. The *Field* had already been going for thirty years and had made a great deal of money for the Cox family since its purchase in 1854.[25] The full title of the paper indicates clearly at whom it was aimed; *The Field, the Farm, the Garden, the Country Gentleman's Newspaper.* Furthermore, although sport and particularly rural sport was to feature prominently in its pages, it was devoted "to the collection of every kind of information calculated to inform and amuse those who take an interest' in the country and rural occupations; the garden, the home farm, the poultry yard, the stable, the dairy, and the household would be considered alongside the field sports.[26] It was to be a family paper which would not, as the *Sporting Times* was later to do, concentrate on the man about London town, but upon the man, and his family, out of town.

Its actual sporting coverage reflected its general policy and outlook. Hunting, shooting, fishing, coursing, and the turf were given the most prominence through the decades but ball games gradually crept into more space and by the early twentieth century there is a hint of some tension between the field sports group on the staff and the ball games group over how much space each should have. In general, though, the paper turned up its nose at professional games players and was openly critical of spectatorism.[27]

The *Field*'s services to its readers ran to thirty-two pages of advertisements and a Sporting Registry which could be consulted at its offices and contained information on shooting, fishing waters to let, hunting boxes, gamekeepers requiring situations, and the sale of a predictable range of items from hounds to yachts. Those thirty-two pages of advertisements necessitating their own index provides an indication of what must have been coming in. Rose points to a steady decline of profits after 1890, but they had been about £75,000 in that year on a circulation of around 19,000. By any standards the *Field,* together with its stablemate the *Queen,* was a very successful family business which the Great War would severely but not fatally damage.

Although there is not anything like the same documentation relating to the *Athletic News,* it was the other most successful weekly sporting paper of this period. Unlike the *Field,* it stuck to sports news only and, even more astonishingly, sporting news without the otherwise ubiquitous horse racing. This was partly because it originated from the Hulton-Bleackley partnership, which also turned out the *Sporting Chronicle,* and in many respects it complemented that paper. It first appeared in 1875 with the aim of covering the sporting activities of amateurs, but it did not neglect the professional element in cricket from the start and allocated a large amount of space to professional football from its formal beginnings in 1885. Athletics (a term denoting all track-and-field sports), cycling, and rugby were also strongly featured. From the middle of the 1880s it came out on a Monday which brought it closer to Saturday's matches. Indeed it became increasingly identified with professional football. From 1893 to 1900 the paper's editor was also president of the Football League.[28] It became a penny paper at the start of the 1887–88 football season and by the middle of the 1890s claimed a circulation of 180,000 a week from September to April. Its match reports were long, critical, and stylish. Although it had a northern and midland focus, reflecting where organized football had grown fastest in the first decade of its existence, its orientation was firmly national as its special correspondents in London and Scotland showed. Long before 1914, it had carved out for itself a special position in the minds of the sports-conscious clerks and skilled workmen, from Birmingham northward, who almost certainly made up the majority of its readers.

From the 1870s, as the numbers playing, watching, and hopefully reading about a variety of sports grew, many specialist weeklies, sometimes devoted to a single sport, sometimes to a variety, began but few stayed long. they were usually begun by sporting or journalistic enthusiasts or both. *Pastime,* for example, survived twelve years from 1883–95 under the editor-ownership of sportsman-journalist, N. A. Jackson. *Cricket,* owned and edited by sporting journalist, Surrey County Cricket Club secretary, and sometime secretary of the Football Association Charles W. Alcock even longer. It was a twopenny weekly throughout the cricket season, monthly during the autumn and winter. It began in 1882. With its biographical articles, historical features, and contemporary descriptions, it provides the most comprehensive account of the game's development before 1914, an essential source for any historian of the game. However, it does not seem to have recovered from the death of Alcock in 1907 and was about to alter its serious approach when the First World War killed it off.[29] In general, though, the specialist sporting press, daily and weekly, was not a victim of the First World War but of the increasing attention paid to sporting news by the morning, evening and Sunday papers.

The trend is clear. Sporting news was taking up a larger portion of the daily press at the end of our period than at the beginning, and the range of sports covered was much wider. Of course, there were differences between individual newspapers in style and in the sports chosen to receive the most space, notably, from the 1890s, between the halfpenny and penny papers, but for all morning papers of whatever ownership or political persuasion sports news and comment had become a regular feature. If we take the *Daily Telegraph* as an example, it was rare for more than 2 percent of the paper to be devoted to sports news, and that almost entirely horse racing, and in season, cricket, with an occasional athletics meeting thrown in. The geographical emphasis was on London and the south. This pattern did not change from the 1850s until the 1890s, save for a brief mention of other sports: football, cycling, tennis, and billiards. By the mid 1890s, however, sports coverage had risen to 7.5 percent, with more football and rugby. With advertising also on the increase sporting news was spread over five columns by 1905, although as a proportion of the paper it was down to 5.8 percent. This was but a temporary setback. On the eve of the war in 1914, sport was straying onto the news pages and total coverage had risen to 11 percent. Seven columns were given over to reports from the Amateur Golf championship alone.

The nineties may be the key decade so far as the sports consciousness of the daily press is concerned. Certainly no paper beginning then and aiming for a popular readership felt that it could neglect sporting news. The *Morning Leader,* a Liberal halfpenny daily produced for artisans and clerks,

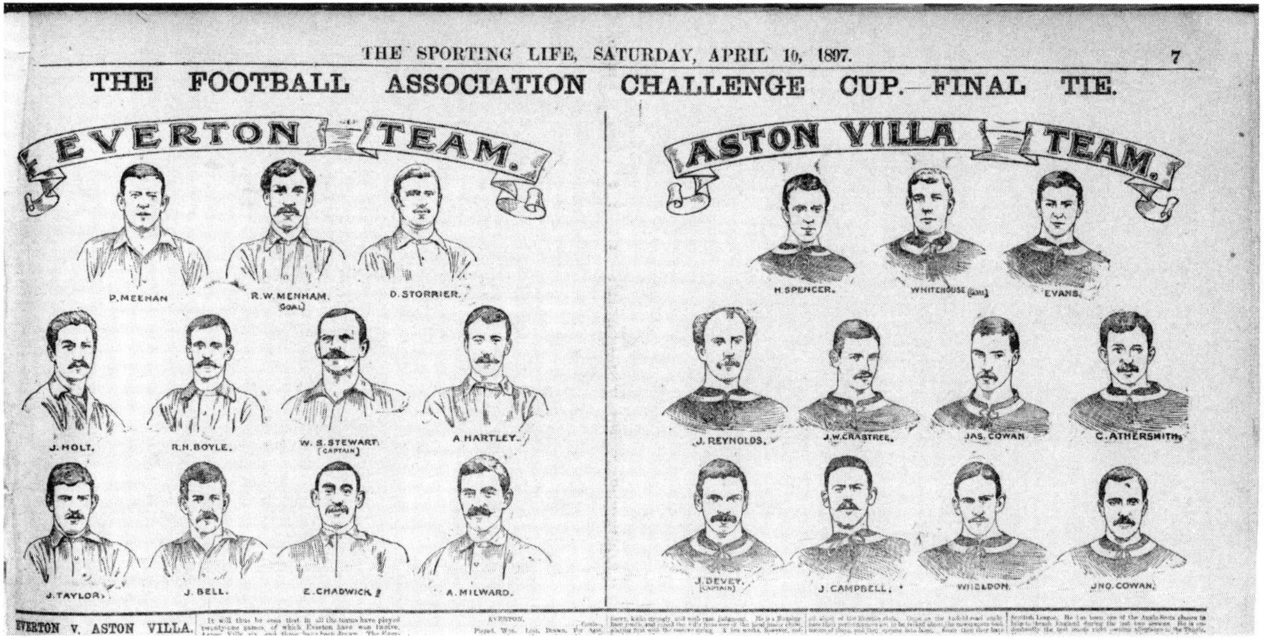

Cup-final teams from the *Sporting Life,* Saturday, 10 April 1897 (British Library Newspaper Library).

began on 23 May 1892 with one of its eight pages devoted to the latest sporting news. By the time the football season had begun in September, sport monopolized not only page seven but three of five columns on page six (*Morning Leader,* 5 September 1892) on the Monday after the Saturday matches. The short paragraphs on many different sports so beloved of the new journalism were a feature of the paper but racing and cricket and football in season dominated the columns.

Similarly the *Daily Mail* gave up at least a page to sports news from its inception, one eighth of the whole.[30] Moreover, at the start of its first football season it was quick to inform interested parties "that the most complete arrangements are being made for the treating of the national and winter sport in a most enterprising and novel manner."[31] Looking at the paper's treatment it is difficult to see what was novel about it, unless it was the excessive space given to the home matches of Woolwich Arsenal.[32] Even the *Daily Herald,* although unhappy about providing racing tips and encouraging its largely working-class readership to bet, ran a sports page, and the language of sport was even used to promote the activities of the Herald League, whose forthcoming events were listed under the heading "Today's Fixtures."[33]

The posher papers were more ambiguous about sport, or at least about including a lot of information about it in their pages. They had never totally ignored it. *The Times,* for example, had long given prominence to such events as the Boat Race, the Derby, and the Eton and Harrow match and had had a cricket correspondent since 1880, though no sports editor.[34] The Anglo-Australian test matches were important news by the 1890s, and the paper could occasionally wax lyrical over the social value of mass sport, as in its editorial on the Monday following the Cup Final of 1899. But in general it distrusted games being played for a living and it offered little publicity to the regular program of professional soccer and rugby matches. Neither did it encourage betting by providing the services of a tipster.

The *Morning Post* adopted a similar policy and even the *Manchester Guardian,* located, as it was, in a football stronghold, gave amateurs more space than professionals, even though, by 1913, it reported the Association game quite fully with a preview of Saturday's program in Friday's paper, together with results and match reports on Mondays. Presumably it did so, at least in part because the editor felt that that was what its regular readers preferred.[35]

A similar pattern is repeated in the Sunday papers, although at least three of those began life with the express intention of specializing in results and accounts of the previous day's sporting activities. The *Referee* first appeared in 1877, founded and edited by a former sportsman and sporting journalist, Henry Sampson, with Ashton Dilke putting up the money. *Mitchell's* characterized it as "a journal of sport and the drama,"[36] and it may have been the first Sunday newspaper to run a football results column.

Both the *Umpire* and the *Sunday Chronicle* also proclaimed their intention to give prominence to sporting news from their beginnings in 1884 and 1886 respectively, hardly surprising in the case of the latter, as it was another Edward Hulton paper.

However, the 1890s appear to be the key decade when papers became larger and the area of sports news really grew. Virginia Berridge has pointed out that sport was still a relatively unimportant part of nonadvertising material in the three papers which she studied, *Reynolds's Newspaper, Lloyd's Weekly Newspaper,* and the *Weekly Times,* in 1886. It comprised 2.8 percent of the content of the first two, and 5.3 percent of the latter.[37] But the *News of the World* was by then already devoting 8.3 percent of its space to sporting news, a figure which had risen to 14.4 percent by 1895. Moreover, the racing monopoly had been broken, largely by cricket, football, and athletics in their seasons. In the *News of the World*'s case these changes are almost certainly related to the change in ownership of that paper which took place in 1891.[38] By 1905, 15.75 percent of an enlarged paper was reserved for sporting news, and association football had dethroned the sport of kings by 7¾ columns to 5. The *Umpire* went even further: 18.75 percent of all the material in the paper including advertising was sport, and football led racing by 9½ columns to 6. To the increasingly comprehensive sporting news service provided by the mass-circulation Sunday newspapers and the extended coverage of the mornings was also added the immediacy of the evening papers. Indeed, the relationship between sport and the press produced a new type of paper, the "football special."

It is often difficult to discover which was the first in a long line, but there is no doubt that the Birmingham paper so aptly named *Saturday Night* was one of the earliest of the genre.[39] It first appeared in the late September of 1882, four large pages for a halfpenny, on the streets and in the shops at 7:00P.M. and claiming a larger circulation than any other newspaper in the Midlands, save the two Birmingham dailies.[40] Early in 1883 it confidently characterized itself as 'spicy without being vulgar—a first class serial tale, a complete novelette, humourous and spicy paragraphs, three or four columns of local chat, the results of scores of athletic events all over the Kingdom, and everything *readable.*"[41] We can agree on the importance of this last feature. The newspaper was not much to look at: the printing usually left something to be desired and the paper did not smack of the best quality, but it filled a real gap and was very successful until the competition of the larger local papers which it had provoked brought about its downfall almost sixteen years after its initial brash appearance.[42]

Outside Birmingham both weekly and evening papers soon began imitating *Saturday Night* with football editions. The *Blackburn Times,* for example, advertised its Saturday Football in September 1883, again aiming to reach the streets at 7:00 P.M. but charging a penny.[43] By November 1884, the *Wolverhampton Express and Star* was publishing a Saturday night special edition, which in effect was the same four-page halfpenny paper as on the other five nights of the publishing week except that on page three, the last two columns were different. Column five was headed "Today's Football" and contained four-hundred-word reports on the most important local matches with several shorter reports and a few local results. The sixth and final column was made up entirely of football advertisements, for kit and even team photographs with fifteen local shops and firms mentioned.[44] By December, the column of reports had become one and a half columns of football and half a column of racing. Similar papers soon appeared in places as far apart as Derby, Glasgow, Sheffield, and Manchester, where the *Sporting Chronicle* put out what was described as a tissue at 6:30 P.M. on Saturday evening containing the results of about thirty football matches in England and Scotland.

These early football specials were somewhat tentative about the market for a Saturday evening sports-only paper. That probably explains why they maintained so many of their regular features as much as the wish to get the paper out once the telegrams were in and the local results collected. But the demand was there. On the day Aston Villa met Queens Park in the FA Cup in January 1884, it reached such proportions that halfpenny papers containing only the result of the match were selling for sixpence on the streets of Birmingham at ten minutes to five in the afternoon. This was bound to encourage proprietors to produce the sports-only evening paper.[45]

The Tillotsons, those energetic newspaper entrepreneurs from Bolton, whose *Evening News* was one of the first provincial evening papers, were probably first in the field with the sports-only Saturday special. Their *Football Field and Sports Telegram* appeared each Saturday night around 7.30 P.M. from 1884. Only the two center pages were devoted to the day's events, with results and match reports clustered together. The remainder of the paper involved comment on the previous week's games, assessment of the form of teams and players, and a multitude of brief paragraphs, *Tit-Bits* style, with gossip and comment intermingled on a variety of sports. *Willing's Press Guide* listed twenty-six sports-only papers by the 1900s, almost certainly an underestimation. They came to look increasing alike though printed on pink, green, and white paper. Only the names of the local professional clubs and players, who received the most attention, were different.

The evening papers were first with the news, and that was especially important so far as sports news was concerned.[46] Well before the Great War an evening paper in Newcastle-upon-Tyne and one in Plymouth would both be able to include the full score and a one-hundred-and-fifty-word description of the play in that day's cricket in the Australia-England Test match in Sydney supplied by the Press Association; the cost was only ten shillings per day including the telegrams.[47]

Some people felt that the evening paper had got its sports news coverage completely out of perspective. On the other hand, a writer in the *Journalist* could look on the bright side: if the betting side of sporting needs was afforded such splendid coverage in the evening papers, perhaps the morning papers could at least leave out that portion of the sports news and still flourish. As we noted earlier, however, few were willing to take the risk.

It is doubtful if many newspapers employed specialist sports reporters before 1870. Before that, it was the age of the freelance and the small agency, and even afterward they played an important role in news collection and distribution. In the early 1850s, for example, most London dailies which required racing news were still obtaining it from William Ruff, editor of the Turf department of *Bell's Life,* who had succeeded his father in both jobs.[48] Similarly, cricket news for the London dailies was being supplied in the 1860s and 1870s by a small agency run by George Kelly King.[49] C. H. Ashley, who later became part owner of the *Sportsman,* left that paper in the late 1860s to set up his own sporting news agency.

The Press Association paid him £1,000 a year for such a service before eventually taking on their own sporting staff in 1883 after Ashley had apparently refused to give an undertaking not to extend his own list of direct newspaper subscribers.[50] Hultons also sold sporting news and there were many more small operations, of which the most famous was probably the Cricket Reporting Agency established by Charles Pardon in 1880. Not only did Pardon's agency provide a range of sporting news to a variety of newspapers; it also provided a training ground for several generations of sports journalists. The Press Association appointed its own sports editor in 1901 and from that time collected its own racing news. By that time more and more morning and Sunday papers were employing their own sports staff.

The collection of sporting news in the nineteenth century could be an arduous business. The press had no privileges or special facilities at Newmarket, for example, as late as the 1860s. Reporters who specialized in sending information about horses in training to London and provincial papers hired the hut of a shepherd who worked on the heath. *Bell's Life* used a brougham with a desk in it as later did the *Field.*[51] Following prize fights in the 1850s and 1860s must have been especially difficult. The venue was often secret until the last minute to confuse the authorities and there were usually no seats, let alone desks, although press representatives were sometimes given privileged ringside positions.[52] A position was reserved for the press at the Scotland-England football match in Glasgow in 1884, as it had been at the recent Rugby match between the two countries, but the fact that the *Atlantic News* saw fit to comment suggests it was not the usual occurrence.[53]

However, reporters often found themselves sitting at a table just in front of the spectators with no cover, exposed both to the vagaries of both crowd and weather. The 1890s began to see improvements, with the first press boxes on football grounds and very comfortable ones on the largest cricket grounds. The one at the Oval even had its own lavatory.[54] It was much harder at the smaller clubs, courses, and grounds.

Moreover, the number of journalists who wanted to see the biggest matches was increasing all the time and took a deal of organizing. By 1899 a press committee was alloting seats to almost one hundred and fifty journalists for the Cup Final at the rather inconvenient Crystal Palace ground.[55] The size and scope of the reporting of a major sporting event had so increased that the chief football reporter of *Sport and Play* was given the responsibility of ensuring that the messages produced by the one hundred and eighty journalists at Villa Park Birmingham for the England-Scotland match of 1899 reached the telegraph offices in the center of the city.

Up to about the end of the nineteenth century the agency reporters sent most of their sports news back to their offices by telegram. Certainly by the 1890s the Post Office had travelling staffs of telegraphists at many racecourses and cricket grounds to handle the traffic.[56] There was still competition to have your telegram sent first. Sports journalists on the daily or specialist sporting papers were not under quite the same pressure. A racing man on the *Daily Telegraph* recalled that there was no need to worry about copy being in either while racing was in progress or as soon as possible after it had finished. Any time up to midnight would do.[57]

The telephone brought about significant changes in the collection of sporting news. One of the earliest examples of a newspaper using it to provide a rapid results service was that of the *Sheffield Evening Telegraph* which on 22 March 1889 had the result of Wednesday's quarter-final Cup-tie at Wolverhampton phoned in. "The match finished at six minutes to five, and at two minutes to the hour the result was received in the office. At five o'clock the machines were running and a minute or two later the papers were being eagerly bought up in the street."[58] The Exchange Telegraph Company adopted the telephone for its news-gathering activities about 1900, and in face of that competition the Press Association introduced their own telephone football results service at the beginning of the 1905–6 season. Racing and cricket quickly followed. Offices equipped with telephones and staff were established in a group of major cities and many phones were installed on sports grounds and racecourses.[59] But the cost was high, especially as a result of the extra manpower needed to cover all the various events. The result was an agreement between the two biggest agencies to cooperate instead of competing. The service did not suffer, although the men who were made redundant probably did not appreciate the contribution to efficiency which they were making.[60] By the 1907–8 season, the joint service offered not only results, but scores at particular times, telephonic descriptive reports of the play, telephoned at the times most convenient to those newspapers buying, which could be just seventy-five words or two thousand. Even those papers sending their own reporters to follow particular teams could make arrangements to use the agencies' telephones for transmission of their own reports.[61] The collection of sports news would never be the same again. Well before the outbreak of war, "every big evening newspaper employs a staff of telephone clerks. . . . On the big majority of first-class grounds private telephones to the local newspaper offices are installed and trained journalists dictate their impressions of the play as it proceeds to the telephone clerks who in turn pass their slips on to the sub-editors . . . (then) the copy has to be set in type."[62]

Who were the journalists, usually writing under an elaborate *nom de plume*, whose actual or believed expertise played some part in keeping and perhaps increasing a paper's readership? Like so many other trades and professions it often ran in families. We have already noted that the editor of *Bell's Life* was the son of a journalist and he was succeeded by his own son.[63] Ruff, Sampson, and Feist also followed in their father's footsteps. Another common route was via a printing apprenticeship. Sampson, C. H. Ashley, and Hulton were among many who graduated to sporting journalism from the printer's shop. However, it was still relatively easy for the inexperienced outsider to break into sporting journalism, especially if he could offer an additional skill.

Charles Blake, for example was a veterinary surgeon who was recruited by the *Sporting Life* in 1868 after a series of professional articles. He edited the paper from 1874 to 1891.[64] For papers who prided themselves on being concerned with the quality of British bloodstock rather than merely in racing and betting, such an expert was very useful.[65]

Luck and knowing the right people were also important qualifications.[66] R. P. Watson met an athletics editor from *Bell's Life* at a London swimming club and was offered half a sovereign a week to visit other baths and collect the club results. He was soon being given work by the *Sporting Life* and the *Sportsman*.[67] Bernard Darwin, of Eton and Trinity, Cambridge was a dissatisfied solicitor in 1907 with a passion for golf. A public schoolmaster whom he knew and who had been writing a golf column in the *Evening Standard* offered the job to Darwin on his move to another paper. *Country Life* and *The Times* soon followed.[68]

Sports administrators and active sportsmen were also finding their names above the columns. Alcock, Pickford, and Sutcliffe all wrote extensively on association football from positions of influence inside the FA and the Football League respectively. The Surrey amateur, W. W. Read, had sent back reports to the *Sporting Life* on the English cricket tour of Australia in 1882–83.[69] Several leading footballers were having their names used by the halfpenny papers well before 1914, and the sporting editor of the *Daily Mail* paid each of the County crickets captains two guineas a match for one-hundred-and-fifty-word accounts of each day's play in 1904.[70]

In fact, all sorts and conditions of men earned money by writing on sport, from students of Jowett's at Balliol like William Allison, scholars like C. B. Fry, and aristocrats like Grantley Berkeley to Edgar Wallace, one-time sports editor on the *Evening Times,* and Edward Aveling who was "Cover Point," the Cricket reporter of the *Star* from 1888 to 1897.[71] Sports reporting was frequently a vocation or real enthusiasm, even if few of the practitioners could afford to take the line of the first *Sporting Times* editorial in 1865 which emphasized that the paper was not out to make money. It was true that the reporters would need paying, but most of the writers, a nice distinction, were doing it, *"con amore."*[72]

The style of the sporting writer in the nineteenth century was long dominated by the technical sophistication and racy language pioneered by the doyen of prize-fighting publicists, Pierce Egan.[73] Fights were "mills," blood "claret," noses "conks," eyes "ogles." Eight years after Egan had died and five after Dowling, *Bell's Life* still reported the "gallant and exciting mill between Tom Sayers and Aaron Jones for Two Hundred Pounds" in exactly the same way. Round two illustrates the method.

> Tom came up much flushed, and the gravy distilling from his damaged squinter. After a little dodging, he tried his double, but did not get it home. He tried a second time, but was stopped, and Jones returned on the left ogle. This led to very heavy counters each on the larboard goggle. Jones now feinted, and popped his left on the nose. They got hold of one another, swung round, broke away, and Sayers then popped his left again on the left eye. Severe exchanges followed at close quarters and both were in the end down.[74]

One contemporary commentator had an explanation for what he called this "poetical grab." Coupled with the enthusiasm of the writer it glorified what plain language clearly showed was a useless and brutal activity.[75] Perhaps it was standard "penny-a-line-ese" and really killed off by the extension of the telegraphs, but it was a tradition a little modified perhaps but recognizable in some of the reports of football matches in the *Athletic News* in the 1880s and 1890s, when the ball was a spherical object or the leather, and the pitch a quadrilateral or parallelogram. Reports would also be sprinkled with classical or literary quotations.

This kind of writing depended on time for composition. The pressures on both space and time which increasingly beset newspapers of all kinds as the twentieth century dawned placed limits on the utilization of other than a most economical style. Straightforwardness became more fashionable and the tendency clearly was for the colorful language and the rhetorical style, along with the literary quotations, to disappear. In their place had come, by the interwar period, according to Bernard Darwin, a more psychological explanation for missed catches, goals, and puts. It was more the pressure of the occasion which led to these catastrophes, whereas in more robust Victorian times it had simply been put down to luck or carelessness. Journalists were also becoming on much more familiar terms with the players, and the trend toward overwriting resulting in devaluation was clear.[76] It would be wrong to say that the more considered and thoughtful piece of sporting journalism was ruled out by the new conditions. With the better-class newspaper gradually allowing sports more column inches on more days of the week, in the case of dailies, the analytical was encouraged. But in the halfpenny papers the whole style revolved around the stark headline, the photograph, increasingly, and the economical paragraph. Turning points, major incidents might still be described but more often it was merely the bare bones of the event which got into the papers. Even there, though, what happened might be briefly described one day and why it happened another. This is a difficult subject which deserves a more considered treatment than the scope of this essay will allow.

Who read the sporting press and in what numbers? What changes took place over time? These are interesting questions, but convincing and detailed answers are unlikely without printers' and publishers' records.[77] If circulation is taken first, *Bell's Life* claimed a total sale of 1,457,607 copies in 1858, or 28,030 a week. In 1859 that weekly average was claimed to have increased to 29,032 with the ratio of the sale of unstamped to stamped papers four to one. The largest weekly circulation was said to be for the issue of 10 April 1859—39,604.[78] This writer has not been able to discover any other figures for *Bell's,* and it may not be without significance that these were published in the paper shortly after the establishment of its first serious competitor, the *Sporting Life.* After it had become a penny paper *Deacon's Newspaper Handbook* for 1885 gives *Bell's* circulation as 60,000: however, we do know that the Hultons, who had bought the paper in that year, sold the name to the *Sporting Life* in the next.

Deacon's 1881 edition also informs the reader that the then twice-weekly *Sporting Life* sold 102,000 copies a week, although it is not clear whether that meant Wednesday and Saturday editions together, during 1880. The weekly *Sporting Opinion* was listed as selling 13,500 copies and the *Sporting Times* 49,000. In 1883 *Deacon*'s suggested 30,000 daily for the *Sporting Chronicle*[79] and two years later gave the Birmingham weekly *Saturday Night* 19,700. The paper itself claimed 21,000 every Saturday in the football season in 1891.[80] *Mitchell's Press Guide* of 1888 quotes a figure of 20,000 for the weekly sales of the *Athletic News,* a figure increased to 50,000 in the 1891 edition. The paper itself claimed a weekly sale of 128,000 during the football season in 1893, which had risen to 180,000 by the autumn of 1896, and 192,000 in 1914.[81] We have already noted Rose's figures for the *Field.* These figures meant that when the dailies did cover sport they would automatically reach a far larger audience than the specialist weeklies or even the specialist dailies after the 1880s.

Who read these papers and the sporting pages of the evenings, mornings and Sundays? *Bell's Life* was clearly aimed at a reader with a bob or two if for no other reason than its price. But that did not mean that it did not penetrate the ranks. Dyke Wilkinson's father kept a public house in Birmingham in the late 1840s and took in several newspapers, including *Bell's Life*. "After these papers had been well read by the 'indoors' for a day or two after publication, they travelled all over the neighbourhood from one to another of the 'outdoors', and toward the end of the week, much the worse for wear and tear, they found their way back home and were at my service. . . ."[82] Similarly the *Birmingham Morning News* claimed that both *Bell's* and the *Sporting Life* could be read in Black Country pubs in the 1870s.[83] *Bell's* also claimed "a large number" of readers on the continent and in America, India, and the colonies, which suggests that it was middle-class men or the gentry and even the aristocracy who were its chief patrons.[84] As late in its life as 1886 it was claiming that its publication was the "event of the week" for Oxbridge undergraduates and the officers of every regiment which, with pardonable exaggeration, indicates where the paper's connections thought its readership lay.[85] Certainly the specialist sporting press was read by public schoolboys. William Allison, for example, said he first read the *Sportsman* while at Rugby, and the headmaster of Harrow, giving evidence to the Select Committee of the House of Lords on betting, said that his boys did read sporting papers, although he thought mainly for the cricket averages.[86]

Some better-off working men and clerks probably were buying occasional copies of dailies, like the *Sportsman* and *Sporting Life,* and if it was football rather than the horses which fascinated them, were among those who splashed out a penny each week on the *Athletic News*. There is no way of finding out. Edward Hulton, Jr., agreed with his questioner on the Betting Select Committee that the *Sporting Chronicle* circulated largely among the working classes.[87] The members of the Lord's Select Committee were convinced that it was largely working men and women who bought the morning racing sheets and the evening papers first out with the results. Moreover, they largely blamed the press in their report for the increase in betting. Not only did the papers provide racing information, they also employed tipsters who forecast the results of races and suggested horses to follow. Worse, unscrupulous bookmakers and tipsters used the press to advertise their wares.[88]

But cricket, too, with little opportunity for gambling had its passionate followers and readers of the sports news. Bernard Darwin once wrote that the number of people who knew *Wisden* better than any other book in the world was immense. Many of them could undoubtedly take a creditable degree in a cricket tripos.[89] By 1914, following sport was a considerable minority activity among all classes. Different types of sporting material clearly appealed to different kinds of sportsmen, but all tastes were catered for by the providers of British sporting news.

The development of sport and the expansion of sporting news obviously fed off each other. Sports news sold papers, or was thought by their owners to do so, and they were prepared to see that it had all the space it needed, much to the chagrin of some leader writers.[90] On the other hand, newspapers contributed to the extension and growth of sport not merely by providing publicity and advertising, but, as we noted earlier, match officials, stakeholders, and administrators too, especially in those early days when knowledgeable and experienced men were few and far between.[91]

Looking back we can see that the 1890s was the decade when the coverage of sport in newspapers really took on its modern size and shape. Why it happened then is another matter. One reason must concern the development of sport itself which, particularly in horse racing and the major team sports of association football, cricket, and rugby, had reached its twentieth-century form by 1890 or soon after. A cheaper press combined with the long run of rising real incomes and growing leisure presumably enabled many more working-class people to buy and read papers, especially evening ones.

We can also see that the specialist sporting dailies and weeklies were destined to disappear or undergo considerable modification. They could not survive, unchanged, the onslaught represented by the wider coverage of sport in the evenings and mornings which had set in well before 1914. Not only could these papers be first with the news, in the case of the evenings, but there were neither economic nor technical obstacles to the production of the more penetrating, thoughtful article, the prematch preview and the postmatch inquest. Moreover, they had the virtues of cheapness and regularity and a variety of content other than sports news that appealed to other members of the family, notably the women. If the absolute numbers interested in sport grew, their requirements could be met by the halfpenny daily plus the Saturday night sports special rather than the paper that dealt only in sports news and no other. The *Sportsman* was taken over by the *Sporting Life* in 1924 and thereafter that paper became more and more monopolized by racing intelligence for the specialist and studious punter. By which time the press room on the racecourse would house representatives of every daily paper and not only those of the three sporting dailies, the Press Association, and a couple of London morning papers as it often did before 1914.[92] The *Athletic News* held out until 1931 when it was swallowed by its roommate the *Sporting Chronicle*, and that paper did not desert its wide sports coverage for the turf and the dogs until after the Second World War.

But sporting news was still a press monopoly in 1914, and *Mitchell's* listed eighty-seven periodicals devoted to various aspects of it in that year, as well as all the newspaper coverage which has been discussed above. No paper could afford to neglect it, and those papers like the *Daily News, Daily Herald, Leeds Mercury,* and *Manchester Evening News* that had experimented by leaving out racing always restored it.[93] Indeed the importance of sporting news to the press perhaps needs no other epitaph than the experience of the *Daily Herald.* The paper condemned betting and stopped tipping horses after Lansbury became editor, effectively from February 1914. However, circulation was lost, and the service was restored to such effect that Basil Thompson could explain the popularity of the paper to a bewildered cabinet in 1919 by noting that "unfortunately the sporting correspondent had the good fortune to spot several winners lately and the men who buy the paper for this reason are reported now to be reading its editorial columns with more care."[94]

9
Imperialism, Illustration and the *Daily Mail*, 1896–1904

Catherine Hughes

> How many millions of years has the sun stood in heaven? But the sun never looked until yesterday upon the embodiment of so much energy and power.
>
> *Daily Mail*, 23 May 1897, on the occasion of the Diamond Jubilee

Imperial enthusiasm was sustained and widespread throughout late nineteenth-century Britain, and probably reached its height in the ecstatic celebration of Queen Victoria's Diamond Jubilee in May 1897. The majority of the population read, or knew of, Henty, Henry Newbold, and Kipling, and doubtless thrilled to news such as Kitchener's glorious revenge on the death of Gordon. Earlier reservations, such as those voiced by *The Times* when it described Queen Victoria's assumption of the title Empress of India as "tawdry imperialism" were dispelled or suspended, and the fear that imperialism implied acts of an arbitrary nature, not in the tradition of British political behavior, slowly disappeared. The dawn of a new technological age involving more rapid transport, the telegraph, and the growth of organizations such as Reuters meant that the urbane literary style that had characterized the established news publications of a leisured age was inevitably subject to change.

It was, however, the newly affluent lower middle classes who were most vociferous and unquestioning in their reception of things imperial, and their new wealth coupled with their recent enfranchisement made them a social and political force of no little importance. Furthermore, their enthusiasm for empire and the implicit, if vicarious, sense of superiority it bestowed, was not tempered by the sincere and sometimes overwhelming sense of responsibility felt by those more directly involved in the administration of vast overseas territories and millions of subject people.

Far from being acquired as J. R. Seeley's famous phrase had it "in a fit of absence of mind," the late Victorians regarded the "White Man's Burden" as something heavy, and incumbent upon a Christian people whose technological development and rapid industrialization had distanced them from the rest of the world. Unfamiliarity with other races also bred misconceptions which, according to Christine Bolt, hampered even those learned societies that were specifically concerned with anthropology.[1] The conventional view was still the Darwinian belief that races were arranged in a strict hierarchy on the ladder of progress and morality, a belief that was hardly conducive to a realistic or sympathetic study of racial distinctions.[2] But to have stood aside from those less fortunate would not have constituted a position of moral superiority, it would have been an abdication of responsibility. This view was reflected in a letter written by Queen Victoria to Lord Derby on hearing of the annexation of New Guinea. She wrote, "It is no doubt a serious step, but she rejoices it will enable us to protect the poor natives and to advance civilisation which she considers the mission of Great Britain."[3]

This sense of destiny and pride was also coupled with a strong conviction of racial and cultural superiority which was evident among even the reflective sections of Victorian Society. Richard Cobden described Islamic Society as being in the grip of "poverty, polygamy and the plague," and as Ronald Hyam points out, even a thinker as enlightened as J. S. Mill believed there was "moral influence and weight in the possession of colonies."[4]

But it was undoubtedly the popular press that felt the least need for refinement or sensibility in imperial matters, and although its first edition appeared only in the year before the Diamond Jubilee, it was the *Daily Mail* that most accurately caught the aggressive, boastful, and euphoric mood of the new "jingoes." It is also beyond dispute that Harmsworth, who boasted that his success derived from his policy of reflecting the ordinary man's opinion rather than directing it, realized that the section of society he was out to woo would respond most readily to empire as a heady outlet for the imagination. Harmsworth wanted a wide-circulation newspaper, one that was easy to read. Its policies and views had to be easily assimilated, and it had to appeal to women. This did not mean that Harmsworth was aiming at the lowest reaches of society. He wanted to draw his readership from the higher-working and lower-middle classes which had sufficient disposable income to attract valuable advertising revenue. Hence the importance of a female readership, since Harmsworth was shrewd enough to realize that it was they who disposed of large parts of the family income.

Although G. M. Young has observed that "the eighteenth century liked women to be fragile, the nineteenth century liked them ignorant,"[5] Harmsworth reasoned more simply. He realized that women liked illustrations, and therefore he ensured that the *Daily Mail*, like his other publications, was enlivened by line drawings. Unlike previous "uplifting" penny papers these illustrations brought glamour and romance to the reader, and there was a deliberate restriction on views of abbeys or pictures of saints. But they were simply illustrations, and not a powerful medium of visual expression. Photography had some impact on everyday life, but the technical problems of reproducing photographs in newspapers were far too difficult and expensive. Therefore the *Daily Mail* employed a largely anonymous team of artists who actually copied photographs. Before photography the draughtsmen had been indispensable as the recording eye, often in difficult or dangerous situations, and they were regarded accordingly. Those who merely copied in the security of their offices were given no such status, and finally the development of the halftone block facilitating the reproduction of photographs made them largely redundant. However, in the early days of the *Daily Mail* they were employed to copy photographs of wars and atrocities, but more usually the latest fashions or events in high society. The weekend editions indulged the Victorian passion for autodidacticism by carrying maps and diagrams of proposed feats of scientific and technical ingenuity, or the inevitable ration of natural history.

The assumptions and opinions of the *Daily Mail* were clear and unwavering, and were to remain so even through the shattering events of the Boer War. However, this absence of a questioning or critical editorial approach coupled with the status accorded to the artists was scarcely conducive to the production of good cartoons. In fact, the nineteenth-century cartoonists had abandoned the vicious, unmerciful, and thoroughly memorable style that had characterized their eighteenth-century forbears. Mr. Gladstone himself had recommended a knighthood for Tenniel,[6] and the policy whereby politicans go out of their way to acquire cartoons of themselves, even those that do not flatter, had already begun.[7] At the end of the nineteenth century there was a resurgence of humor and actual caricature in the work of such cartoonists as Will Dyson, resulting in a simplification of line which was very different from the work of Tenniel and his contemporaries.

Most famous nineteenth-century cartoonists were usually trained in, or influenced by, traditional Academy style. Despite the popularity of Art Nouveau, the cartoonists working for the "quality" press invariably produced allegorical set pieces in the classical style, heavy with emblems and symbolism which would not be lost on the classical education of the subscribers. Yet as the increased use of book illustration for the popular market was proving, the minds of those predisposed to buy publications such as the *Daily Mail* usually preferred a more literal interpretation. This can be explained by the fact that they did not feel comfortable with heavy symbolism except in such acceptable and familiar contexts as decorations on public buildings, or on coins of the realm. Doubtless these prejudices against the fanciful were reinforced by the horrid revelations concerning Oscar Wilde, and his doctrine that art had no moral responsibility.

The development of photography and of communications such as the

LONDON: SATURDAY, APRIL 25, 1896.

UGER HAS REPLIED, AND SAYS HE WON'T COME

WAITING!

The reinforcements hurrying from Mafeking to Buluwayo cannot arrive until the end of next week: meantime the Matabele, "thick as bees," are within four miles of the little garrison.

"Waiting." From the *Daily Mail*, Saturday, 25 April 1896 (British Library Newspaper Library).

telegraph led to a growth of interest not only in the conduct of foreign policy but in the statesmen concerned, and in September 1896 the *Daily Mail* ran a series of articles describing the "youthful custom of employing artists." It emphasized the role of the artist in familiarizing the public with the features of prominent men, adding "the day has long gone by when a political candidate can be elected without first making the public acquainted with his physiognomy." The *Daily Mail* conceded the importance of cartoons in other older publications, as evidenced by the reverence for Tenniel and the frequent reproduction of work by F. C. Gould. However, it does not appear to have been editorial policy to allow a cartoonist to pursue an independent or forceful line on any particular issue. In fact, it emphasized that it was the duty of the editor to discover those areas which were best suited to the artists' skills. The boast of the artist that he was capable of diversification was attributed to the "pardonable egotism in his artistic nature."[8]

Therefore the cartoons that appeared in the *Daily Mail* were usually simple and rather uninspired drawings. They did not summarize or interpret, but usually illustrated a widely held point of view. The sentiments that Britain needed more ships, that Dr Jameson should not have been castigated for his abortive raid, that Cecil Rhodes was an indefatigable and invincible builder of railways (using British components, of course) were beyond question or doubt and did not demand, or expect, to be reflected upon. Because they were simply reinforcing a popular and conventional view they were not animated by the energy and vitality which characterized work that was more impassioned or contentious.[9]

This was shown in a cartoon by Rip (Rowland Hill) which appeared in the experimental issue for 25 April 1896 and was typical of much of his work. It showed a garrison at Bulawayo surrounded by the advancing Matabele, but it could easily have been an illustration to a well loved Victorian "ripping yarn." It depicted the steadfast and tenacious pioneer supported by a courageous wife whose classical features and patrician bearing clearly indicated that she was not to be intimidated by hordes of frenzied, bloodthirsty savages.[10] The situation was undoubtedly complicated by an apprehensive child, female and almost at puberty. The horrid implications of this would presumably not have been lost on the more prurient imaginations among the *Daily Mail* readership. Instead of neatly summarizing the predicament of the beleaguered garrison the cartoon comes much closer to the tradition of Victorian narrative painting, as exemplified by Yeames in "And When Did You Last See Your Father?" in which the onlooker is left in a state of permanent uncertainty.

There were occasional attempts at wit and inventiveness. For example, in the issue of 16 April 1896 Chamberlain was portrayed as the Right Hon. Joseph Svengali, teaching Trilby O'Kruger to sing "Rule Britannia"—and meeting with very little success. But attempts to caricature politicians, in

LONDON: THURSDAY, APRIL 16, 1896.
WILL LITTLE TRILBY COME?
Rip
Right Hon. JOSEPH SVENGALI: Come to me, Trilby, and I will teach you to sing—(aside) "Rule Britannia."
TRILBY O'KRUGER: Oh—mai—eye. All—mai—eye. Altogether.

"Will little Trilby Come?" From the *Daily Mail*, Thursday, 16 April 1896 (British Library Newspaper Library).

this instance by depicting the relationship between Chamberlain and Kruger through the characters of George du Maurier's best-selling novel,[11] were rare. It might have been thought that Chamberlain with his pallid face, pursed lips, impeccable frock coat, and the inevitable orchid in his button hole[12] would have been ideal material for the cartoonist, but these characteristics were never used except for identification. The *Daily Mail* printed an advertisement on 2 March 1903 which showed Chamberlain, and his evident appreciation for Mackintosh's Extra Cream Toffee. This drawing, lacking both expression and vigor, was typical of the usual depiction of Chamberlain in *Daily Mail* cartoons, which were vastly different from the drawings of cartoonists such as F. C. Gould.

As Britain became more grimly embroiled in the Boer War, levity and even irony became more conspicuously absent from *Daily Mail* illustrations. The artists throughout this time were chiefly employed drawing maps to show the progress of the war. These maps undoubtedly increased in detail and complexity, presumably on the correct assumption that the readers' familiarity with the geography of South Africa was steadily growing. But there was no attempt to use powerful or emotive drawing to comment on any aspect of the war. In fact, an example of the paper's suspicion of visual communication and its preference for the written word occurred on 13 October 1899 when a verbal vignette of Kruger was specifically provided as an antidote to the "more or less flippant pen and pencil drawings that have appeared during the last few weeks." This totally disregarded the possibility that Kruger's sometimes overbearing manner, his wild gesticulations and weakness for extremely strong tobacco, could be more vividly portrayed by a cartoonist.

Another example of the newspaper's preference for the use of prose occurred on 13 November 1899, when it reported the allegations of Dreyfus against Count Esterhazy. The short report concluded, "The Count is tall, lean and nervous looking and inclined to baldness with a sallow complexion and a luxuriant black moustache of the Hungarian type."

At the outbreak of war the *Daily Mail* preserved a certain degree of ambivalence toward the Boers. They were after all partly redeemed by their irreproachable Dutch Protestant ancestry and the fact that for all their obduracy they did represent white supremacy in South Africa. As the war progressed to undreamt-of lengths and the British losses became too significant to ignore, the courage and fighting skills of the Boers had to be acknowledged. Therefore the paper did not mete out to them the thinly veiled contempt it accorded to "foreigners" in general. It was the Europeans who in the main qualified for this treatment. Those further away were usually insufficiently civilized to incur anything more than amusement or patronizing pity. This was not effective against the arrogant posturings and sometimes insufferable behavior of our European neighbours. Here the popular press undoubtedly went to excesses. Unlike those who subscribed to the more prestigious publications, the readers of the *Daily Mail* were unlikely to have cultural ties with, or taste and affection for, the continent at this time, although there was a continental edition published later.[13]

The *Daily Mail* frequently used illustrations to point out common racial characteristics, or what a phrenologist had deduced from studying the imperial cranium of Kaiser William II.[14] To the readers of the paper there was obviously nothing distasteful or sinister in this random aggregation of physical traits.

The paper frequently bemoaned the lack of imagination and (probably justified) lack of national pride which prevented other countries from inventing an embodiment of these supposed characteristics, such as John Bull, a well loved and familiar figure throughout the British press. As if to demonstrate this dearth of foreign imagination, the *Daily Mail* began a series called "As Others See Us" which regularly produced cartoons from the foreign press. Because of its own apparent conviction of the invincibility of the written word, the *Daily Mail* obviously saw little or no danger in reproducing what were in fact good examples of the considerable skills of the foreign cartoonists. The quality and flair of these cartoons put them in a separate category from anything produced by the *Daily Mail.* It was obviously assumed—no doubt correctly—that their heretical interpretation of John Bull as brutal and half-witted, would so offend the reader that they would certainly not wish to seek, or be predisposed to find, artistic merit in such scurrilous depictions. Foremost among these, and certainly among the most distinctive and subtle, was the work of the famous French cartoonist Caran d'Ache.[15] He had in fact been given an exhibition by the Fine Art Society in 1898, and familiarity with his drawing did much to show English artists an alternative to the all-powerful *Punch* style.

But even if Caran d'Ache's incisive skills were recognized elsewhere, they could not hope to penetrate the implacable convictions of the "penny dreadfuller."[16] The paper was magnanimous enough airily to acknowledge the skills of Caran d'Ache in an article placed casually yet obtrusively near to his cartoons. It damned with faint praise and concluded by cursorily dismissing the relevance of his undeniable linguistic skills by observing that he not only hated the English but that "He rarely, if ever, visits our shores, and knows I fancy very little about us gleaning—as his work shows—most of his notions as to British manners and dress from the Easter visitors by the Agence Cook."[17]

On 16 December 1899, when the Boer War was providing a fruitful outlet for exasperation, anger, or plain venom against Britain, the *Daily Mail* reproduced a cartoon from *Figaro.* It showed a totally uncoordinated John Bull sinking into the surrounding morass, his feet of clay unable to support his bloated body, and the entire spectacle being much enjoyed by more agile international onlookers. An article on the same page, ostensibly unrelated, explained that "the average Frenchman is ready to fly off at a tangent as soon as a fresh sensation presents itself, that he can hardly be said to be capable of lasting feelings of any kind." The article then sagely concludes, "The French journalist possesses most of the characteristics of his nation."

The *Daily Mail* was still oblivious of the power and vitality of these drawings, and once again attempted to combat them by the heavy and ponderous use of words. On 4 November 1899 an article did concede that the efforts of foreign cartoonists in their treatment of English subjects was always of interest, but concluded, "Now that the war has begun in grim earnest there is a chance for some ambitious cartoonist to make a great reputation. A political cartoonist is the rarest of all artists."

The halfpenny *Morning Leader* also frequently reproduced foreign cartoons but, as was to be expected from a newspaper which also published articles by H. W. Massingham[18] its purpose was not to show how misguided ignorant foreigners could be, but to alert its readers to the truths contained in these cartoons. On Wednesday, 7 February 1900, it reproduced a cartoon from *L'Asino* of Rome showing an obese John Bull staked down and powerless, being leapt on by a frock-coated top-hatted Kruger. The paper commented, "This cartoon is very typical of the attitude which the war has enabled continental journalists to take towards British power."

On 17 February 1900 under the heading "How They Love Us," an article in the *Morning Leader* concluded, "It is to the Jingoes and the Jingoes alone that we owe this demonstration in the cartoons of newspapers abroad of the unpopularity of Great Britain among the nations of the world." However, despite its earnest and heartfelt attempts to make the public reassess the imperial role, the *Morning Leader* was preaching to the converted, who were insufficient in number to keep it solvent, and it was absorbed by the *Daily News* in 1912. The paper could not, however, be accused of lack of sympathy toward the fighting men. On Thursday, 4 January 1900, it promised, "A gratis box of Beecham's Pills will be sent postage paid to any individual soldier now on active service in South Africa."

One thing the *Morning Leader* did have in common with the *Daily Mail* was its attitude to cartoons from the American newspapers. In 1900 it carried an article which asserted that "This wretched war has given some of the American Press the opportunity of indulging in candid friendship by cartoon."[19] Although never referring to what was later termed the "special relationship" quite so directly, the *Daily Mail* too was far more indulgent of North American cartoons, even though some of them could be brutally frank and did not hesitate to attack the revered figure of John Bull. A cartoon reproduced from the *Philadelphia Times Herald*[20] showed a gluttonous and coarse John Bull seated before a pile of clean picked bones like some dreadful old troll. The bones are variously labeled "India," "Egypt," "Sudan," and "South Africa." His gorging repast had obviously been insufficient for this old monster, who was demanding that "Tommy" now bring him another slice of India. The homely sampler on the wall bears the incongruous message

The Earth
This belongs to me
I bought it of
Adam
J.B.

Yet most American cartoons reproduced in the *Daily Mail* were not so direct in their attack on Britain's imperial posturings. They usually showed a senile, bumbling, hopelessly incompetent, and shabby John Bull being effortlessly and cleanly outwitted by a mature, yet vigorous and healthy Uncle Sam in the battle for world trade and exports.

If we accept that the assumption of racial superiority was fundamental to the values and prejudices of the *Daily Mail,* it seems likely that the indulgence extended to North America was founded upon a belief in racial and cultural similarity. This view was supported by a short article which appeared in the paper in 1898 pointing out that it is important that its readers realize that the term *Yankee* was originally used "by the aborigines to describe the white colonists of Massachusetts"—that is, those settlers who were most indisputably of sound, Puritan Anglo-Saxon stock.[21] This "curious fact" should be widely recognized, because it further reinforces "Anglo-Saxon Unity."

However, even indulged offspring had to be occasionally reprimanded. An article which appeared in the *Daily Mail* on Friday, 31 August 1900, presented the reader with a rather astonished account of the American political system, and a description of a people who "like to wear their party heart on their sleeves, so they bedeck themselves with badges, and hang their town halls with banners." A series of sketches then illustrated what the *Daily Mail* obviously regarded as bizarre, if not primitive, political behavior. The underlying message was clearly that, although American cartoonists might appear to strike hard at British traditions and institutions, there was little to fear from a rude republic still so immature and gullible in its own political organization.

But the presumption of our partners in Anglo-Saxon Unity obviously overreached itself when the *Daily Mail* saw fit to reproduce a drawing from the *New York Herald* entitled "A.D. 2,000—An American Forecast."[22] Coming at a time when the humiliations of the Boer War were making the maintenance of raucous imperialism a strain even for the *Daily Mail,* this drawing was as disconcerting as a prophecy of the end of the world. It showed the United States controlling South America, Greenland, and the Philippines, with Russia dominating Asia and Turkey. Australia and Africa were republics, but the most unacceptable and unthinkable prophecy of all was at the conclusion of the article: "Britain, bereft of India owns nothing outside her island limits." This chilling prediction struck a note of unease. Gradually, but very perceptibly, it became evident that even such certainties as the continuing occupation of India could no longer be relied upon, and this struck deep at the heart of the imperial spirit.

Edgar Wallace had scooped the news of the final peace agreement of the Boer War for the *Daily Mail,*[23] but the reception of this news was relatively subdued compared with the boisterous reception of the Relief of Mafeking two years previously.[24] Attention was diverted from exploits and victories in the far-flung reaches of empire to a threat nearer home—the increasing menace of the German empire, personified by Kaiser William II.

There had always been warnings about maintaining the supremacy of Britain's naval power, and the *Daily Mail* had contributed to this. An early cartoon[25] by Rip (Rowland Hill) showed Mrs. Britannia visiting Dr. Goschen,[26] who advises her to take a prolonged course of shipbuilding. The doctor is shown wearing an anchor-shaped tie pin, his medicine cabinets are filled with models of warships, and his chair back is shaped like Britannia's shield.

The message of the consulting room is clear and what is also conveyed is that Mrs. Britannia's condition gives no cause for alarm; she is fundamentally in very good health. A similar sentiment was expressed by Rossi Ashton in a cartoon which showed two infants representing France and Russia gazing desparingly at their shoddy and fragile toy battleships.[27] Little Master Goschen, smartly attired in his sailor suit, is more fortunate and has a whole pile of gleaming, seemingly indestructible, toy battleships.

These warnings were really more like the cautionary tales beloved of the Victorian nursery—an almost pleasurable shiver of apprehension and then back to the reality of the warmth and security of the fireside. But it was not very long before realization began to dawn: the vastness of the imperial possessions did not make Britain impregnible; it rendered her vulnerable. In fact, in 1896 when William II sent his notorious Kruger telegram, and just one year before he joined the fulsom tributes to his Grandmother's Golden Jublilee celebrations, the Kaiser was drafting the first German war plans for a possible swift strike against Britain.

As we have seen, the chauvinism of the *Daily Mail* was just as resolute against Europe and such restraint as existed was largely prompted by the fact that attacks on European institutions did not excite wonder or fire the imagination. Attention was, however, frequently drawn to displays of arrogance and pomposity perpetrated by Kaiser William. He could be easily identified, and there was interest in his activities, both political and social. But attacks upon him in the *Daily Mail* were neither virulent nor sustained. The reason is not hard to find. Despite the fact that he represented a way of life that was not British and that his imperial aspirations were obvious, he was still the grandson of Queen Victoria. He could not be cowed into submission along with the numerous strange and uncivilized despots and potentates throughout the globe. He would not subscribe to the myths surrounding the British Imperial Monarch and because he was, when all was said and done, a branch of that monarchy, it was right and proper that this should be so. Hence the ambivalence of which the *Daily Mail* was painfully and continually aware.

Yet as the imperial outlook slowly and steadily darkened, ideas which would have been unthinkable a mere ten years previously were horribly feasible during the opening years of the twentieth century—hence the phenomenal success of Erskine Childers's *The Riddle of the Sands.*[28] Adventure in the cold gray vicinity of the Frisian Islands lacked the glamour of the exotic locations of Henty, but it certainly gained in feasibility. Proximity and familiarity had rarely appealed to the popular press, which is one reason why Ireland was so frequently ignored.

The *Daily Mail* attempted to keep its old standards intact. A comment in Sir Harry Johnston's exhaustive work on the Uganda Protectorate observes, "Some of his photographs, especially those of the native races are scarcely beautiful, though doubtless their scientific value depends upon their absolute truthfulness."[29]

The illustrations to an article on Tibet showing the inhabitants wearing strange masks was jauntily captioned, "A strange festival in Tibet, where our Next Little War Might Be."[30]

The regular illustrators followed the established *Daily Mail* line, but from 1903 onward the captions heading the introduction of foreign cartoons recognized the individuality of their creators and had captions such as "opinions as reflected by the cartoonists." They were in the same vein as before, but the shadow of the Boer War, and the steady realization that the Empire might not be invincible made their thrusts and gibes harder to dismiss.

On 7 January 1902 two cartoons were reproduced from the *New York Tribune* by F. Opper.[31] The one showed a bewildered and mangy lion caught in the talons of American trade enterprise, and the other showed a decrepit lion cowering in abject terror as the comet of American Business Rivalry screeched overhead. In both cartoons the unfortunate lion was accompanied by a shabby, heavy, shambling figure—that of John Bull. A particularly pathetic touch is that both lions wear bedraggled Union Jack ribbons round their tails—which are just asking to be pulled, with no possibility of effective retaliation.

A more realistic but nevertheless somber note was struck by the *Daily Mail's* own cartoons, some of which were produced by Haselden.[32] In 1904 he showed an empty House of Commons with the caretaker placing a huge ball marked "British Empire" in the center. The caption reads, "There it is ready for them to kick off again! Ah! but I can remember when they didn't make a game of it. I suppose those good old days'll never come back again now."[33]

RMS ON WHICH "DR. JIM" SURRENDERED.—SEE
BRITANNIA'S HEALTH.
NAVAL ESTIMATES INCREASE £10,000,000
Mrs. BRITANNIA (who has called to consult her adviser, Dr. Goschen): "You know, doctor, my recent attacks of German measles and Franco-Russian fever have shown me that my constitution is not, perhaps, so strong as I thought it was. What do you recommend?"
Dr. GOSCHEN: "Ironclads, my dear madam. A prolonged course of shipbuilding is what you want. It is an expensive treatment, but, believe me, it is vitally essential. If you do not take the matter in hand now you will one day awake to find it is too late."

"Britannias Health." From the *Daily Mail*, Monday, 16 March 1896 (British Library Newspaper Library).

Haselden was right. About that time the *Daily Mail* turned its attention to such matters as Mr. Chamberlain's call for colonial preference (which failed to capture the public imagination) and the trumpetings against the cartels of J. P. Morgan, which lacked the marketable violence and bravado of earlier stories. Chamberlain was eloquently castigated in a raging and ominous article by G. W. Steevens[34] in which the commercial creeds of the New Imperialism were described as having affected the British so that "Where they had once resolved to possess, they now aspired but to trade! As a consequence of this . . . the proud spirit of Empire sank into the narrow greed of the shareholder."

There were many who passionately agreed with Steevens. Deprived of the sense of moral rectitude, high principle, and responsibility which lent a certain stature to the imperial position of innate superiority, what the imperialists were left with was the mere posturings of the imperial attitude. Posturings, moreover, that grew less realistic and more distasteful as the century progressed, particularly as they still retained the potency to influence many minds at a very basic level.

It has been recently pointed out that probably the worst heritage of empire was not Dean Acheson's "damagingly misleading" and famous remark on Britain's inability to find a role, but the fact that even in the domestic policies of the late twentieth century the nation is divided into restless natives and white men with burdens, a form of internal imperialism resulting in showy, inefficient, piecemeal reforms, which work too slowly to produce any conspicuous political advantage.[35]

Such an insular and destructive diminution of the imperial spirit could never have been envisaged by Lord Northcliffe when he first conceived the idea of a mass-circulation daily to bring the proud and vital spirit of empire to the breakfast tables of the queen's fiercely loyal, lower-middle-class subjects. The fact that this imperial participation was vicarious did not detract from the hearty contempt felt for things not British, or diminish the brutal assertion of British racial and cultural superiority.

The prejudices thus continually reinforced, even throughout the Boer War, were not easily reversed by later events, nor did they allow easy or painless adaptation to sudden and bewildering shifts in the world order. The incomprehension and imperturbability that met the skilful and perceptive criticisms contained in the contributions submitted by foreign cartoonists is an indication of this.

The inescapable conclusion seems to be that, even at the height of imperialistic fervor, the *Daily Mail* never fully harnessed or realized the potency of the visual image. But such images as there were, and the sentiments they illustrated, were sufficient to ensure that even when flag-waving ceased to be a widespread or public activity, it was still very much part of the public consciousness.

10
Content Analysis and Historical Research on Newspapers

Virginia Berridge

Those who write about the history of the press generally lament the lack of fellow workers. Newpapers are doubly neglected. There is a dearth of histories of the press; and newspapers are still underutilized as a source for other areas of historical research. The complex and miscellaneous character of the newspaper has meant that much work, at least until recent years, has tended to concentrate on a narrow section of its content, primarily the development of editorial opinion on specific issues. The implication—dubious from the standpoint of "effects research" in media sociology—is that such editorial content adequately represents the opinion of individual readers and that changes in editorial opinion are linked to shifts in readership attitudes. This type of approach, suggesting an individual effect at a particular time, is being superseded by a broader conception and theoretical justification of the uses of newspaper content and by a more sophisticated ideological analysis of the newspaper's role in society. With this altered perspective in mind, this chapter will look at how the idea and practice of content analysis has developed from its origins in the social sciences, and at its subsequent application to historical research. It will conclude with a brief case study of some findings from the popular Sunday press in the second half of the nineteenth century.

"The content analyst," wrote Kaplan and Goldsen in 1943, "aims at a quantitative classification of a given body of content, in terms of a system of categories devised to yield data relevant to specific hypotheses concerning that content."[1] Bernard Berelson, one of the leading figures in communications research in America of that period, defined the method: "Content analysis is a research technique for the objective, systematic, and quantitative description of the manifest content of communication."[2] Such a definition was based on a number of assumptions, chiefly that quantification of content in this way could reveal both the purposes and characteristics of the communicators as "reflected" in content and also the effect of the content upon the attitudes of readers or listeners. At a subsidiary level, the content analyst assumed that the meanings he ascribed to the content, by placing it in certain categories, also corresponded to the meanings intended by the communicator and understood by the audience, and that the frequency of occurrence of the various categories of content was itself important both to the communicator and the readership. Content analysis defined in this way was first used as a research tool in the 1930s. It formed part of the general attempt to quantify and measure social influences. Early opinion polls, market research, and social surveys were part of this trend and while Political and Economic Planning made its early surveys in England in this decade, Mass Observation also carried out a number of its investigations in the prewar period.[3] Content analysis, in its assumption that attitudes and reactions could be specifically quantified and measured, was an example of the "scientism" of the thirties, a belief that apparently scientific methods of this type would provide an objective analysis. At this time there was little conception of the social construction of scientific ideas and methodology. Content analysis seemed to be simply a method of counting and measuring fact, and doubts cast by a later generation of Marxist social scientists on whether facts indeed had any independent existence apart from the social situation which structured them and the class perceptions which defined them, bothered the early practitioners of content analysis not at all. It was a means of measurement adopted in a particular area—that of mass culture and mass communications.

By contrast the Frankfurt School in the United States and a number of European social and literary critics shared a revulsion against mass culture in general, and American culture in particular. The advent of radio and film as means of mass communication brought a concern for what was happening to cultural standards and an awareness of the relatively new phenomenon of the mass audience. In pre-war England, critics like the Leavises decried the cultural products offered to this audience but also set about analyzing them. Queenie Leavis's *Fiction and the reading public* is perhaps the best known example of this work.[4] Members of the Frankfurt School on the other land saw the mass media as instruments of social dominance, "controlling the public in the interest of capital." The overt content of any radio program, film, or newspaper was involved in the process and therefore required detailed scrutiny along with the general structure of the media and its use.

This sort of ideological concern continued to stimulate forms of content analysis although, by the 1960s, the areas of interest had shifted. Debates within the 'New Left' about minority and democratic culture brought an interest in the development and establishment of popular, rather than mass, culture, and how this was represented, and distorted by the media. The press was still seen as an agency of social control, with more emphasis on how the news was selected and represented to structure a particular form of reality. Within both the "scientific" and ideologically motivated approaches "media bias" had already become the central issue. It dominated, for example, the findings of the post war Royal Commission on the press which organized a comprehensive analysis of the content of a range of English newspapers published between 1927 and 1974. Did the individual newspapers in dealing with politically controversial news items, the survey inquired, distort or overemphasize this kind of news or suppress important parts of it. . . ? If inaccuracy occurred was it correlated with the views expressed in the newspaper's editorial comment, and was it designed with political ends in view. . . . ?" Although the conclusions drawn from such material were muted, there was little doubt from the Commission's report that the press did distort its representation of the news in order to suit particular political ends.[5]

While the distinction between the two lines of approach has become increasingly blurred, media bias has remained the major preoccupation. Much recent analysis has concentrated on television news presentation although the findings have clear implications for the newspaper press. The work of the Glasgow University Media Group has bought the issue of distortion to the forefront—the way in which television structures a particular form of social reality which favors social consensus rather than conflict, and which represents the views of those in positions of power rather than others whose views are not in accord with the dominant ideology.[6] The analysis by the Leicester Mass Communications Research Centre of the reporting of the 1968 Vietnam demonstration in London brought another set of biases into focus. In this study, media content was examined alongside such topics as news values and production processes. Reporting of this large and mainly peaceful demonstration was shown to have been structured by the 'event-as-news'; that is, the demonstration was predetermined to be potentially violent, even revolutionary, by newsmen, who were then compelled to find incidents to fulfill their predictions and to structure news stories in this light.[7] More recent research and controversy about the media and the Falklands War and the television reporting of the 1984–85 miners' strike, has continued these lines of inquiry.

Other analysts of media content have had a slightly different purpose in mind. They have looked at newspapers as purveyors of a form of cultural reality which was assumed to have a direct impact on its readers. Francis Balle's analysis of French newspapers from 1946 to 1965 in *Annales* sought to look at the political and popular culture they conveyed.[8] Analyzing developments in the coverage of political news, leisure, culture, and advertising, one of his conclusions was that political coverage in the French press had indeed declined in substance and depth, not only in quantifiable terms of number of pages or column inches devoted to political matters, but also in the way political news was presented. The connection he made with French society under de Gaulle was direct—"la dépolitisation des quotidiens nous ramène constamment à l'examen de celle de la société française elle-même." But perhaps the best-known content analysis of the press from the cultural point of view was that made by Raymond Williams in *Communications.* Williams's concern for cultural forms, for popular and democratic culture as opposed to minority culture, and for the debasement of working-class culture by the commercial interests represented in the media, was fully displayed in a wide-ranging analysis of its content. This took in women's and children's magazines as well as the "quality" and "popular" press and indicated an increasingly close connection between the methods and content of advertising and editorial material, as well as a marked degree of cultural specialisation. The analysis showed that "the formulas seem to be hardening: 'the masses'—crime, sex, sport, personalities, entertainment, pictures; 'the minority'—traditional politics, traditional arts, briefings on popular trends."[9]

The issues which have prompted the investigation of contemporary mass communications through forms of content analysis have also begun to stimulate a similar process in relation to historical materials. There is a growing body of work, to which the present volume bears witness, on the history of the press and in particular on changes and developments in its content. Issues peculiar to press history, such as the influence of advertising, the concentration of press ownership, and the development of the popular press, are beginning to be looked at. However, at a more theoretical level, the function of the newspaper in society has also begun to attract attention. This has placed newspaper content firmly in the area of popular culture and has led to the emergence of a dual approach to the press as an institution. In one interpretation, newspapers have appeared as "organised centres of cultural production over which 'the people' have no control," with the hegemonic function of passing on the dominant ideology to readers in subordinate classes. In the other, the press is seen as reflecting and mediating forms of cultural practice among oppressed groups and classes, as a means of cultural opposition, finding a coherent form in the popular press.[10]

Content analysis has been used as a research tool in both areas—press history and popular culture—and its use has raised, in particular in relation to the latter, some serious problems. Content analysis in the examination of trends in press history is relatively unproblematic. My own work on the mass circulation Sunday press in the nineteenth century shows a variety of points of interest from the press history point of view. Take, for instance, the increased importance of advertising. In *Reynolds's Newspaper,* this increase was most marked after the removal of the newspaper stamp in 1855, and an even more pronounced trend appeared in *Lloyd's Weekly Newspaper,* the prototype of the modern, popular publication. In *Lloyd's,* the volume of advertising content also increased from the 1850s well into the 1880s. By 1886, nearly 40 percent of the paper was composed of advertising.[11] Looked at more closely, the disparity in types of advertising was notable. For example, *Reynolds's*, as the more radical, less reputable paper (and consequently less attractive to advertisers), continued to accept a large number of patent medicine advertisements while these declined in importance in the more up-market and less politically extreme *Lloyd's*.

Questions concerned with such topics as this can easily be settled by the techniques of content analysis. The message the paper actually conveyed to its readers is another matter. Reliance on editorial attitudes is dubious as an indicator of audience reaction or even of the views of the readership. Louis Galambos's study of the public image of big business in America in the late nineteenth and early twentieth centuries is open to criticism on this point. Galambos, critical of the unrigorous techniques employed by historians of 'social perception,' and in particular the reliance on isolated quotation, based his study on a computer-organized content analysis of magazines directed to particular occupational groups. The assumption was that 'some relationship existed between circulation and support for the publication's ideas.' But this raises the question of the representativeness of editorial opinion, a problem aggravated in his study by the case of trade-union journals which were deliberately produced to strengthen union feeling. By aggregating his data on the basis of the respective size of three broad occupational groups—farmers, skilled workers, and professional people—in the American population at the time, he made the further assumption that readership of these journals was representative of those broader groups.[12]

More successful content analysis work of this type avoids Galambos's equation of editorial opinion with readership attitudes. The presentation of particular themes in the press and the possible effect on audience perception can be examined more rigorously by an analysis of all forms of newspaper content. O'Malley's examination of the presentation of religious content in this volume extends into advertising as well as editorial and news material and is an example of this type of work. Perhaps the most extensive content analysis of a single issue was made by Alvar Ellegard in his study *Darwin and the general reader*.[13] Ellegard analyzed the reaction to, and the presentation of, Darwin's theories of natural selection and evolution as they appeared (or failed to appear) across a wide range of newspaper and periodical literature in the 1860s and 1870s. His method involved the construction of quantitative scales both for the amount of information provided, and for attitudes taken toward Darwinian theory. Periodicals and papers were classified according to their type of readership and assessed according to contemporary estimates and internal evidence as educationally highbrow, middlebrow, and lowbrow (scale 1 to 3) and various correlations were made. A 5-point scale was constructed for the evolution theory in general, and a 3-point scale for the theory in its application to Man; Ellegard then noted, for each periodical, every instance where it expressed or endorsed any opinion on aspects of Darwinian theory. Scores were also awarded for attitudes to the theories; one diagram showed yearly changes in attitude, with the average position for each year given as the arithmetical mean of the highest and lowest position taken during the year. This analysis represents perhaps the high point of the 'scientific' approach to content analysis in a historical context. However, Ellegard's assumption was, like that of other earlier content analysts, that a direct correlation could be made between newspaper presentation and readership attitudes; he made a connection between published information on Darwin and consequent reactions among the different social classes reading the papers. This was the view of the early content analysts and students of the mass media of the 1930s. 'Effects research' in the 1960s cast serious doubt on whether the media did indeed have any effect at all, let alone such a specifically measurable individual effect on attitude. Recently, a more sophisticated analysis of possible media effect has taken the place of these negative conclusions. There has been a shift away from the emphasis on individual attitude formation to questions of social perception, of newspapers as cultural products which mutually reinforce systems of belief and outlook of their readers. This new emphasis is best summed up by Denis McQuail, who suggests that such research should "pay more attention to people in their social context, look at what people know (in the widest sense) rather than in their attitudes and opinions, take account of the uses and motives of the audience member as mediating any effect, look at structures of belief and opinion and social behaviour rather than individual cases, take more notice of the *content* whose effects are being studied."[14] Certainly the impact of the media cannot be identified directly from their content. But, as John Westergaard has pointed out, "it is hardly conceivable that long-term exposure to the media themselves has no significant part to play among the sources for those predispositions by which people make sense both of the world and, in turn, of the particular interpretation of the world on offer from the media."[15]

The press must be seen as a constructor of social reality for its readers, but also as part of a process of "reciprocal symbolic interaction" with its audience. Some historical work involving content analysis is beginning to approach the subject from this potentially more rewarding perspective. Louis James's study of the Victorian periodical press and his specific content analysis of the *London Journal* sees the periodical as a form of "cultural outlook." Content analysis itself he sees, despite its limitations, as a "useful finger-print," encapsulating a particular style of living expressed for readers at that particular time.[16] The most extensive work of this type has been the study by Smith, Immirzi, and Blackwell of the content of two popular papers, the *Daily Express* and *Daily Mirror* from the 1930s to the 1960s. The method here was to use a combination of content analysis of "manifest" content where that seemed appropriate, together with literary, linguistic, and stylistic analysis which was found more useful in penetrating the latent meanings of a text. This latter approach preserved something of the complexity of language and connotation sacrificed by the more routine methods of content analysis. The authors wished, they wrote, "to get behind the broad distribution of manifest content to the latent, implicit patterns and emphasis." By this means they demonstrated how the *Mirror* not only promoted, but also responded, to a mood of popular radicalism among its readers in 1945. Yet the postwar years saw the deformation of this relationship. The paper's radicalism hardened into a mere formula, and its notable articulation and reinforcement of the mood for social change in 1945 receded, to be replaced by paternalism and demands for leadership.[17]

The combination, in this study, of content and linguistic analysis, to arrive at some assessment of the deep structures of meaning inherent in a paper's presentation and selection of the news, offers a fruitful way forward for content analysis and for historical research on newspapers. Clearly the total content of a newspaper is not seen by all readers in the same way—nor does the simple frequency of occurrence of a particular item of content necessarily reflect its importance. But the paper nevertheless presents a particular form of reality to its readership, albeit they make sense of it, or "decode" it, in different ways. The "world view" of readers is both reflected and reinforced by newspaper content.

The rest of this paper will look, using content analysis methods, at the particular world view or perception of society articulated in one popular Sunday paper of the latter half of the nineteenth century, *Reynolds's Newspaper,* and how this both shaped and reflected the attitudes and responses of its readers as well as revealing some of the changes in their material circumstances and expectations. The period under examination stretches from the 1850s to the 1880s, encompassing, in a political sense, the change from Chartism through to the reformism of the third quarter of the century, with the beginnings of socialism in the eighties. The purpose of looking at the paper in this period was to examine not simply what was happening to the press, but the perceptions and experience of its readers as reflected in content. Comparisons were made with *Lloyd's Weekly Newspaper,* a Sunday paper of a similar type, but with a significantly different class of readership, lower middle class rather than working class.[18] *Reynolds's* qualifications for this role were important. The paper, established in 1850 by G. W. M. Reynolds, found its origins both in the Chartist political press and in the commercial traditions of popular literature. The paper arose out of Reynolds's smaller-circulation *Reynolds's Political Instructor* (1849), edited at one stage by Bronterre O'Brien. It was also the culmination of Reynolds's career in cheap publishing and popular fiction. His fiction series, "The

Mysteries of London" and "The Mysteries of the Court of London," had made him famous as a novelist; to these were added his editorship of such popular weeklies as the *London Journal* and his own magazine, *Reynolds's Miscellany.* The paper therefore combined political with commercial traditions; Reynolds was a business entrepreneur as well as a Chartist.[19]

Nevertheless, the paper retained the strong identification and close relationship with its readers which had marked the smaller-circulation unstamped and Chartist papers. Its circulation was a mass one by the standards of the day—rising from 50,000 to 150,000 a week after the abolition of stamp duty, and stabilizing at between 200,000 and 300,000 after the repeal of paper duty in 1861. The readership was still a strongly working-class one and remained so to a remarkable degree over the thirty-year period studied. All the available secondary evidence about the paper suggests this conclusion. Internal evidence, primarily correspondence columns and appeal fund lists but also employment and trade advertising and reports, adds some detail. The paper had a strongly artisan readership, and the general "skilled" category always formed a high proportion of those writing in or responding to appeals. For example, correspondence columns show that, in the 1850s, the paper was popular among the older well-established, skilled, clothing workers. Appeal fund lists gave similar results, although these varied according to the type of interest generated in a particular cause. In the 1860s, the emphasis within correspondence columns altered, with a shift of interest away from the "old" skilled trades toward apprentices and miners. However, the former type of skilled workers were still sending money to the paper's appeals, although not corresponding to such a degree as before. But newspaper content also reveals the existence of a stratum of unskilled readers not mentioned by contemporaries. Chief among these were members of the armed forces, most of whom wrote to the paper with queries (in 1862 and 1866, as much as 25 and 39 percent of all "named" queries came from them). *Reynolds's* was known for its virulent opposition to flogging in both army and navy. That there was also a general unskilled readership, appears in queries from agricultural laborers, and also factory and mill hands. The latter sent money quite generously to the appeals of the 1850s and continued to send large sums in the 1870s. Changes in the class structure in the period, in particular the expansion of the lower-middle class stratum in the last quarter of the century and the increase in clerking and office occupations, affected the readership profile of *Reynolds's* very little. The paper did publish a high proportion of queries (25 percent in 1874) dealing with clerking jobs; but most were from people hoping to become clerks, not actually working as such. Tradesmen and shopkeepers in increasing numbers were writing in and there was more evidence, too, of property ownership in the 1870s and 1880s. But the development of lower-middle-class commercial and shopkeeping groups never really made a major impact on the paper's readership in this period. There is certainly little internal evidence to support the claim that *Reynolds's* changed its appeal in the post-Chartist years to cater for what James Curran has called a "coalition of middle-class and working-class readers"; its readership profile indicated by an analysis of the content remained relatively static.[20]

The paper retained a lively two-way relationship with this readership. The Chartist publications, the *Northern Star* most notably, had acted as centers of agitation, organization, and education; *Reynolds's* continued these functions for its readers.[21] Whether or not the paper was financially dependent for survival on advertising revenue, it certainly carried relatively little advertising, even in relation to a paper like *Lloyd's*. The post-1855 increase was not maintained, and throughout the 1860s and 1870s, only 14–15 percent of content was devoted to advertising, in contrast to 25–28 percent in *Lloyd's*. There are many examples of the reliance of readers on *Reynolds's* in the political sense—not least the response to its appeal funds, and the paper's direct political involvement, in particular in the 1850s, in causes like antisabbatarianism and opposition to the Poor Law. The paper's "Labour and Wages" column, at least in the early years, provided firsthand information about strikes and lockouts, and trade disputes involving readers. But the readership participation extended into the nonpolitical sphere, in particular through the paper's correspondence columns. Although readers' letters were given in full elsewhere in the contemporary press, in Sunday papers participation was limited almost entirely to one- or two-line replies to queries which were not themselves printed. The paper could therefore publish replies weekly to a considerable number of readers. From the mid-1880s onwards, the percentage proportion of nonadvertising content composed of queries never fell below 2 percent and the average number was well over 45 per issue. In 1882 and 1886, there were averages of over 130 per issue—a yearly correspondence total of over five thousand readers writing in, approximately 2 percent of total readership. Readers' concerns—although admittedly biased toward the literate and more articulate—ranged across a variety of issues, from political, historical, and social matters to advice on landlord and tenant disputes, savings, and points of law. The paper was a guide and mentor to its readers on these details of everyday life. Clearly certain features which appeared in the paper—the column of friendly society advice, and that offering information about emigration—were connected with the considerable interest shown in such matters in readers' correspondence (over 14 percent of queries dealt with life insurance and savings in 1854, for example), not primarily with a need to attract advertising revenue from friendly societies.[22]

Given the close extended relationship between reader and read across a wide range of nonpolitical as well as political interests, what does analysis of content indicate about changes within the working class in the thirty-year period? The results presented here will concentrate on five areas—self-help; leisure activities; the home and consumer goods; the "world view" of readers; and readers' perceptions of the structure of society. In a limited space, a full analysis cannot be made of every tendency represented by newspaper content, so the following sections represent merely a sampling and brief synopsis of some general tendencies. These years were indeed a time when the collective aspirations of the Chartist period were giving way to an interest in individual betterment. The popular radical tradition had always contained within it an emphasis on self-education and cooperation through friendly societies and similar organizations; but seen more as collective means of resistance to class domination rather than as societies for personal advancement. Interest in friendly societies—and in education—are the two areas where attention will concentrate in this analysis, although the self-helping impulse also manifested itself in the paper's content in such areas as emigration and funeral provision.[23] There were two distinct periods of particular activity, the first coming in the 1850s. *Reynolds's* paid a tremendous amount of attention to this relatively new possibility. Of the paper's advertising content in 1854, 12.5 percent dealt with some form of friendly society (excluding loan companies) and over 14 percent of readers' queries asked advice about them. The paper published a special column of general information, the "Friendly Societies' Advocate" written by "Unitas" (or Mr. W. Watkins), which accounted for over 2 percent of nonadvertising content.[24] There was a second period of lesser interest in the 1870s; at the same time as advertisements for consumer goods began to fill the columns of the three papers, advertisements offering a wider, and more sophisticated, variety of savings opportunities, boosted percentage figures—from 1 percent in 1874 to over 6 percent of advertising content in *Reynolds's* in 1878. News reports, too, stressed the gradual move towards more businesslike and commercially efficient forms of self-help. The local affiliated societies mentioned in *Reynolds's* in the 1850s gave way in the 1860s to the more financially sound and solidly based general societies and to general reports on the idea of friendly societies, which stressed efficiency and good business conduct. Life insurance companies made their appearance in the advertising—but unlike *Lloyd's* (which appealed to a lower-middle-class rather than a working-class-readership), *Reynold's* published little or nothing either on building societies or on savings banks. For much of the period, interest concentrated on a much more basic institution, the loan society or company. Virtually never mentioned in the paper's news sections, which concentrated their attention on the more "respectable" forms of institutional self-help, their preponderance in advertising material was striking with, in *Reynolds's* in the sixties, seventies, and eighties, between 3 and 4 percent of advertising content devoted to them. Self-help in a financial sense was still relatively limited even for skilled workingmen, and the preponderance of the loan society could also have represented mistrust of a more generalized form of saving.

Self-help in educational matters was also strong, even after the "landmark" of the 1870 Education Act. Both advertising and news material indicates a good deal of interest in the subject, but stresses the continuing importance of voluntary education well past 1870. But this interest was beginning to take rather different forms with the lower-middle-class readers of *Lloyd's*. In the news sections of the papers, over 26 percent of all social reform reports in *Reynolds's* and 20 percent in *Lloyd's* dealt with the new Education Act in 1870. However, working-class interest, as represented in *Reynolds's,* suffered a rapid decline in the following two decades, and attention did not revive until 1886. The developing state system appears to have made little impact on either working- or lower-middle-class consciousness, and advertisers in both papers offered to teach writing, book-keeping and dressmaking. After 1870, such advertisements in *Lloyd's* gave way to more generalized advertising of private schools offering all-round 'good education'. These also received attention in the paper's new columns, and thereby diverged significantly from *Reynolds's,* which published nothing of the type at all. All this does not mean that readers of both papers were deprived of coverage of state educational matters. There was a real interest in the subject and 15/33 reports on education in *Lloyd's* and 9/15 in *Reynolds's* in the 1870–86 sample years, dealt with state education in some form. However, the continued importance of earlier voluntary and self-helping preoccupations also needs to be stressed. Working-class interest in state education only revived after Mundella's introduction of compulsory school attendance in 1880; in the 1886 issues of *Reynolds's,* the themes of Church school indoctrination and the demand for free education received much attention.[25]

Increased opportunities and availability of leisure time were part of the move away from the political interest of the 1830s and 1840s. The gradual provision of longer holidays, the weekly half holidays, and even holidays with pay (Lubbock's 1871 Bank Holiday Act), were symptomatic of a tendency to control and regularize practices which already existed. Working people had in any case found the oportunity for sport, singing, and so on even before they were legally entitled to, by simply staying away from work. But material published in *Reynolds's* news and advertising columns does suggest something of the changing patterns of interest in leisure—and can also be used to indicate how these were altering in comparison to the parallel interests of the lower-middle-class readership of *Lloyd's.* In fact there appears to have been little class basis to the expansion in the volume of leisure-oriented material; there were differences of emphasis between *Reynolds's* and *Lloyd's* but the interests of both strata of readers appear generally similar.[26] Both papers reported and advertised leisure activities such as excursions, theaters and music halls and reading matter. Two particular areas—changing patterns of sporting interest and the possession of a musical instrument—illustrate some of the developments. Sports reports, even in 1886, were a relatively unimportant section of general news content—2.8 percent of the content in both *Reynolds's* and *Lloyd's,* although the seventies and eighties were the decades when interest developed. *Lloyd's* percentage figures were smaller than *Reynolds's* in 1882 because, from mid-1878, that paper was publishing its sports reports in smaller type on the front page, probably to maintain its much vaunted news coverage, while accommodating the increased readership interest in sport. Most striking in both papers, but particualrly in *Reynolds's* is the continued preference for professional forms of sport rather than the amateur variety and for a range of activities other than football. Three sports can illustrate the "professional" emphasis. *Reynolds's* continued to report pugilistic bouts (the bare-knuckle form of fighting) through the 1860s and little attention was paid to amateur boxing before the 1880s.[27] In athletics, too, the emphasis in the seventies and eighties was not on amateur versions, but a continuing interest in the professional forms—pedestrianism and rowing, for example, predominated until the eighties. Nor did cricket and football assume quite the popularity often ascribed to them. The bulk of sports reports in *Reynolds's* until the eighties dealt with racing. Cricket was less important—and even the phenomenal rise in football reports in *Lloyd's* (from 3 percent of sports reports in 1874 to 43 percent in 1886) was not matched in *Reynolds's.* What was noticeable, however, was a rapid expansion in the range of sports considered worth reporting in the 1880s. *Reynolds's* reported only two (racing and rowing) in its 1874 editions, while by 1882, there were reports on ten or more different activities.

The possession of a musical instrument was also part of the expansion of leisure possibilities. Advertising of musical instruments in *Reynolds's* began to increase in the 1860s, and was accompanied by reference to a widening range of instruments. The "easy to play" instrument of the 1850s gave way to two types in particular—concertinas and brass band instruments.[28] At some point in the 1860s, horizons further widened to encompass the possible purchase of a harmonium, both cheaper than a piano and easier to play. Hire purchase arrangements became possible at this time, and the harmonium advertisements to some extent paved the way for purchase of a piano, the ultimate badge of respectability. In *Reynolds's,* piano advertisements were not common before the late sixties and early seventies, when figures rose to over 20 percent of all musical instrument advertising (in 1870 and 1878). Hire purchase payments—first mentioned separately in the mid-1860s—were clearly established by the eighties as the main means of buying a piano. Without them prices would have been beyond the reach of most readers, although most of the instruments advertised appear to have been—at fifteen to eighteen guineas in *Reynolds's*—lower than others mentioned in more respectable papers.[29]

The advertising columns of the paper make it clear that consumer choice and material standards in general were improving for a proportion of the working and lower-middle-class and that the 1870s were the crucial decade for this development. But a fair amount of spending was still within a limited range. A high proportion of goods advertised for the home were of the more basic kind—washing materials, soap, starch, and blue. Such products comprised up to 70 or 80 percent of household-item advertising in the paper in most of the years analyzed. But some more substantial goods did begin to find a place there. The acquisition of better-quality cutlery appears to have been one of the first signs of expanding consumer choice in the 1850s and 1860s. In the next two decades, more elaborate furnishings and labor-saving devices were more widely advertised. Mangles were popular purchases, and also furniture. Beds and bedding were advertised in *Reynolds's* from 1854 to 1866; the iron bedsteads sold from around 8*s*. 6*d*. upward and there was no mention of any hire purchase arrangement.[30] But the 1870s saw a change in furnishing habits-*Reynolds's* began to carry advertisements by large general furniture firms, offering complete house furnishings at low prices. Hire purchase arrangements were common and virtually all the companies offered them, although prices appear to have dropped considerably by the 1880s. However, there was more of this type of advertising in *Lloyd's,* directed at the better-off lower-middle-class readership.

Personal possessions, it is clear, both in the form of clothing and miscellaneous consumer durables, were also becoming more widespread in the 1870s and 1880s. Earlier working-class papers had been noted for their unprincipled insertion of advertisements for slop-shop tailoring firms and *Reynolds's* followed in this tradition. Until the mid-1860s, well over 60 percent of its clothing notices dealt with firms like Moses & Son, Hyam & Co. of Oxford Street, B. Benjamin of Regent Street, and Roberts & Co. of Shoreditch, selling cheap men's clothing. Cheap, ready-made hats and boots, according to the volume of advertising, were part of this expansion. In the eighties firms selling better class secondhand clothing and outfits for hire also began to advertise. The sewing machine became an indispensable item in the home of some readers as early as the 1860s. In the next two decades, it spread much more widely. Average numbers of sewing machine advertisements in a single issue of *Reynolds's* jumped from 1.7 in 1867 to 8.7 in 1871. Improved standards of personal appearance thereby made possible for some were completed by the purchase of better-quality watches, especially gold and silver ones. Watch advertising was fairly limited until the mid-seventies. Most of those advertised were of the cheaper Swiss or American type selling at between one and three shillings, and it was not until the late 1870s that more expensive English watches were advertised in increasing numbers. Made of gold or silver, such watches were naturally more expensive. Over 30 percent of watch advertisements in *Reynolds's* in the late seventies and eighties dealt with watches selling for over £1 and sometimes over £5. Toilet goods—soaps, toothpaste, breath fresheners among them, indicative of poor skin and teeth—were increasingly prominent and even home medication shared in the tendency to improvement. *Reynolds's* had long been noted for its inclusion of dubious patent medicine advertising—thinly disguised abortifacients, cures for 'spermatorrhoea' and other sexual diseases. There was a well established connection between political radicalism, sensationalism, and disreputable advertising, and this remained the case into the 1870s. But the continuing and increased importance of relatively straightforward self-medication advertisements emphasizes how important self-healing was to working people. The 1870s saw an increased number of such medicines on offer to a working-class public. Average figures for "straighforward" medicines in *Reynolds's* (Holloway's or Beecham's pills, Keating's cough lozenges and others) leapt from ten per issue in 1870 to twenty-one in 1874. Home doctoring was stimulated along with the general expansion of consumer spending.

Much of this expansion was only made possible by two factors—the lowering of prices and the widespread introduction of hire purchase. With the household goods advertised in the papers, credit buying and hire arrangements first became common with the purchase of sewing machines in the 1860s. From there the habit spread until by the 1870s mangles, furniture, watches (through watch clubs) could all be bought in this way. In 1875, for example, Dyer's were advertising their "Cooperative Clubs" in *Reynolds's* enabling the members to obtain at wholesale cash prices "Dyer's celebrated watches by paying 1/– a week."[31] Even without H.P., the prices of many consumer goods had fallen considerably over the period. Sewing machines advertised in *Reynolds's* were cheaper than most accounts suggest. The well-known companies—Singer, Wheeler & Wilson, Wilcox & Gibbs—still sold at between four and six guineas for a domestic machine. But a cheaper one could be had through a cut-price dealer like S. Davis & Co. of the Borough and Hackney Road, or by purchasing one of the cheaper machines, many imported from the U.S. available at £1 or 30*s*.[32] Furniture could be obtained from £1 upwards. But working people were prepared to pay higher prices for better-quality English watches—and high prices, too, for medical goods like galvanic bands and necklaces, which were often utterly worthless.

Analyzing advertisements in this way can provide useful pointers to the character of newspaper readership. No direct inferences are possible about the actual purchases made by the paper's readers—but the range of advertisements do indicate what was on offer and presumed attractive by the advertisers themselves. But content can also be used, as in the Smith-Immirzi-Blackwell study, to examine the "collective mind" of the people who read the paper. This is not just a question of editorial attitudes on specific issues, but of perceptions across the whole range of content. *Reynolds's* presented its own particular version of "reality" to its readers. Although not all of them would take in the content, or read and assess it, in the same way, their perception of events was in some way confirmed, reinforced, and molded by what they saw in their chosen paper. In the present study, content of this type has been looked at in two ways—in an examination of the working-class "world view"—perceptions of foreign and colonial events and military affairs, and in an analysis of views of the structure of society in the post-Chartist period. What is important here is not differences in editorial attitude over particular issues—*Reynolds's* support for the South, for instance, in the U.S. Civil War, against *Lloyd's* guarded approval of the Northern cause[33]—but in the way in which broad issues and themes were treated as a whole.

The 1870s were the decade when leisure activities and consumer spending appear to have become more important in working-class life. Were these material changes paralleled by shifts in perceptions of the world about them? This does in some senses seem to have been the case. International as well as domestic politics had figured largely in the working-class world of the 1850s. Working-class international sympathies traced their ancestry back to the days of the French Revolution and the English Jacobins. This strong interest in foreign news was initially maintained. The Crimean War attracted particular attention in 1854 (nearly 30 percent of news content in *Reynolds's* and *Lloyd's*), and the 1860s saw continued interest. Front page coverage, too, taken as an index of particular interest, showed foreign news and editorials generally comprising around 40 percent of content in both papers. But after 1870 interest was on the wane, and the seventies and eighties were decades when foreign news provided a declining proportion of content. The long period of internationalism was coming to an end. The focus of interest in the paper was also shifting. Analysis of the distribution of foreign news and editorial reports in both *Reynolds's* and *Lloyd's* indicates that there were clear differences between lower-middle-class and working-class perceptions of world events, but that increasingly both strata were presented with a similar world view. In *Reynolds's*, interest in those countries where events demonstrated the failings of monarchs and the rise of popular liberal or nationalist reforming movements and governments, remained strong until the 1870s. There was a good deal of interest in the U.S., as the "great example of a working democracy" and news from this area generally provided between 10 and 30 percent of the total number of news items, with regular editorial coverage in the sixties, seventies and eighties. But most attention was reserved for European affairs. Within Europe, much reporting was directed toward France and Italy, continuing the long-established radical tradition of interest in French affairs. Around 25 percent of foreign affairs coverage in *Reynolds's* in the fifties and sixties dealth with French news, and this continued into the seventies and eighties. There was clearly also intense interest in the progress of Italian nationalism—Garibaldi's defeat and capture at Aspromonte attracted much attention, accounting for over 45 percent of foreign reports in *Reynolds's* in 1862.

The pattern and intensity of reporting makes it clear that, for many readers, interest in foreign events must have been based on battlefields, military campaigns, and "blood and thunder," rather than, or as well as on, radical commitment to the issues involved. Both *Reynold's* and *Lloyds* for the most part concentrated their attention on events effectively combining a radical cause with maximum sensation; the Crimean War was a particular case in point. There were some differences in the perception and presentation of foreign affairs in the two papers. For *Reynolds's* readers, news from other countries within Europe was restricted because of the paper's concentration on radical causes; and the working-class view of the world outside Europe was also more limited. *Lloyd's* carried a much broader range of reports in the fifties and sixties. In the following two decades, however, these distinctive differences disappeared, and the world outlook provided for readers from both strata became almost identical. There was still a continuing interest in Western Europe, and in France in particular. But the main focus of attention shifted further away—to Eastern Europe and the Eastern Question and to areas where imperialism rather than nationalism was the dominant concern—to Asia and to Egypt.

However this broadening of interest did not make for an upsurge of enthusiasm for the empire. It is notable how limited was nonadvertising content devoted to the colonies in *Reynolds's.* Even after 1870, the peak of attention was 5 percent of news content in 1878. The appeal of sensationalism as much as pro-imperial sentiment appears to have dictated the focus and emphasis of colonial news stories. The Indian Mutiny attracted a great deal of attention, and India continued to receive most emphasis as far as colonial news went.[34] *Reynolds's* perception of colonial events prior to 1870 focused almost exclusively on that country. It was only in the 1870s that the paper began to expand its colonial coverage and a wider range of reports and editorials was published.[35] This broader, if not greater, interest in the colonies, was not accompanied by any growth of enthusiasm for the army and military matters. Military reporting did increase in both *Reynold's* and *Lloyd's* and it might have seemed that the earlier radical opposition to a corrupt and aristocratic-led army was evaporating. However, much of the increased interest concentrated instead on the volunteer movement, with both *Reynolds's* and *Lloyd's* publishing separate columns of volunteer news. Editorially, these papers welcomed the movement as providing the germ of a citizen army.[36] The pattern of reporting—the Aldershot maneuvers and the rifle championship meeting at Wimbledon—

suggests that the outdoor, sporting aspect of volunteer activity had some appeal as well.

The coverage of foreign news offered to the working-class readers of *Reynolds's* up to the 1870s contained, in a sense, the foreign counterpart of the "old analysis" of society offered to readers as an explanation of domestic politics and class structure. The paper continued a Jacobinical "old corruption" line of attack until late in the nineteenth century at a time when the language of "ranks and orders" was in any case applied in favor in working-class politics.[37] Nor was this "old analysis" simply a matter of editorial content. It was not just political commentary read only by the most politically conscious readers. This type of outlook also pervaded the news content of the paper. Nowhere was this more obviously the case than in the type of sensational news presented. About 20–25 percent of the paper's news and editorial material could be classified in this way. Police and crime news were as important as they had been in *Cleave's Weekly Police Gazette,* in the chapbooks and last dying speeches. But scandal was also particularly important in *Reynolds's.* The proportion of "scandalous" news in *Reynolds's* was always higher than in *Lloyd's* and it was used in an explicitly radical way. James Curran has recently stated that the new Sunday papers of this period, *Reynolds's* especially, "concentrated upon sensationalism *rather* than taxing political commentary, and consequently secured a large audience."[38] But this is not the point; sensationalism was *part* of the paper's political commentary and a continuation of it. Personalized revelations were used to heighten the appeal of the analysis. An affair at Portsmouth in 1854, for example, when two officers had thrown a drunken, local girl overboard after they had beaten and abused her was "typical of those indulged in by a large portion of the upper orders".[39] In this way, elements of the "old analysis" reached even the politically unsophisticated readership. This perception of social structure, however archaic and misplaced it was in its targets of attack, did thereby serve a dual function—widening the appeal of the paper itself through a threadbare but easily marketable appeal and consolidating a form of class solidarity for its readers by employing the type of rhetoric with which they were familiar. To see this analysis, as Curran does, rather as a means of uniting a coalition of working- and middle-class readers for the paper is to misunderstand both the cultural significance of the rhetoric and the pattern of *Reynolds's* readership. There is little evidence of any significant middle-class readership of the paper, nor did the analysis hold any particular appeal for lower-middle-class readers. *Lloyd's* pattern of social comment was nothing like that in *Reynolds's.*[40] The language of the "old analysis," although far from everyday working-class speech, had a social meaning for a working-class readership; it both expanded and continued the type of attacks on 'privilege' with which they were already familiar through the highly miscellaneous forms of popular theater and popular literature.[41]

CONCLUSIONS

The conclusions to be drawn from this examination of trends in the uses of content analysis and its specific application to the nineteenth-century Sunday press are varied. So far as the analysis of *Reynolds's* content goes, the pattern of advertising and of editorial and news material demonstrates a shift of focus in the 1870s as some of the divergences between working- and lower-middle-class perceptions began to disappear. The analysis of advertising content provides an adjunct to work done on the expanding possibilities for leisure activities, consumer spending, and saving in the last quarter of the century. But the "world view" presented in editorial and news sections, and the social framework of reference which structured perceptions of class relationships and the possession of power, are difficult to analyze by other means. Patterns of working- and lower-middle-class consciousness are still an elusive focus of historical research, primarily through lack of evidence; the analysis of the content of newspapers read and relied on within these strata give some approximation to the image of society they held. *Reynolds's* itself fulfilled a dual function in terms of popular culture. It purveyed, in news, editorial, and advertising content, a social reality which acted as a form of social control—conveying the notion of individual betterment, nonpolitical leisure activities, and an archaic world view, both domestic and foreign. But this form of social reality also reflected the cultural attitudes of its readership, and the paper could not have flourished in this period without doing so.

Content analysis itself as a method therefore has its uses as a means of historical research on newspapers. If used to excess it can be a sledgehammer to crack a nut; but it is perhaps the only means of getting to grips with and drawing conclusions from the "manifest content" of the paper. Some of the statements about *Reynolds's* refuted in this analysis show how easy it is to come to the wrong conclusions about trends in content and in newspaper readership without some form of quantitative examination. However the assumed contrast between 'scientific' and 'objective' content analysis and impressionistic literary and linguistic examination does not hold good. Quantitative methodology and the statistical approach is as ideologically structured as any other means of research.[42] Content analysis methods are historically specific, rooted in the social situation and preoccupations of the 1930s, which were repeated and expanded upon during the wave of 1960s radicalism. The most fruitful approach could be the use of the two methods in combination. Content analysis can be used even in the analysis of language and rhetoric (as in the analysis of *Reynolds's* references to social class in this essay).[43] It needs also to be combined with some more traditional literary and stylistic examination. The two methods taken together can help penetrate the latent meanings and patterns of newspaper content and provide a means of analyzing the perceptions and consciousness of newspaper readers of differing social classes.

Notes

GENERAL INTRODUCTION

1. G. Boyce, J. Curran, and P. Wingate (eds.), *Newspaper history: from the seventeenth century to the present day* (London: Constable/Sage, 1978).

2. A. J. Lee, *The origins of the popular press 1855–1914* (London: Croom Helm, 1976).

3. R. Harrison, G. B. Woolven and R. Duncan (eds.), *The Warwick guide to British periodicals 1790–1970* (1977): M. Wolff, J. S. North, and D. Deering (eds.), *The Waterloo directory of Victorian periodicals 1824–1900*, Phase 1 ([Waterloo, Ontario]: Wilfrid Laurier University Press, n.d.).

4. For a recent example of the approach see J. Shattock and M. Wolff (eds.), *The Victorian periodical press: samplings and soundings* (Leicester: at the University Press, 1982).

5. For comments on this see J. Curran, M. Gurevitch, and J. Woollacott, (eds.), *Mass communication and society* (London: Edward Arnold/Open University, 1977), pp. 1–4.

6. This characteristic was particularly marked in the Victorian period, see A. J. Lee, *op. cit.* (1976), p. 18.

PART ONE: INTRODUCTION

1. For an account of the London press and the booksellers in the eighteenth century, see M. Harris, 'Periodicals and the book trade,' in *The development of the English book trade, 1700–1899* (Oxford: at the Polytechnic Press, 1981).

2. Some analyses of these forms of newspaper content appear in G. A. Cranfield, *The development of the provincial newspaper, 1700–1760* (Oxford: Clarendon Press, 1962), pp. 93–116; R. M. Wiles, *Freshest advices: early provincial newspapers in England* (Ohio State University Press, 1965), pp. 303–38; J. H. Plumb, 'The public literature and the arts in the eighteenth century,' in P. Fritz and D. Williams (eds.), *The triumph of culture: eighteenth century perspectives* (Toronto: Hakkert, 1972), pp. 27–48; M. Harris, "The London newspaper press, 1725–1746," (Ph.D. thesis, University of London, 1973), pp. 314–33.

3. For the range of distribution early in the century, see M. Harris, 'Newspaper distribution during Queen Anne's reign, *Studies in the Book Trade* (Oxford Bibliographical Society, 1975), pp. 139–51. For the seasonal fluctuation in the midcentury, see J. Brewer, *Party ideology and popular politics and the accession of George III* (Cambridge University Press, 1976), p. 143.

4. C. Blagden, 'The distribution of almanacks in the second half of the seventeenth century,' *Studies in Bibliography* 11 (1958), Table 1.

5. See, for example, D. Cressey, *Literacy and the social order: Reading and writing in Tudor and Stuart England* (Cambridge: at the University Press, 1980), pp. 147–49.

6. Mist's *Weekly Journal* in particular seems to have made a strong appeal to the lower levels of readership.

7. The earliest of the cut-price papers were William Heathcote's *London Post* and George Parker's *London News*, both published in 1717 at ½*d.* rather than the conventional 1½ *d.*

8. For an attempt to place some of this material against the general background of popular literature, see M. Harris, 'Trials and criminal biographies: A case study in distribu-

tion, 1670–1780,' in *The sale and distribution of books in England from 1700* (Oxford: at the Polytechnic Press, 1982).

9. Contemporary estimates put the total circulation of the unstamped papers during the late 1730s at 50,000 per week or more. See, for example, *London Evening Post,* 2 December 1738; *Daily Post,* 4 December 1738.

10. The continuity of this involvement appears clearly in J. A. Downie, *Robert Harley and the press* (Cambridge: at the University Press, 1979), M. Harris, *op. cit.* (1973), and J. Brewer, *op. cit.* (1976).

11. For an analysis of the political ideas of Walpole and Bolingbroke based largely on a reading of the major London weeklies, see I. Kramnick, *Bolingbroke and his circle* (Cambridge, Mass., 1968).

12. D. Read, *Press and people* (1961), a study based on papers published in Leeds, Manchester, and Sheffield.

13. Contemporary estimates are highly impressionistic but, for example, in 1711 each issue of the *Spectator* was claimed to pass through about twenty hands, while in the early 1730s the figure for a single copy of the weekly *Craftsman* was said to be at least forty, M. Harris, *op. cit.* (1973), p. 62. For the distribution networks of the provincial papers, see G. A. Cranfield, *op. cit.* (1962), pp. 190–206 and R. M. Wiles, *op. cit.* (1965), pp. 95–146.

14. E. R. Turner, 'The excise scheme of 1733,' in *Essays in eighteenth century history* (1966), pp. 21–24; T. W. Perry, *Public opinion, propaganda and politics in eighteenth century England* (Cambridge, Mass.: Harvard University Press, 1962). For an analysis of the role of the press in the careers of Pitt and Wilkes, see M. Peters, *Pitt and popularity* (1981), and J. Brewer, *op. cit.* (1976).

CHAPTER 1. RELIGION AND THE NEWSPAPER PRESS, 1660–1685: A STUDY OF THE *LONDON GAZETTE*

1. The *London Gazette* (known for its first 23 issues as the *Oxford Gazette*) was first published in 1665. This chapter deals only with the religious content of the paper, not with its political, foreign or trade coverage. For a history of the paper, see P. M. Handover, *A history of the* London Gazette (London: H.M.S.O., 1965).

2. I am grateful to Dr. H. McLeod for introducing me to the work of C. Field on religious practice in this and subsequent periods.

3. See M. Watts, *The dissenters* (Oxford: at the University Press, 1978); J. Miller, *Popery and politics in England, 1660–88* (Cambridge: at the University Press, 1973).

4. In 1715, out of an estimated population of 5,441,670, Presbyterians numbered 179,350 (3.3%), Catholics 60,000 (1.1%), Independents 59,940 (1.1%), Particular Baptists 40,520 (0.74%), General Baptists 18,800 (0.35%), and Quakers 39,510 (0.73%). Based on a collation of figures in Watts, *op. cit.* (1978), p. 270, and J. Bossy, *The English Catholic community, 1570–1850* (London: Darton, Longman and Todd, 1975), pp. 189, 422.

5. I. M. Green, *The re-establishment of the Church of England, 1660–63* (Oxford: at the University Press, 1978); R. A. Beddard, 'The restoration church,' in J. R. Jones (ed.), *The restored monarchy, 1660–1688* (London: Macmillan, 1979), pp. 155–75.

6. For a list of newspapers published between 1660 and 1685, see *The Times, Tercentenary handlist of English and Welsh newspapers* (London: The Times, 1920), pp. 26–31, and *The New Cambridge Bibliography of English literature,* 2 (Cambridge: At the University Press, 1971).

7. J. B. Williams, *A history of English journalism to the foundation of the* Gazette (London: Longmans and Co., 1908; G. Kitchin, *Sir Roger L'Estrange* (London: Kegan Paul and Co., 1913); J. Frank, *The beginnings of the English newspaper, 1620–1660* (Cambridge: Harvard University Press, 1961); A. N. B. Cotton, "London Newsbooks in the civil war: their political attitudes and sources of information," (D.Phil. thesis, Oxford University, 1971); R. B. Walker, 'The newspaper press in the reign of William III,' *Historical Journal* 17 (1974); T. J. Crist, "Francis Smith and the opposition press in England," (Ph.D. thesis, University of Cambridge 1977).

8. Kitchin, *op. cit.* (1913), p. 149; J. P. Kenyon, *Stuart England* (London: Allen Lane, 1978), p. 349; J. C. Muddiman, *The king's journalist* (London: John Lane, 1923), p. 195; J. R. Western, *Monarchy and revolution* (London: Blandford, 1972), p. 64.

9. For details of Tudor and Stuart attempts to control the product of the printing presses, see F. S. Siebert, *Freedom of the press in England, 1476–1776* (Urbana: University of Illinois Press, 1965); T. Hobbes, *Leviathan* (Harmondsworth: Penguin, 1981), p. 379; R. Baxter, *The Worcestershire petition to the parliament* (1653), p. 37; R. L'Estrange, cited in Kitchin, *op. cit.* (1913), p. 413.

10. On illegal Nonconformist publication networks in the period, see Crist, *op. cit.* (1977), and my 'Defying the powers and tempering the spirit: A review of Quaker control over their publications, 1672–1689,' *Journal of Ecclesiastical History,* 33 (1982), pp. 72–88. On the government's attempts to control the press after 1660, see Siebert, *op. cit.* (1965), pp. 237–302. On the licensing of almanacs in this period, see B. S. Capp, *Astrology and the popular press: English almanacs, 1500–1800* (London: Faber, 1979), pp. 47–51.

11. For details on the origins of the *Gazette,* see Handover, *op. cit.* (1965), *London Gazette* (hereafter *LG*), 9 August 1666; 17 June 1672, 30 December 1675; R. Steele, *Tudor and Stuart proclamations, 1485–1714* (Oxford: at the University Press, 1910), 1, p. 450; *LG,* 12 May 1680.

12. N. Luttrell, *A brief historical relation of state affairs from September 1678 to April 1714,* 1 (Oxford, 1857), p. 141; see also Muddiman, *op. cit.* (1923); P. Fraser, *The intelligence of the secretaries of state and their monopoly of licensed news, 1660–88* (Cambridge: at the University Press, 1956); J. P. Kenyon, *The Stuart constitution* (Cambridge: At the University Press, 1966), pp. 492, 496; Western, *op.cit.* (1972), pp. 59–61.

13. Siebert, *op.cit.* (1965), p. 301.

14. *Public Record Office Calendar of State Papers Domestic* (hereafter *CSPD*) (1671), pp. 298, 318.

15. *CSPD* (1665–66), p. 497; (1678), p. 345.

16. See Fraser, *op.cit.* (1956). A list of Williamson's correspondents is in W. D. Christie (ed.), *Letters addressed from London to Sir Joseph Williamson,* 2 (Camden Society, 1874), pp. 161–65; *CSPD* (1665–66), p. 280.

17. J. Nickalls (ed.), *The journal of George Fox* (Cambridge: at the University Press 1975), p. 147; W. L. Sachse (ed.), *The diurnal of Thomas Rugg, 1659–1661* (London: Camden Society, 1961), pp. xii—xiii.

18. My calculations are based on information in *CSPD* (1666–67), pp. 187, 193–34 compared with data on the size of paper and reams in P. Gaskell, *A new introduction to bibliography* (Oxford: Clarendon Press, 1974), p. 59, and in H. L. Snyder, 'The circulation of newspapers in the reign of Queen Anne,' *Library,* 5th series, 23 (1968), pp. 207, 217, 226.

19. *CSPD* (1666–67), pp. 193–94; (1667), p. 260.

20. Christie (ed.), *op.cit.* (1874), 1, pp. 30–31; F. M. G. Evans, *The principal secretary of state* (Manchester: University of Manchester, 1923), p. 217.

21. A. Ellis, *The penny universities: A history of the coffee houses* (London: Secker at Warburg, 1956), p. xv; M. Harris, 'Newspaper distribution during Queen Anne's reign: Charles Delafaye and the Secretary of State's office,' in *Studies in the book trade in honour of Graham Pollard* (Oxford Bibliographical Society, 1975), p. 146; Muddiman, *op.cit.* (1923), pp. 192–97; *CSPD* (1666–67), pp. 255, 511; (1667), p. 260; (1667–68), p. 102; *Historical Manuscripts Commission* (hereafter *HMC*), 3d report, p. 270, 5th report, p. 37.

22. D. Cressy, *Literacy and the social order* (Cambridge: at the University Press, 1980), p. 72; Christie, *op.cit.* (1874), 2, pp. 161–65.

23. Cressy, *op.cit.* (1980), pp. 118–19; Christie, *op.cit.* (1874); *CSPD* (1666–67), p. 6.

24. See M. Spufford, 'First steps in literacy: the reading and writing experiences of the humblest seventeenth century spiritual autobiographies,' *Social History* 4, no. 3 (1979), especially p. 434.

25. *CSPD* (1678), p. 575; *LG,* 16 December 1678; *CSPD* (1665–66), p. 193; (1666–67), p. 129; (1672), pp. 201–2; *LG,* 20 April 1682, 23 October 1682; P. Latham and W. Matthews (eds.), *The Diary of Samuel Pepys* (London: Bell and Hyman, 1970–83), 2, p. 194.

26. *CSPD* (1667), p. 427; (1665–66), p. 562.

27. *HMC*, 4th report, p. 250; *LG*, 23 October 1679; A. Browning (ed.), *Memoirs of Sir John Reresby* (Glasgow: Jackson Son and Co., 1936), p. 235; *CSPD* (1671), p. 59; (1666–67), p. 85.

28. *CSPD* (1671–72), p. 388; (1671), p. 59; (1666–67), p. 85; Christie *op.cit.* (1874), 2, pp. 94–95; *LG*, 20 January 1678/9; *Commons Journals* (1678), pp. 533–35, 539, 541, (1680), pp. 665–67, 688–89.

29. A. MacFarlane (ed.), *The Diary of Ralph Josselin, 1616–1683* (Oxford: at the University Press, 1976), pp. 310–11, 573; *CSPD* (1666–67), p. 465; Dr. Williams Library, London, R. Morrice MSS Entring Book 1, pp. 372–75.

30. Luttrell, *op.cit.* (1857), 1, p. 175; Friends House Library, London, (hereafter *FHL*) Meeting for Sufferings MSS 2, p. 209; on Smith see Crist, *op.cit.* (1977).

31. W. Warwick, *Truth's pursuit after falsehood* (1664), p. 1.

32. K. L. Carroll, *John Perrot: Early Quaker schismatic* (London: Friends Historical Society, 1971), p. 77; Fox, *op.cit.*, pp. 551–52; *FHL*, Crosse MSS p. 45, Thirnbeck MSS 11, Meeting for Sufferings MSS 3, p. 189; 5, p. 276.

33. *LG*, 15 January 1682/3; C. E. Whiting, *Studies in English Puritanism from the Restoration to the Revolution, 1660–1688* (London: S.P.C.K., 1931), p. 181.

34. Beddard, *op.cit.* (1979); on almanacs and religion, see Capp, *op.cit.* (1979), pp. 173–79.

35. On the doctrine of Providence, K. Thomas, *Religion and the decline of magic* (Harmondsworth: Penguin, 1973), pp. 108, 111, 126–32.

36. *Oxford Gazette*, 23 November 1665, 27 November 1665; *LG*, 22 March 1665/6, 7 June 1666, 10 January 1666/7, 10 September 1666.

37. *Oxford Gazette*, 14 November 1665, 8 January 1665/6.

38. E. P. Thompson, 'Patrician society, plebeian culture,' *Journal of Social History* 7, no. 4 (1974): 389.

39. *LG*, 2 May 1670.

40. *LG*, 9 September 1667, 11 June 1677.

41. *LG*, 3 February 1675/6, 8 November 1677, 12 November 1677, 17 August 1682, 7 April 1684.

42. *LG*, 17 September 1666, 19 March 1682/3.

43. For example, *LG*, 8 April 1667, 14 May 1677.

44. *LG*, 28 May 1683.

45. Thomas, *op.cit.* (1973), p. 234; *LG*, 23 August 1677.

46. Thomas, *op.cit.* (1973), p. 228; *LG*, 9 April 1683, 29 May 1682.

47. Thomas, *op.cit.* (1973), p. 234; *LG*, 20 November 1684; M. Sylvester (ed.), *Reliquiae Baxterianae* (1696), iii, p. 199.

48. R. B. Walker, 'Advertising in London newspapers, 1650–1750,' *Business History* 15 (1973), does not cover the *Gazette* in any great detail in these years; but see Sarah Tyacke, *London map-sellers, 1660–1720:* 7 (Tring: Map Collector Publications, 1978), based on advertisements for maps in the *Gazette*.

49. Kitchin, *op.cit.* (1913), p. 150. The following is a list of those booksellers, arranged in declining order of importance, who between them accounted for more than 40% of the adverts which I examined: R. Chiswell, H. Brome, T. Basset, B. Took, H. Herringman, T. Cockerhill, R. Boulter, J. Baker, M. Pitt, T. Parkhurst, J. Starkey, J. Collins, J. Martyn, R. Pawlet, J. Edwin, D. Newman.

50. *LG*, 28 June 1675, 15 October, 1677, 16 May 1678, 26 March 1683.

51. *LG*, 4 March 1666/7, 1 June 1668, 2 July 1677.

52. C. J. Sommerville, *Popular religion in restoration England* (Gainesville: University Presses of Florida, 1977), p. 30.

53. For examples of the range of pro–Church of England publications offered, see *LG*, 14 February 1675/6, 12 March 1676/7, 29 January 1684/5.

54. *LG*, 20 June 1670; D. R. Lacey, *Dissent and parliamentary politics in England, 1661–1689* (New Brunswick: Rutgers University Press, 1969), p. 62.

55. *LG,* 27 October 1673, 10 November 1673; Lacey, *op.cit.* (1969), pp. 68–71.
56. *LG,* 16 December 1678, 24 April 1679, 9 June 1679, 17 July 1679.
57. See H. Horwitz, 'Protestant reconciliation in the exclusion crisis,' *Journal of Ecclesiastical History* 15 (1964); *LG,* 12 May 1679 (Baxter), 11 August 1679 (Owen).
58. *LG,* 13 March 1681/2, 28 June 1683.
59. *Oxford Gazette,* 23 November 1665; *LG,* 5 February 1665/6.
60. *Oxford Gazette,* 22 January 1665/6; *LG,* 3 November 1670, 7 September 1682.
61. *LG,* 28 May 1666, 8 April 1678.
62. J. P. Kenyon, *The Popish Plot* (Harmondsworth: Penguin, 1974), p. 110; *LG,* 31 October 1678, 4 November 1678.
63. *LG,* 21 November 1678, 8 May 1679.
64. *LG,* 13 February 1667/8, 18 March 1671/2. Early hostile references in the form of official statements are in *LG,* 12 March 1667/8, 19 July 1669, 8 November 1669, 16 June 1670.
65. Beddard, *op.cit.* (1979), p. 174; *LG,* 11 October 1683.
66. *LG,* 12 July 1683.
67. *CSPD* (1679–80), p. 592; *LG,* 8 June 1682.
68. *CSPD* (1680–81), p. 533; Luttrell, *op.cit.* (1857), 1, p. 85; *The Weekly Pacquet of Advice from Rome* 3 (July 1681): 448.
69. *LG,* 26 July 1683, 6 August 1683.

CHAPTER 2. POLITICS AND THE PRESS

1. G. A. Cranfield, *The development of the provincial newspaper 1700–1760* (Oxford: Clarendon Press, 1962), chapter 1; R. M. Wiles, *Freshest advices: early provincial newspapers in England* (Ohio State University Press, 1965), appendix B.
2. J. A. Downie, *Robert Harley and the press* (Cambridge: at the University Press, 1980).
3. L. Hanson, *Government and the press 1695–1763* (Oxford: Clarendon Press, 1936), p. 14.
4. P. M. Chapman, "Jacobite political argument in England 1714–1766," (Ph.D. thesis, Cambridge University, 1984).
5. M. Harris, "Print and politics in the age of Walpole" in *Britain in the age of Walpole* ed. J. Black (London: Macmillan, 1984), pp. 202–03.
6. R. L. Haig, *The Gazetteer 1735–1797* (Carbondale: Southern Illinois University Press, 1960).
7. Cranfield, *op. cit.* (1962), pp. 126–27.
8. Quotations from the *Review* are cited from *Defoe's Review reproduced from the original editions. . . . by Arthur Wellesley Secord* (22 vols. New York: Facsimile Reprint Society, 1938).
9. *Rehearsal* 26 May–2 June 1705.
10. It has been suggested to me by Alan Downie that Defoe himself actually wrote these editorials, which was an unusually deep game even for so devious a journalist.
11. Leslie was technically correct, for there was no mass admission of freemen in Ipswich immediately before the general election. However, since the previous general election in 1702 some 133 men had been granted the right to be admitted, 40 of them on 24 August 1703. These were Tories almost to a man, including several Tackers. P. E. Murrell, "Suffolk: the political behaviour of the county and its parliamentary boroughs from the Exclusion Crisis to the accession of the House of Hanover" (Ph.D. thesis, University of Newcastle upon Tyne, 1982), pp. 149–152.
12. *A collection of several paragraphs out of Mr. Dyer's letters* (1705).
13. For an objective account of the county contest see Murrell, *op. cit.* (1982), pp. 90–92.
14. *Craftsman,* 6 October 1733.
15. *Free Briton,* 30 May 1734.
16. P. Langford, *The excise crisis* (Oxford: at the University Press, 1975), p. 106.
17. Quoted in the *Newcastle Courant,* 6 July 1734.

18. Langford, *op. cit.* (1975), p. 111.

19. Cranfield, *op. cit.* (1962), p.

20. *Newcastle Courant*, 16–23 May 1734; *Newcastle Journal*, 23 May 1734.

21. J. Cannon, *Parliamentary reform 1640–1832* (Cambridge: at the University Press, 1973), pp. 278–89. Miss Pat Murrell informs me that, although both exaggerated, Tutchin was nearer to the truth than Leslie, some freemen being created in Ipswich by the Tories in the run up to the election of 1705. Coverage of contested elections by London newspapers improved steadily in the early eighteenth century. They provided the results, including votes cast for all candidates, for only 13 out of a total of 86 contests in 1702. This compares with 33 out of 109 in 1705, 33 out of 97 in 1708, 71 out of 130 in 1710, and 41 out of 97 in 1713. I owe the information in which this analysis is based to Dr W. R. McLeod. Although coverage was not complete by 1734, *Cote's Weekly Journal, or The English Stage Player* for 25 May listed votes cast for candidates in 79 contests, alphabetically by constituency, when the election was not quite over, and when in the end it was to produce a total of only 107 contested elections in England.

CHAPTER 3. THE BRITISH PRESS AND EUROPE IN THE EARLY EIGHTEENTH CENTURY

1. There is very little available in print on this subject. The best work is by G. Gibbs, 'Newspapers, Parliament and foreign policy in the age of Stanhope and Walpole,' *Mélanges offerts à G. Jacquemyns* (Brussels: Universite Libre De Brusselles, 1968), and 'The role of the Dutch Republic as the intellectual entrepôt of Europe in the seventeenth and eighteenth centuries,' *Bijdragen en Mededelingen Betreffende de Geschiedenis der Nederlanden* 86 (1971): 323–49.

2. Glenorchy to Townshend, Secretary of State for the Northern Department, 7 August 1728, n.s., Public Record Office, State Papers (hereafter SP), 75/51, f. 184.

3. Glenorchy to Townshend, 24 August 1728, n.s., SP 75/51, f. 202.

4. M. Harris, 'Newspaper distribution during Queen Anne's reign,' *Studies in the book trade: essays in honour of Graham Pollard* (Oxford Bibliographical Society, 1975), pp. 139–51.

5. On 6 September 1715 Dudley Ryder recorded in his diary, 'I went to Toms's coffe house, where I read a French paper from Holland.' Transcripts from the *Shorthand journal of Dudley Ryder*, material omitted from the published edition, Ryder Papers, Sandon Hall.

6. The *British Journal; or, The Censor*, 20 July 1728, was sarcastic about ' those infallible oracles the Dutch prints.'

7. For example, *Fog's Weekly Journal*, 17 April 1731.

8. The *Craftsman*, 24 October and 5 December 1730, are good examples of this.

9. The *Craftsman*, 19 April 1735.

10. J. Black, 'The Challenge of Autocracy: The British Press in the 1730's,' *Studi Settecenteschi* 3–4 (1982–83): 107–18. The conflict between the French government and the Parliament of Paris in 1732 provided a good occasion for such material.

11. Ryder diary, see note 5.

12. The *Daily Post Boy*, 29 May 1729, noted contradictory reports from Vienna and Warsaw about whether there was trouble in Poland; the *London Journal*, 12 June 1736, printed incompatible accounts of the Corsican troubles; the *York Courant*, 3 November 1741, noted that there were contradictory reports from Leghorn and in the Paris newsletter as to whether Britain was to aid Austria.

13. Another instance of a courier being the source of false news, in this case of the fall of Cardinal Fleury, occurred in 1732. Thomas Robinson, British envoy in Austria, to Earl Waldegrave, British envoy in France, 9 April 1732, n.s. Chewton Manuscripts.

14. *Original Mercury, York Journal; or, Weekly Journal*, 17 December 1728.

15. *Original Mercury*, 6 February 1728.

16. For the difficulty of discovering Venetian policy, the *Present State of Europe,* April 1730. The *Craftsman,* 26 July 1729, argued that it was difficult to discover the 'secret springs' because statesmen deliberately concealed their real purposes.

17. Possibly the sharpest attack in the Walpolean period upon press debates of foreign policy occurred in the *Daily Gazetteer,* 18 October 1740, which argued that press discussion represented 'the mob ready to sit in judgement on the legislature.'

18. Newcastle to Horatio Walpole, 20 June 1728, British Library, Additional Manuscripts (hereafter Add. MSS) 32756, ff. 349–56.

19. Townshend to Glenorchy, 25 June 1728, SP 75/51, ff. 155–56; Townshend to Waldegrave, 4 June 1728, Chewton Manuscripts. These orders had some effect; see Holzendorf to Tilson, 2 July 1728, SP 84/301, f.3; Waldegrave to Townshend, 3 July 1728, SP 80/61, f. 19; Waldegrave to Tilson, 22 October 1729, Chewton Manuscripts; Castres to Delafaye, 20 October 1731, n.s., SP 94/108. When the *Daily Gazetteer* of 17 October 1740 printed several accounts of the death of the emperor it gave pride of place to that in the *Gazette.*

20. R. Hatton, 'The *London Gazette* in 1718; supply of news from abroad,' *Bulletin of the Institute of Historical Research* 17 (1940–41): 108. Buckley did have problems in obtaining sufficient news; see Buckley to Delafaye, n.d., SP 35/68, ff. 99, 115.

21. It is interesting that 'Franc. Careless,' the fictional rural correspondent of the *Universal Journal,* claimed that he and his friends read that paper, *Stanley's Letter,* and the *Gazette* in the *Universal Journal,* 13 June 1724. In 1729 Charles Delafaye was not terribly impressed by the *Gazette;* see Delafaye to Tilson, 24 June 1729, SP 43/78; and in the following year, Tilson referred to it as 'the most harmless paper in the world'; see Tilson to Waldegrave, 27 March 1730, Chewton Manuscripts.

22. *Hyp Doctor,* 23 December 1735.

23. Charles Delafaye, under secretary of state and a former editor of the *Gazette,* to Stanyan, 29 August 1724, SP 35/51, 123; *The Post-Man and the Historical Account,* 5 September 1724; *The Flying Post; or, Post Master,* 5 September 1724, for a good instance of this process that was discovered by the government. For an attempt to insert pro-Spanish material in the press, apparently with Zamboni's help, see Examinations of Christopher Perry and Deposition of Richard Nutt, both 29 May 1726, SP 35/62, ff. 79–81. *Fog's Weekly Journal,* 29 November 1729, mentions reports of Spanish links with the British press. It was believed in 1730 that the Prussian resident Reichenbach had inserted material in the *Daily Post Boy;* see Tilson to Hotham, 10 April 1730, Hull University Library, Hotham Papers (DDHO 3/1). For the Austrians supplying information to the *Utrecht Gazette,* sse Finch to Tilson, 22 February 1726, SP 84/289, f. 117, and to the *Delft Gazette,* see James Dayrolles to Townshend, 22 February 1726, SP 84/287. On pamphlets see J. Black, "Foreign inspiration of eighteenth century British political material: an example from 1730," *Trivium* (1986).

24. *London Evening Post,* 26 January 1740. The *London Evening Post* in 1728 accused the *Post Boy* of the reverse procedure, of copying from the Holland mail material it inserted 'under the London article,' *London Evening Post,* 17 December 1728.

25. *York Courant,* 27 October 1741.

26. Zamboni to Le Coq, 17 June 1727, n.s., Bodleian Library; Rawlinson MSS Letters (hereafter Rawlinson), 120, f. 6. *Daily Post,* 5 June 1727; *Post Boy,* 6 June 1727; Mist's *Weekly Journal,* 10 June 1727; *Wye's Letter,* 6 June 1727; L'Hermitage, Dutch Agent in London to the States General, 20 June 1727, n.s., Add. MSS 17677.

27. *Whitehall Evening Post,* 10 June 1727; *Wye's Letter,* 10 June 1727.

28. Newcastle to Horatio Walpole, 12 June 1727, Add. MSS 32750.

29. Finch to Tilson, 18 November 1727, n.s., SP 84/294, f. 276.

30. Townshend to Herman, 7 May 1728, SP 75/51, f.65. This action was due to Dutch prompting, see Chesterfield to Townshend, 11 May 1728, n.s., SP 84/300, f.21, and orders were sent to the British envoy in Hamburg, to insert denials of it in the press there; see Townshend to Chesterfield, 7 May 1728, SP 84/300, f. 47; Townshend to Wych, 7 May 1728, SP 821/45, f.

194; Wych to Townshend, 4 June 1728, n.s., SP 82/45. For complaints about the British Press in 1770 see J. Black, '"A Contemptible Piece of Ribaldry": *The Gazetteer and New Daily Advertiser* Offends the Bourbons,' *Publishing History* 12 (1982): 77–86.

31. The outbreak of war with Spain in 1739, and the operations against the French in Nova Scotia in the War of the Austrian Succession led to much interest in American news. Both the Newcastle and the York press printed fairly detailed accounts of the American territories as background information, for example, the account of Cuba in the *York Courant,* 13 October 1741. The British agent in Paris was skeptical about the accuracy of West Indian news: 'We have news here from Carthagena every day as regularly, and given out with as much assurance, as if it was only ten leagues distant: see Thompson to Weston, 7 July 1741, n.s., SP 78/225, f.357.

32. For the difficulty of producing accurate reports about Persia, see *Daily Journal,* 25 January 1734.

33. The accounts of Tamas Kuli Khan's invasion of India were certainly incredible by the standards of contemporary European warfare.

34. J. R. Jones, *Britain and the world 1649–1815* (London: Fontana, 1980), pp. 13, 184.

35. Ryekhoff, the 'Directeuor de la Gazette d'Amsterdam,' suggested that fear of governmental action was a major factor affecting the publication of material in Britain; see Ryekhoff to Zamboni, 17 September 1744, n.s., Rawlinson, 128, ff.225, 227.

36. The Swiss visitor César de Saussure noted in October 1726, 'La plupart des artisans commencent la journée par aller au café, pour y lire les nouvelles. J'ai souvent vu des décroteurs et autres gens de cette étoffe s'associer pour acheter tous les jours la gazette. . . .'; see *Lettres et voyages de Monsr. César de Saussure 1725–1729* (Lausanne, 1903), p. 167.

37. *Weekly Register,* 3 April 1731.

38. *St. James's Evening Post,* 1 September 1726.

39. *Post Boy,* 29 August 1728.

40. *London Evening Post,* 17 December 1728, 25 November 1729.

41. See the comment on London readers in *Original York Journal; or, Weekly Courant,* 19 December 1727.

42. *Newcastle Courant,* 3 March 1733.

43. *London Journal,* 6 November 1731.

44. Zamboni to Manteuffel, 3 February 1730, 120, f.94; Edward Finch to Newcastle, 24 June 1730, SP 95/55, f.57; Walther, 'secretaire de cabinet' of Augustus II of Poland, to Zamboni, 16 August 1730, n.s., 3 February 1731, n.s., Rawlinson, 129, ff. 215, 217; Fagal to Hop, Dutch envoy in London, 19 September 1730, SP 107/2. Benjamin Keene, British envoy in Spain cited a report of Philip V of Spain reading the *Craftsman;* see Keene to Delafaye, 20 May 1731 n.s., SP 94/107.

45. These are filed in the Correspondance Politique Angleterre Series in the Archives Etrangères. The French war minister Dangervilliers received a regular report upon the contents of the British press; See Captain Glascoe to James III, 14 December 1732, n.s., Royal Archives, Stuart Papers, 157/129.

46. C. Quazza, *Il problema italiano e l'equilibrio europeo 1720–1738* (Turin, 1965), pp. 455–63. Black, '1733—Failure of British diplomacy?' *Durham University Journal* 74 (1982): 202.

47. A typical example of such views was expressed by the Sardinian envoy at The Hague; see A. Ruata, *Luigi Malabaila di Canale, riflessi della cultura illuministica in un diplomatico piemontese,* (Turin, 1968), p. 104.

48. De Bourgay, British envoy at Berlin, to Townshend, 22 February 1729, SP 90/24; Waldegrave to Horatio Walpole, 12 April 1731, n.s., Chewton Manuscripts.

49. *The Flying Post: or, Post Master,* 3 September 1726. See Chesterfield to Townshend, 23 November 1729, SP 84/302, f. 133. In 1749 the King of Sweden issued a formal denial of press reports of plans to introduce despotism in Sweden; see *Newcastle Courant,* 13 May 1749.

50. Molesworth to Newcastle, 10 February 1725, n.s., SP 92/31, f. 422. Tilson believed that

the 'spawn of the authors of the *Craftsman* . . . will make little or no impression on people of sense'; see Tilson to Waldegrave, 6 January 1730, Chewton Manuscripts.

51. Waldegrave to Newcastle, 2 August 1733, Add. MSS 32782, ff.13–14. In 1730 Reichenbach believed that the government encouraged the printing of complaints against Spain in the government press in order to prepare their readers for the ending of the Spanish alliance; see Reichenbach to Frederick William I of Prussia, 18 September 1730, SP 107/2.

52. The *Original Mercury,* 22 October 1728. A similar report, appearing in the *Dublin Journal,* 12 December 1727, was noted by the government; see copy in SP 36/4, f. 92.

53. For the relationship between 'public opinion' and the press, R. B. McDowell, *Irish public opinion 1750–1800* (London: Faber and Faber, 1944), p. 263; R. Munter, *History of Irish newspapers 1685–1780* (Cambridge: at the University Press, 1967), Robinson complained that the Austrians believed that the opposition press represented 'the true interest and disposition of the people.' See Robinson to Harrington, 18 November 1730, SP 80/69.

54. On the mass of newspapers available in Britain, see the *Freeholder's Journal,* 18 May 1723. Saussure was very impressed by the number of newspapers available in London; see *Lettres et voyages, op. cit.,* p. 167.

55. V. S. Doe (ed.), *The diary of James Clegg of Chapel-en-le-Frith 1708–55,* Part 1 (Derbyshire Record Society, 1978); E. Hobhouse (ed.), *The diary of a West Country physician* (London: Simpkin Marshall, 1934).

CHAPTER 4. NEWSPAPERS AND INDUSTRY: THE EXPORT OF WOOL CONTROVERSY IN THE 1780s

1. For a detailed study of these theses see J. Money, *Experience and identity: Birmingham and the West Midlands 1760–1800* (Manchester: at the University Press, 1978).

2. G. A. Cranfield, *The development of the provincial newspaper, 1700–1760* (Oxford: Clarendon Press, 1962) provides much the best guide for the early country newspapers. Unfortunately he stops in 1760. There is also useful information in R. M. Wiles, *Freshest advices: Early provincial newspapers in England* (Ohio State University Press, 1965); D. Read, *Press and people, 1790–1850: Opinion in three English cities* (London: Edward Arnold, 1961); R. K. Webb, *The British working class reader* (London: George Allen and Irwin, 1955); and G. Boyce, J. Curran, and P. Wingate (eds.), *Newspaper history: From the seventeenth century to the present day* (London: Constable/Sage, 1978). M. J. Murphy, *Cambridge newspapers and opinion, 1780–1850* (Cambridge: at the University Press, 1977) is a good local study, and J. Brewer, Party, ideology and popular politics at the accession of George III (Cambridge: at the University Press, 1976) provides a lively account of the burgeoning of the provincial press in the 1760s.

3. Cranfield, *op.cit.* (1962), pp. 90–91.

4. The fullest accounts are to be found in the old classics, J. Smith, *Rusticum commerciale, or Memoirs of wool* (1747); J. Bischoff, *A comprehensive history of the woollen and worsted manufacturers* (1842), and J. James, *A history of the worsted manufacture* (1857). J. de L. Mann, *The cloth industry in the west of England from 1640 to 1880* (Oxford: Clarendon Press, 1971) provides the best up-to-date discussion of the wool trade and its literature in this period.

5. This paragraph is based on a box of papers in the Hailstone Collection (Box 5.29) in the Minister Library at York. See also the *Journal of the House of Commons* for January–February 1752.

6. *Report from the Committee Relating to the False Winding of Wool and the Marking of Sheep with Pitch and Tar* (1752).

7.'Circular' letter of John Hustler (?) on the proceedings of the Lincolnshire MPs on 12 February 1752 in the Hailstone Collection.

8. Ibid., D. Stanfield to R. G. Sawrey, 15 February 1752.

9. See I. R. Christie, *Wilkes, Wyvill and reform* (1962), pp. 25–67; also the Introduction to L. Werkmeister, *The London daily press, 1772–1792* (Lincoln, Nebraska: University of Nebraska Press, 1963).

10. *Leeds Mercury,* 1 March, 19 April, 27 September 1774; 3, 25 January, 7 February, 24 October, 7 and 14 November, 12 December 1775; 24 August 1779; 14 and 21 May 1782. *Leeds Intelligencer,* 10 February 1778.

11. I. R. Christie, *op.cit.* (1962), pp. 222–31.

12. *Leeds Mercury,* 14 December 1779.

13. T. S. Ashton, *Economic fluctuations in England, 1700–1800* (Oxford: Clarendon Press, 1959), pp. 62, 130; R. G. Wilson, *Gentlemen merchants* (Manchester: at the University Press, 1971), pp. 48–51.

14. See E. C. Black, *The Association: British extraparliamentary political organisation 1769–1793* (Cambridge, Mass.: Harvard University Press, 1963), pp. 31–130.

15. I. R. Christie, *op. cit.* (1962), pp. 105, 117, 136, 140, 167, 190, 192–96, 207, 209, 220–21. See also N. C. Phillips, *Yorkshire and English national politics, 1783–1784* (Christebuch, New Zealand: University of Canterbury, 1961). The West Riding worsted manufacturers used the technique of sending letters to and making announcements in the Leeds papers while promoting the Worsted Committee legislation in 1776. See *Leeds Intelligencer,* 10, 24 September, 29 October, 26 November 1776.

16. The best background account, especially good on the technical niceties of sheep and wool, is to be found in J. A. Perkins, 'Sheep farming in eighteenth and nineteenth century Lincolnshire,' *Occasional Papers in Lincolnshire History and Archaeology,* no. 4 (Sleaford, 1977). H. B. Carter (ed.), *The sheep and wool correspondence of Sir Joseph Banks, 1781–1820* (London: British Museum (Natural History), 1978) is essential reading. From the correspondence it is possible to gain a detailed view of the export controversy. It also provides the basis of the editor's *His Majesty's Spanish flock* (Norwich: Angus and Robertson, 1964). But the original Banks manuscripts in the Sutro Library, University of San Francisco (hereafter Banks (Sutro) MSS) contain much more material, especially price data, printed ephemera, and Banks's copious press cuttings taken both from the London and country newspapers. (A microfilm is in the Natural History Museum General Library, see *His Majesty's Spanish Flock,* Introduction.)

17. *Leeds Intelligencer* and *Mercury,* 6 November 1781; *Stamford Mercury,* 8 November; also *Cambridge Chronicle* cutting in Banks (Sutro) MSS III, section 11.

18. Carter, *op.cit.* (1978), Letters of Charles Chaplin, 30 November 1781, and Benjamin Stephenson, 28 January 1782.

19. Banks (Sutro) MSS III, section 11; also Carter, *op.cit.* (1978), Letter of Charles Chaplin, 19 January 1782.

20. *Stamford Mercury,* 15 and 29 November 1781.

21. J. Bischoff, *op.cit.* (1862), 1: 206–40, gives a précis of the chief pamphlets. See also under J. Dalrymple and A. Young in Carter, *op.cit.* (1978), and the Rev. J. Sheepshanks, *Plain reason addressed to the people of Great Britain against the (intended) petition to Parliament* (Leeds, 1782).

22. Carter, *op.cit.* (1978), Letter of Benjamin Stephenson, 12 December; Charles Chaplin, 15 and 18 December 1781.

23. Ibid., Charles Chaplin to Sir Joseph Banks, 7 February 1782.

24. Ibid. Letter of Sir Joseph Banks, 31 January 1782, and Appendix II, p. 528 from 'My Pamphlet.' The apathy of the landowning interest and the superior organization and ability of the merchants and manufacturers in pressing their interests is a constant theme in the writings of Lord Sheffield and Arthur Young. Their opinions were largely formed from this experience in 1781–82.

25. *Leeds Intelligencer* and *Mercury,* 6 November 1781; see also Bradford University Archives, WC/1/1 Worsted Committee Book, (1777–86), minutes of meeting at Halifax, 31 December 1781.

26. *Leeds Mercury,* 27 November 1781; also printed in the *Intelligencer.*

27. *Leeds Mercury,* 1 January 1782.
28. Ibid., 4 December 1782; also *Intelligencer* (same date).
29. The resolutions were printed in both Leeds papers on 25 December 1781 and 1 January 1782.
30. R. G. Wilson, *op. cit.* (1971), pp. 48–9.
31. Ibid., Appendix II, pp. 524–30. The same points were made in H. Butler Pacey's pamphlet address to Sir George Savile (never published) in Banks (Sutro) MSS III, section 8. There are several references to the severe competition from cotton. See the two pamphlets cited in note 32, also letter of Mercator in the *London Courant* in Banks (Sutro) MSS III, pp. 11, 42, and letter of John Parkinson, 21 January 1782, in Carter, *op.cit.* (1978).
32. These were used, rather clumsily, to lever a split between the struggling worsted clothiers and the wealthy export merchants in Leeds and Wakefield. See Carter, *op.cit.* (1978) Benjamin Stephenson to Sir Joseph Banks, 28 January 1782.
33. *Leeds Intelligencer,* 1, 8 January 1782.
34. Ibid., 8, 15, 22 January 1782; there are press cuttings about these meetings in Banks (Sutro) MSS III, pp. 11 and a list in J. Bischoff, *op.cit.* (1842). 1:210–14.
35. *Leeds Mercury,* 12 February 1782.
36. J. de L. Mann, *op.cit.* (1971), pp. 260–64.
37. *Norwich Mercury,* 26 January 1782. The Colchester resolutions caused 'universal and merited disgust' amongst the government party. Pelham was so incensed by the resolution which stated 'this meeting will *resist and oppose* with their utmost power any attempt that may be made to repeal the laws now in force' that he went straight to Lord North to protest. See the *Lincoln Courant,* 9 February 1782.
38. *Salisbury and Winchester Journal,* 4, 11 February 1782.
39. J. James, *op.cit.* (1857), p. 300; *Cambridge Chronicle,* 18 January 1782.
40. *Leeds Intelligencer,* 19 March 1782.
41. Banks (Sutro) MSS III, Section 11, comprises a volume almost entirely of pasted press cuttings covering the 1781–82 controversy. Many were taken from the London daily papers.
42. Carter, *op. cit.* (1978), Letter dated 31 January 1782.
43. West Suffolk Record Office (Bury St. Edmunds), Diary of James Oakes, entry for 7 February 1782.
44. This paragraph is based upon material in Banks (Sutro) MSS III, section 11, and letters printed in Carter, *op. cit.* (1978).
45. *Ibid.,* letter dated 13 April 1782.
46. A collection of these are pasted in Banks (Sutro) MSS III, section 11, and so labeled in Banks's hand.
47. For a full discussion of this see Werkmeister, *op.cit.* (1963), passim.
48. *Norwich Mercury,* 23 February, 2, 16, 23 March, 11 May 1782. Sir Joseph Banks extracted many cuttings from the *Cambridge Chronicle;* see Banks (Sutro) MSS III, section 11.
49. This was Charles Chaplin's view. See his letter of 13 April 1782 in Carter, *op.cit.* (1978).
50. A. Young, *The farmer's tour through the East of England* (1771), IV, p. 362, had already predicated that 'if ever unfortunate questions should be started, in which a preference must be given to one, none but a fool can imagine that the land-lords of this great empire of about fourscore millions of acres are to yield to the transitory sons of trade and manufacture.'
51. Carter, *op.cit.* (1978), p. 60, letter dated 28 January 1781.
52. Banks (Sutro) MSS III, section 6, pp. 2–3.
53. R. G. Wilson, 'The supremacy of the Yorkshire cloth industry in the eighteenth century', in N. B. Harte and K. G. Ponting (eds.), *Textile history and economic history* (Manchester: Manchester University Press, 1973), pp. 243–4.
54. W. Bowden, *Industrial society in England towards the end of the eighteenth Century* (New York: Macmillan Co., 1965), pp. 164–92.
55. See evidence of John Anstie in 'Report from the committee on the illicit exportation of wool, live sheep, worsted and yarn' (June 1786) in *Reports from Committees of the House of*

Commons (1800), 11, pp. 300–302. Also *Norfolk Chronicle,* 8 May 1786.

56. Ibid. See Anstie's evidence in 'Report from the committee on the laws related to the exportation of live sheep and lambs, wool, wool fells etc.' printed in the same volume, pp. 303–17.

57. Carter, *op.cit.* (1978), letter dated 31 May 1786.

58. James Oakes's diaries, entries for 10 April and 26 May 1786 (see note 43).

59. *Norfolk Chronicle,* 14 October 1786.

60. Carter, *op.cit.* (1978), P. Milnes to Rev. Beveridge, 14 October 1786.

61. *Leeds Intelligencer,* 2, 9 January 1782; *Leeds Mercury,* 9, 16 January 1782.

62. Carter, *op.cit.* (1978), letter dated 27 June 1787.

63. The *General Advertiser,* 19 May 1787. In the meetings during February 1788 Anstie was still worried about criticism of his conduct and was threatening to resign; see the *General Advertiser,* 20 March 1788.

64. See various articles scattered in volumes 7, 8 and 9 (1786–88) of Arthur Young, *Annals of agriculture.* See also Young's evidence before the Committees mentioned in notes 55–56 above and his letters to Sir Joseph Banks in Carter, *op.cit.* (1978).

65. *Norfolk Chronicle,* 9 February 1788; also letters of J(ohn) T(aylor) addressed to Young in same, 17, 24 February 1787.

66. The various versions of the bill are to be found in Banks (Sutro) MSS IV, pp. 1–5. See *Cobbett's Parliamentary history of England,* 27 (1788–89), pp. 382–90, and *The Parliamentary Register* 23 (1788): 258–59, 495–97, 527–28 for accounts of the bill's passage through Parliament.

67. The *Norwich Mercury* and *Norfolk Chronicle* together provide the best accounts. There was less interest in the West Riding.

68. Carter, *op.cit.* (1978), letter dated 28 November 1786.

69. *The Parliamentary Register* 23 (1788): 528. At a personal level William Windham's diaries show how bored he was as T.P. for Norfolk with the whole wool business. See *The diary of the Rt. Hon. William Windham, 1784–1810* (1866), pp. 134–36.

70. *Cobbett's parliamentary history of England,* 27 (1788–89), p. 480.

71. The best account is in the *Leeds Intelligencer,* 8 July 1788.

72. Bischoff, *op.cit.* (1842), still provides a good summary of the furore over the wool duty of 1819–24 and a reasonable one of the declining quality of English wool.

PART TWO: INTRODUCTION

1. A sophisticated version of the 'fresh start' view of 1855, involving a considerable downgrading of previous newspaper developments, appears in S. Koss, *The rise and fall of the political press in Britain,* 1 (London: Hamilton, 1981), pp. 1–3, 31, and passim.

2. For the working-class publications see, for example, P. Hollis, *The pauper press* (Oxford: at the University Press, 1970); J. N. Wiener, *The war of the unstamped* (Ithaca, New York: Cornell University Press, 1969); S. Coltham, 'English working-class newspapers in 1867,' *Victorian Studies* 3 (1969–70): 159–80; A. Jones, 'Workmen's advocates in ideology and class in the Labour newspaper system,' in J. Shattock and M. Wolff (eds.), *The Victorian periodical press: samplings and soundings* (Leicester: at the University Press, 1982), pp. 297–316.

3. B. Harrison, 'Press and pressure groups in modern Britain,' in Shattock and Wolff, *op.cit.* (1982), p. 282. For a brilliant analysis of the temperance press see the same authors '"A World of which we had no conception": Liberalism and the English temperance press: 1830–1872,' *Victorian Studies* 13 (1969–70): 125–58.

4. V. S. Berridge, 'Popular Sunday papers and mid-Victorian society,' in G. Boyce, J. Curran, and P. Wingate (eds.), *Newspaper History: From the seventeenth century to the present day* (London: Constable/Sage, 1978), pp. 247–64.

5. There were, for example, periodicals directed at women, lawyers, farmers, and gardeners.

6. A. J. Lee, *The origins of the popular press, 1855–1914* (London: Croom Helm, 1976), p. 70.

7. Harrison, in Shattock and Wolff, *op.cit.* (1982), p. 277. The estimate is taken from the *Quarterly Review.*

8. Woodcut illustration had been a feature of the popular street literature since the seventeenth century and was adopted extensively in the cheap periodicals from the 1820s.

9. The first issue of the *Daily Mail,* 4 May 1896, though quite conservative in general appearance, offered a combination of material which was beyond the scope of the established dailies. This included a full page taken up with serialized fiction and several 'magazine' features.

10. A guide to circulation figures can be obtained through the advertising lists and directories of which Charles Mitchell's *Newspaper Directory* is the most useful. However, their reliability is doubtful, see A. J. Lee, *op.cit.* (1976), p. 67. For a collection of miscellaneous estimates drawn from a variety of sources see R. D. Altick, *The English common reader* (London and Chicago: University of Chicago Press, 1957), Appendix C, pp. 391–96. See also A. P. Wadsworth, 'Newspaper circulation, 1800–1954,' *Transactions of the Manchester Statistical Society* 4 (1955): 1–40. Although the total readership was increasing during the later nineteenth century, much of this growth was apparently centered on such proliferating service-sector groups as clerks and shop assistants whose potential spending power drew in the advertisers. The popular Sundays were alone in creating and maintaining a genuinely working-class readership profile before 1900.

11. Shattock and Wolff, *op.cit.* (1982), pp. XIV–XV.

12. See V. S. Berridge, in Boyce, Curran, and Wingate, *op.cit.* (1978), pp. 260–66 and P. Bailey, *Leisure and class in Victorian England* (1978), pp. 59–60.

CHAPTER 5. THE RELIGIOUS PERIODICAL AND NEWSPAPER PRESS, 1770–1870

1. S. Durden, 'A study of the first Evangelical magazine, 1740–1748,' *Journal of Ecclesiastical History* 27 (1976): 255–78. See also S. J. Royal, 'Religious periodicals in England during the Restoration and eighteenth century,' *Journal of Rutgers University* 35 (1971): 27–33; F. E. Mineka, *The Dissidence of Dissent* (Chapel Hill: University of North Carolina Press, 1944), pp. 27–84.

2. The *Weekly History,* cited in Durden, *op. cit.* (1976), p. 258.

3. Durden, *op. cit.* (1976); *The christian history, containing accounts of the revival and propogation of religion in Great Britain and America . . . 1743 and 1744* (Boston, Mass.: 1744–45), 2 vols.; A. Fawcett, *The Cambuslang revival: the Scottish Evangelical revival of the eighteenth century* (London: Banner of Truth Trust, 1971), pp. 92–3; E. S. Gaustad, *The great awakening in New England* (New York: Harper & Bros., 1957).

4. Henceforth all magazines and newspapers cited are published in London unless otherwise indicated. *Royal Spiritual Magazine; or Christian's Grand Treasure* (1751); W. Wilson, *The history and antiquities of Dissenting churches . . . in London. . . .* (1808), 4, pp. 426–28; J. M. Bumstead and C. Clark, 'New England's Tom Paine: John Allen and the spirit of liberty,' *William and Mary Quarterly,* 3d series, 21 (1964): 560–70.

5. *Christian Magazine,* (1760–67). For Dodd see P. Fitzgerald, *A famous forgery, being the story of 'the unfortunate Doctor Dodd'* (1865) and sources cited, p. vi.

6. Durden, *op. cit.* (1976), p. 274; W. T. Whitley, *A history of British Baptists* (London: C. Griffin and Co., 1923), pp. 214–15.

7. The *Gospel Magazine; or Spiritual Library* (1766–72); the *Gospel Magazine or Treasury of Divine Knowledge* (1774–83); continued as the *New Spiritual Magazine; or Evangelical Treasury*

. . . (1783–85). For circulation, see *Gospel Magazine* 2:1; and for Toplady see W. Winters, *Memoirs of the life and writings of the Rev. A. M. Toplady* (1872).

8. *Theological Repository; Consisting of Original Essays . . . to Promote Religious Knowledge (1769–71.* See also H. McLachlan, *The Unitarian movement in the religious life of England* (London: G. Allen & Unwin, 1934), pp. 165–223 for this and other early Unitarian periodicals.

9. The *Arminian Magazine* (1778–97), then the *Methodist Magazine* (1798–1812), then the *Wesleyan Methodist Magazine* (1822–1913).

10. W. R. Ward, *Religion and society in England, 1790–1850* (1972), pp. 1–176; A. D. Gilbert, *Religion and society in industrial England: Church, chapel and social change, 1740–1914* (London: Longman, 1976), pp. 1–125.

11. Brief outlines can be found in G. J. Stevenson, *City Road Chapel, London and its associations* (1872), pp. 271–85, and F. Cumbers, *The Book Room: the story of the Methodist publishing house and Epworth Press* (London: Epworth Press, 1956). MS Minutes of the Book Committee, Letter Books and correspondence of editors and book stewards can be found in the Methodist Archive Centre, John Rylands Library, University of Manchester.

12. MS Minute Books, Book Committee, 5 July 1826.

13. MS Minute Books, Book Committee, 24 February 1823, 20 November 1834, and many other entries. See also MS Letter Book, Book Committee, 21 January 1841, and related entries.

14. MS Minute Books, Book Committee, 5 July 1826 and 26 February 1835; T. Jackson, *Recollections of my own life and times* (1878), pp. 179 and 210; R. Chew, *James Everett: A biography* (1875), pp. 172–75.

15. *Arminian Magazine* (1778–90), and F. Cumbers, 'The *Methodist Magazine,*' *Proceedings of the Wesley Historical Society* 37 (1969–70): 72–6.

16. W. F. Swift, 'The women itinerant preachers of early Methodism," *Proceedings of the Wesley Historical Society* 8 (1951–52): 89–94; *Methodist Magazine* (1800–1820). Also see J. T. Wilkinson, 'The rise of other Methodist traditions,' in R. Davies, A. R. George, and G. Rupp (eds.), *A history of the Methodist Church in Great Britain,* 2 (London: Epworth Press, 1978), pp. 304–9 for American and English revivalists who were condemned by and excluded from the *Methodist Magazine.*

17. Stevenson, *op. cit.*(1872), pp. 388–90 for the scholarly Joseph Benson as editor. See also J. MacDonald, *Memoirs of the Rev. Joseph Benson* (1822).

18. H. F. Mathews, *Methodism and the education of the people, 1791–1851* (London: Epworth Press, 1949); Stevenson, *op. cit.* (1872), pp. 388–90.

19. F. J. Jobson, MS Memo of Book Room Affairs. This is a financial history of the Book Room written by Jobson, who became book steward in 1864. See also MS letter of John Mason, London, 22 January 1827, claiming that on taking over as book steward he found 'the Periodicals pay well,' Mason Correspondence, Methodist Archive Centre. Printing figures are given in the MS Minute Books, Book Committee, 18 January 1827.

20. See MS Minute Books, Book Committee, 5 July 1826, and numerous other entries for debts.

21. Wilkinson, in Davies, George, and Rupp *op. cit.* (1978), pp. 276–329, gives a recent account of these groups. For their publishing operations see Cumbers, *op. cit.* (1956), pp. 22–63.

22. Cumbers, *op. cit.* (1956), pp. 22–24, 57–58, 101–3; T. D. Crothers, 'Historical sketch of the Methodist New Connexion,' in G. Packer (ed.), *The centenary of the Methodist New Connexion, 1797–1897* (1897), p. 80; *Methodist Monitor* (Leeds, 1796–7); The *Methodist Magazine or Evangelical Repository* (Manchester, 1798–1811), then the *New Methodist Magazine* (1812–32).

23. H. B. Kendall, *The origin and history of the Primitive Methodist Church,* 2 (n.d.), pp. 1–14; F. Baker, 'James Bourne (1781–1860) and the Bemersley Book Room,' *Proceedings of the Wesley Historical Society* 30 (1956): 138–50; J. Walford, *Memoirs of the life and labours of . . . Hugh Bourne,* 2 (1856), pp. 167–68.

24. T. Shaw, *The bible Christians, 1815–1907* (1965), pp. 50–52, 62; S. L. Thorne, *Samuel Thorne, Printer* (1875), pp. 133.

25. Bibliographical details can be found in Cumbers, *op. cit.* (1956), p. 148. For examples of contents see 'The Remarkable Accounts' and 'Memoirs' which run through the *Primitive Methodist Magazine* (Bemersley, near Tunstall) 8 (1827) and any volume of the *Arminian Magazine,* then the *Bible Christian Magazine* (Launceston, Stoke Damerell and Shebbear, 1822–27).

26. H. Bourne's, 'Ecclesiastical history from the creation to the present time' was serialized in the *Primitive Methodist Magazine* from 1825 to 1843, and his 'History of the origins of the Primitive Methodists' appeared in the *Primitive Methodist Magazine* 2 (1821). Early volumes of the magazine are full of rules and regulations. For W. O'Bryan's 'The rise and progress of the connexion of people called Arminian Bible Christians,' see the *Arminian Magazine* 2 (1823).

27. J. Vickers, *History of Independent Methodism* (1920), pp. 33–35 and 271–17; and the *Independent Methodist Magazine or Repository of Religious Knowledge* (Glasgow, 1823–29), quarterly.

28. See, for example, K. P. Russell, *Memoirs of the Rev. John Pyer* (1865), pp. 2–102 for George Pocock, the Tent Methodists and the *Tent Methodist Magazine* (1824–25), no copies of which have been located.

29. For membership see Gilbert, *op. cit.* (1976), p. 31, and for circulation see sources cited above, notes 22–28, and *Primitive Methodist Magazine,* 3d series, 10 (1852): 111.

30. *Evangelical Magazine* (1793–1904); W. T. Owen, *Edward Williams, D.D. 1750–1813: his life, thought and work* (Cardiff, 1963), pp. 64–65 and 162–64; A. S. Wood, *Thomas Haweis, 1734–1820* (1957) pp. 191–94; G. Collison, *The pastor's tomb. A sermon occasioned by the death of the Rev. Matthew Dilks* (1829). I have used the little-known *Index to the first twenty-four volumes of the Evangelical Magazine. . . .* (1817) as a guide to sampling the contents. The preface to volume 9 (1801) discusses the original purposes of the magazine at length. *Evangelical Magazine* (1829), pp. 89–94 and 133–40.

31. Trustees and contributors were listed on the title page of each volume. They included many prominent Dissenters and a few Anglicans. For the first editor, J. Eyre, see *Evangelical Magazine* (1803), pp. 225–30 and 273–87; p. 281 indicates a circulation of 12,000 copies a month. For George Burder, see W. Wilson, *op. cit.* (1808), 3: 467–71, and H. F. Burder, *Memoir of the Rev. George Burder* (1833).

32. See *Evangelical Magazine* 4 (1797) for reference to advertisements.

33. See, for example, the *Biblical Magazine* then *Theological and Biblical Magazine* (1801–7). The *Protestant Dissenters Magazine* (1794–99), on the other hand, had much Unitarian support.

34. Some claims about circulation came out of conflict between the *Evangelical Magazine* and the *Edinburgh Review,* which ridiculed evangelical piety and advertisements for religious tradesmen and servants; see *Edinburgh Review* (1807–8), pp. 341–62; *Evangelical Magazine* (1809): 183–89. *Evangelical Magazine* (1841) claimed 16,000 copies distributed, but by then it was only one of many similar magazines. Profits were distributed twice yearly and listed in the magazine.

35. *Gospel Magazine* and *Theological Review* (1779 to date). The quotation is from 1806, p. 512.

36. R. Hindmarsh, *Rise and progress of the New Jerusalem Church in England and America . . .* (1861), pp. 108–9, 139, 180, 213–14.

37. W. Jones, *Autobiography of the late William Jones* (1846), pp. 44–138; and R. Taylor, 'English Baptist periodicals, 1790–1865,' *Baptist Quarterly,* n.s., 27 (1977–78): 50–82. For general Baptist periodicals see also A. Taylor, *The history of the English General Baptists,* 2 (1818), 1, pp. 333 and 456.

38. The best account of the early Catholic press is to be found in a series of articles by J. Gillow in the *Tablet,* 29 January 1881–19 March 1881. See also J. Gillow, *A literary and biographical history, or bibliographical dictionary of the English Catholics from 1534 to the present* (1895–1900), 1:43–52

39. *Christian Observer* (1802–77); M. Hennell, *John Venn and the Clapham Sect* (1958), pp. 190–95; E. M. Howse, *Saints in politics* (1952), pp. 105–8.

40. See, for example, *Christian Observer* (1804), pp. 55–56, 370–73, and 640–43, and the reply in *Evangelical Magazine* (1804), p. 423.

41. For the *British Critic* see E. S. Houghton, 'The *British Critic* and the Oxford Movement,' in F. Bowers (ed.), *Studies in bibliography*, 16 (1963), pp. 119–37. The *Critic's* principal backer and the promoter of other High Church magazines like the *Christian Remembrancer* (1819–68), was Joshua Watson, see A. B. Webster, *Joshua Watson, the story of a layman, 1771–1850* (London: S.P.C.K., 1954); and E. Churton, *Memoir of Joshua Watson* (Oxford, 1861).

42. McLachlan, *op. cit.* (1934), pp. 178–84, and Mineka, *op. cit.* (1964), discuss the well-known *Monthly Repository*. This and other literary and intellectual magazines which have been well explored will only be touched on in this article. For the *Eclectic Review*, see E. R. Conder, *Joshua Conder: a memoir* (1857), p. 125.

43. *Christian Guardian* (1802–53); *Christian Reformer* (1815–63).

44. *Baptist Annual Register* (1790–1803); Taylor, *op. cit.* (1977–78), p. 54; E. A. Payne, *The Baptist Union: A short history* (London: Baptist Union, 1950).

45. *Baptist Magazine* (1809–65); Taylor, *op. cit.* (1977–78), pp. 56–7; Payne, *op. cit.* (1950), pp. 18–138; S. J. Price, 'Early years of the Baptist Union,' *Baptist Quarterly* 4 (1928–29): 53–178.

46. *London Christian Instructor or Congregational Magazine* (1818–45); A. Peel, *These hundred years: a history of the Congregational Union of England and Wales, 1831–1931* (London: Congregational Church, 1931), pp. 13–18 and 413. For the Countess of Huntingdon's Connexion see *Evangelical Register*, (1824–1907).

47. Only a sample of specialist periodicals can be cited here. Most of the denominational magazines had extensive missionary supplements, the *Evangelical Magazine*, for example, becoming the *Evangelical Magazine and Missionary Chronicle* in 1813. Baptist magazines are described in Taylor, *op. cit.* (1977–78), pp. 54, 57–62. The Church Missionary Society issued the influential *Missionary Register* (1813–55), see E. Stock, *History of the Church Missionary Society*, (1899), pp. 126–28. The SPG had *Occasional Quarterly Papers* from 1830 and the Wesleyans had *Missionary Notices* from 1816.

48. *Missionary Magazine and Chronicle Relating Chiefly to the Missions of the London Missionary Society* (1836–37), p. iv, discussed the advantages of separate publications. Baptist juvenile magazines are described in Taylor, *op. cit.* (1977–78), pp. 60 and 68. The Wesleyan *Cottager's Friend*, which was aimed at the young, contained several pages of 'missionary facts and anecdotes' as did many of the other children's papers. See also MS Minute Books, Book Committee, 18 October 1836 and 8 November 1842. By the 1850s most of the major missionary societies had monthly magazines for adults and children.

49. For Baptist and Congregational Home Missionary Societies see my article 'Popular Religion and Social Reform: A study of revivalism and teetotalism,' *Journal of Religious History*, 10 (1978–79), pp. 286–91; and Taylor, *op. cit.* (1977–78), pp. 59–61.

50. *City Missionary Magazine* (1836 to date); J. M. Weylland, *These fifty years: Being the jubilee volume of the London City Mission* (1884); J. Campbell, *Memoirs of David Nasmith* (1844), pp. 313–68. Other cities besides London had their own magazines by the 1840s.

51. See, for example, the *Revivalist* (1832–44), and Billington, *op. cit.* (1978–79).

52. There is a very extensive literature of this kind, see, for example, the *Cottager Magazine* (1811–47); the *Friendly Visitor* (1824–1912); the Wesleyan *Cottager's Friend* (1837–45); and the High Anglican *Cottager's Monthly Visitor* (1821–56). For background to some of the literature see P. R. Mountjoy, 'The working class press and working class conservatism,' in G. Boyce, J. Curran, and P. Wingate (eds.), *Newspaper history from the seventeenth century to the present day* (London: Constable/Sage 1978).

53. *Youth's Magazine or Evangelical Miscellany* (1805–67); *Youth's Instructor (1817–55);* MS Minute Books, Book Committee, 18 January 1827 and 7 May 1855, show the print run of the *Youth's Instructor* declining from 12,250 to 3,500. For readership, see J. R. Gregory (ed.), *Benjamin Gregory, D.D. autobiographical recollections . . .* (London: Hodder and Stoughton, 1903), pp. 13, 33, 118, and 389.

54. *Child's Companion* (1824 to date); W. Jones, *The Jubilee memorial of the Religious Tract*

Society (1850), pp. 134–35. The United Society for Christian Literature had MS Minute Books and other material which throw light on the working of the Religious Tract Society. Also see *Child's Magazine,* (1824–45); and MS Minute Books, Book Room Committee, 10 April 1834.

55. Shaw, *op. cit.* (1965), p. 49; D. A. Beckerlegge, 'Bibliography of the Bible Christians,' *Proceedings of the Wesley Historical Society* 38 (1965–66): 46; Kendall, *op. cit.* (see note 23), 2 : 10–12. See *Primitive Methodist Magazine* 3 (1852) for a circulation figure of 4,000 for the *Child's Magazine* in the early 1840s. Also see Packer, *op. cit.* (1847), p. 93; Taylor, *op. cit.*, (1977–78), pp. 50–60.

56. This is based on files of the *Child's Companion,* the *Child's Magazine,* and *Baptist Children's Magazine.*

57. The *Children's Friend* (Kirby Lonsdale, 1824–1930); and for Carus Wilson see Mountjoy, in Boyce, Curran, and Wingate *op.cit.* (1978) and W. K. L. Clarke, *Eighteenth-century piety* (London: S.P.C.K., 1944), pp. 135–37. For a typical hyper-Calvinist child's magazine see the *Little Gleaner* (1854–94).

58. T. W. Laqueur, *Religion and respectability: Sunday schools and working class culture, 1780–1850* (New Haven: Yale University Press, 1976), pp. 116–17, indicates the range of teachers' magazines, though his comments on the general religious press and circulations are suspect. The Wesleyan Book Room circulated the unofficial *The Catechumen Reporter sabbath-school teacher's guide* from 1840 and eventually bought it out in order to publish its own Sunday school magazine. See MS Minute Books, Book Committee, 3 November 1856; and A. M. McAuley, *Extracts and outlines of . . . Book Room affairs* (privately printed, n.d.), p. 8, for a critical history of this event. For local preachers' magazines see, for example, the short-lived *Primitive Methodist Preacher's Magazine* (1827–32), and the much more successful *Local Preacher's Magazine* (1851 to date), which circulated among the Wesleyans. Evangelical women had their *Christian Lady's Magazine* (1834–49), edited by Charlotte Elizabeth Tonna, but lack of space prohibits discussion of the religious press for women here. For a brief introduction to Mrs. Tonna see E. Moers, *Literary women* (London: W. H. Allen, 1977), pp. 24–26 and 316.

59. *Philanthropic Gazette* (1817–23); the *Catholic Advocate of Civil and Religious Liberty* (1820–21).

60. The *Truth Teller,* 11 February 1825. For Bible Christian and Primitive Methodist newspapers, see the *Western Herald* (1837); Shaw, *op.cit.* (1965), p. 51; *Primitive Standard* (1853–54).

61. The *Record,* (1828–1923); G. R. Balleine, *A history of the Evangelical party in the Church of England* (London: Church Book Room Press, 1951), pp. 162–63; *A biographical sketch of Alexander Haldane,* (London: Spottiswoode and Co., 1882); *The Watchman* (1835–84); W. R. Ward (ed.), *Early Victorian Methodism: the correspondence of Jabez Bunting,* 1830–1858 (Oxford: at the University Press for the University of Durham, 1976), is a convenient introduction to the background of the paper.

62. W. S. Tarrant, 'Some chapters in the story of the *Inquirer,*' *Transactions of the Unitarian Historical Society* 4 (1927–30): 35–44; R. H. Tener, 'R. Hutton's editorial career 1, the *Inquirer,*' *Victorian Periodicals Newsletter* 7 (1974): 9–10; Conder, *op.cit.* (1857), p. 273; the *Watchman,* 7 January 1835.

63. Tarrant, *op.cit.* (1927–30), pp. 37–38; Balleine, *op.cit.* (1951), p. 162; the *Tablet,* 19 February 1881.

64. Conder, *op.cit.* (1857), p. 273; A. Miall, *Life of Edward Miall* (1884); B. A. Smith, *Dean Church: The Anglican response to Newman* (Oxford: at the University Press, 1958), pp. 74–81; Tarrant, *op.cit.* (1927–30), pp. 39–40.

65. Conder, *op.cit.* (1857), p. 273; C. Binfield, *So down to prayers: Studies in English Nonconformity, 1780–1920* (London: Dent, 1977), p. 110; the *Inquirer,* 3 September 1842. Circulation figures which indicate a decline for these religious newspapers by the 1860s are given in A. Ellegard, 'Readership of the periodical press in mid-Victorian Britain,' *Victorian Periodicals Newsletter,* no. 13 (1971), pp. 3–22.

66. Tarrant, *op.cit.* (1927–30), p. 36; the *Primitive Standard,* 1 October 1953.

67. Ward, *op.cit.* (1972), pp. 20, 32–33, 128–29, 168, 398; Benjamin Gregory, *Sidelights on the conflicts of Methodism* (1899), pp. 129–32; D. A. Gowland, *Methodist secessions: The origins of Free Methodism in three Lancashire towns: Manchester, Rochdale, Liverpool* (Manchester: Cheetham Society, 1979), pp. 32–33; R. Currie, *Methodism divided: A study in the sociology of ecumenicalism* (London: Faber, 1968), p. 67.

68. *Wesleyan Times* (1849–67); the *Western Herald* (1837); *Primitive Standard* (1853–54).

69. The *Patriot* (1832–66); the *Nonconformist* (1841–84); the *Inquirer* (1842 to date).

70. The *Nonconformist* and its editor Miall have received much attention, see Binfield, *op.cit.* (1977), pp. 101–24 and sources cited pp. 265–66; M. C. Haines, 'The Nonconformists and the Nonconformist periodical press in mid-nineteenth century England' (Ph.D. thesis, University of Indiana, 1966); and for American connections see L. Billington, 'Some connections between Britain and American reform movements, 1830–60' (M.Phil. thesis, University of Bristol, 1966), pp. 193–351.

71. The *Guardian* (1846 to date), was the more popular alternative to the *Record.* For the Catholic press, in addition to the sources already cited see J. J. Dwyer, 'The Catholic press 1850–1950,' in G. A. Beck (ed.), *The English Catholics, 1850–1950* (London: Burns Oates, 1950), pp. 475–514.

72. The *Watchman,* 7 January 1835 and 15 April 1835; The *Inquirer,* 18 November 1843; Dwyer, in Beck *op.cit.* (1950), p. 483.

73. *Ecclesiastical Gazette* (1838–1900). Issues cited here after 14 July 1846 and 13 June 1848. See also Clarke, *op.cit.* (1944), pp. 146–50.

74. Anti-Catholic titles include the *Protestant Journal,* the *Protestant Magazine, British Protestant,* the *Bulwark of the Reformation Journal,* and the *Bristol Protestant.* There were many more, especially at a local level. The *Record* was also active in this field; see S. Gilley, 'Protestant London, No-Popery and the Irish poor,' *Recusant History* 10 (1970): 210–30, and 11 (1971): 21–46.

75. Bibliographical details in Gillow, *op.cit.* (1895–1900), 1: 49–50. I have examined the *London and Dublin Orthodox Journal* (1835–42), and the *Weekly and Monthly Orthodox* (1849), both published by Andrews and his family.

76. Gillow, *op.cit.* (1845–1900), 2: 89; the *Tablet,* 12 and 19 February 1881.

77. The *Dublin Review* and the *Rambler* are both well known to scholars. The Nonconformist *British Quarterly Review* is examined in F. P. Unrich, 'A historical study of Robert Vaughan and his views . . . as reflected in the *British Quarterly Review*' (Ph.D. thesis, University of Missouri, 1962). Haines, *op.cit.* (1906), has some discussion of the Wesleyan 'serious' quarterly, the *London Quarterly Review,* which never attracted a wide audience. See also W. Strawson, 'The *London Quarterly* and the *Holborn Review* 1953–1968,' *Church Quarterly* 1 (1968): 11–52.

78. The *Friend* (1843 to date), and the more liberal *British Friend* (1843–1913), are the key periodicals. The Moravians had the short-lived *Moravian Magazine* (1854), and later the *Messenger* (1864 to the 1890s[?]).

79. The *Watchman's Lantern* (Liverpool, 1833–35); the *Illuminator* (Liverpool, 1835–36); Gowland, *op.cit.* (1979), p. 96; MS Minute Books, Book Committee, 23 June 1835 to 25 April 1836; the *Wesleyan Protestant Methodist Magazine* (Leeds, 1829–34); the *Wesleyan Methodist Association Magazine* (1838–57).

80. The *Wesley Banner and Revival Record* (1849–54); the *Wesleyan and Christian Record* (1846–48); *Wesleyan Vindicator and Constitutional Methodist* (1850–57); *Wesleyan Methodist Penny Magazine (1851–52); Wesleyan Review and Evangelical Record* (1850–51); *United Methodist Free Church Magazine* (1858–91). D. A. Beckerlegge, *The United Methodist Free Churches: A study in freedom* (London: Epworth Press, 1957), places the more important of the above journals in context. For other Dissidents and their magazine see W. H. Jones, *History of the Wesleyan Reform Union* (London: Epworth Press, 1952).

81. *Evangelical Reformer and Young Men's Guide* (1837–39) and the *Christian* (1845–47) were Barker's most important periodicals in his religious phase. The latter contains the earliest

version of his autobiography. For the Primitive Methodist schismatics and their periodicals see Billington, *op.cit.* (1978–79), pp. 278–81; and the *Original Methodists' Record* (1850 to the 1860s[?]).

82. In addition to the *Gospel Magazine,* the *Spiritual Magazine* ran from 1825 to 1852 and the same publisher issued *Zion's Trumpet, or The Penny Spiritual Magazine* (1834–68). There was also the curious *Spiritual Wrestler* (1847–54). See also P. Scott, '*Zion's Trumpet:* Evangelical enterprise and rivalry, 1833–35,' *Victorian Studies* 13 (1969): 119–203.

83. P. Toon, *The emergence of hyper-Calvinism in English Nonconformity* (London: Olive Tree Press, 1967), provides a background. Much work has been done at a local level; see, for example, G. A. Weston, 'The Baptists of North West England 1750–1850' (Ph.D. thesis, University of Sheffield, 1969), pp. 119–30; and A. J. Klaiber, *The story of the Suffolk Baptists* (London: Kingsgate Press, 1931), pp. 128–30. One group is covered in outline in A. F. Paul, *Historical sketch of the Gospel Standard Baptists* (Congdon, Surrey: C. J. Farncombe and Co, n.d.), but the best sources are the magazines themselves and numerous biographies and autobiographies.

84. Bibliographical details are provided in Taylor, *op.cit.* (1977–78), pp. 63–73.

85. An amusing outsider's view of this milieu can be found in C. M. Davies, *Unorthodox London and phases of religious life in the metropolis* (1875), pp. 117–34.

86. The *Primitive Communionist,* then the *Primitive Church Magazine,* (1838–65), is the best known of the less rigid Strict Baptist journals. For details see Taylor, *op.cit.* (1977–78), p. 66. Spurgeon commenced *The sword and the trowel: A record of combat with sin and labour for the Lord* in 1865.

87. The *Gospel Standard* published a supplement throughout the 1860s which included sermons, poetry, obituaries, and advertisements. These throw light on the economic and social background of the sect. From first to last they also include advertisements for eighteenth- and early nineteenth-century Calvinist periodicals, including Allen's *Spiritual Magazine* and Toplady's *Gospel Magazine.*

88. *Latter Day Saints Millennial Star* (Liverpool, 1840–1944); R. L. Evans, *A century of Mormonism in Great Britain* (Salt Lake City, The Deseret News Press, 1937); P. A. M. Taylor, *Expectations westward: the Mormons and the emigration of their British converts* (Ithaca, New York: Cornell University Press, 1965).

89. L. Billington, 'The Churches of Christ in Britain: A study in nineteenth-century sectarianism,' *Journal of Religious History* 8 (1974): 21–48, indicates their periodicals. The Associated Christadelphians published the *Ambassador of the Coming Age* (Birmingham, 1864–68), then the *Christadelphian.* See R. Roberts, *Dr. Thomas: His life and work* (Birmingham,: R. Roberts 1925), for the key figures. On millenarian movements see L. Billington, 'The Millerite Adventists in Great Britain, 1840–1850,' *Journal of American Studies* 1 (1967): 191–212; and J. F. C. Harrison, *The second coming: Popular millenarianism 1780–1850* (London: Routledge and Kegan Paul, 1979).

90. Lack of space prohibits a full discussion but key periodicals are indicated in P. E. Shaw, *The Catholic Apostolic Church sometimes called Irvingite: A historical study* (New York,: Kings Crown Press, 1946), pp. 74–75; and R. Coad, *A history of the Brethren movements* (London: Paternoster Press 1968), pp. 67, 183, and passim.

91. R. K. Webb, *The British working class reader, 1790–1848: Literary and social tension* (London: George Allen and Unwin, 1955), pp. 60–82; R. D. Altick, *The English common reader: A social history of the mass reading public 1800–1900* (London and Chicago: University of Chicago Press, 1957); V. E. Neuberg, *Popular literature: A history and guide* (Harmondsworth: Penguin, 1977), pp. 193–206. For the appeal of the new magazines see, for example, A. Rushton, *My life as farmer's boy, factory hand, teacher and preacher* (Manchester: S. Clarke, 1909), pp. 70–71; and G. Eayrs, *William John Townsend, D.D., Methodist preacher, Free Church leader* (London: Andrew Crombie, 1916), p. 22.

92. Altick, *op.cit.* (1957), is unreliable on the *Family Herald* which commenced in 1842. A

better account, but concerned with very specific themes, is S. Mitchell, 'Forgotten woman of the period: penny weekly family magazines of the 1840s and 1850s,' in M. Vicinus (ed.), *A widening sphere: Changing roles of Victorian women* (Bloomington: Indiana University Press, 1980), pp. 29, 51.

93. T. Pearson, *Infidelity: Its aspects, causes and agencies* (1863), p. 268. Originally published 1853.

94. Leicester Domestic Mission, *5th Annual Report* (Leicester, 1850).

95. 'New and cheap forms of literature,' *Eclectic Review* (1845), pp. 74–78; *Primitive Methodist Magazine* (1843), pp. iii–iv; 'Cheap literature,' *British Quarterly Review* (1859), pp. 313–45; Pearson, *op.cit.* (1863), pp. 252–73.

96. Webb, *op.cit.* (1955), pp. 73–78; *Saturday Magazine* (1853–54).

97. Jones, *op.cit.*, (1854), p. 135; *Weekly Visitor* (1833–36), priced ½d.

98. *Christian's Penny Magazine* (1848), the preface indicated that a trust fund enabled a large free distribution to be undertaken.

99. Taylor, *op.cit.* (1977–78), pp. 65–72 describes many of the cheap Baptist magazines. The *Tablet,* 26 February 1881, summarizes the Catholic cheap press.

100. *Zion's Trumpet* (1834), pp. iii–iv, indicates a circulation of 2,438 copies. *Church of England Magazine* (1836–75).

101. *Cottager's Friend* (1837–45), then the *Christian Miscellany* (1846–1900). MS Minute Book, Book Room Committee, 11 April 1837, indicates a print run of 36,000, and 14 July 1857 shows the *Christian Miscellany* selling 40,000 copies, when the combined sales of the shilling and sixpenny magazines were only 7,000.

102. MS Minute Books, Book Room Committee, are the best source for the Wesleyans. In spite of revisions the sales of the more expensive magazines declined. F. J. Jobson, MS Memo of Book Room Affairs, cited in note 19 above, claimed that the total periodical sales were still high but admitted that it was difficult to compete with the nondenominational press. F. Baker, 'John Flesher and the Bemersley Book Room,' *Proceedings of the Wesley Historical Society* 30 (1956): 171–78, reproduces a key document concerning the Primitives' move to London, but their circulation problems occurred later. See J. Atkinson, *Life of Rev. Colin C. McKechnie* (1898), p. 220, for the low point to which the magazines had sunk by the early 1870s because of commercial competitors.

103. *Christian Witness* (1844), pp. v–viii and 44; R. Ferguson and A. Morton Brown, *Life and labours of John Campbell, D.D.* (1867), pp. 205–227 and 363–405; Peel, *op.cit.* (1931), pp. 222–35.

104. Taylor, *op.cit.* (1977–78), pp. 67–75; K. R. Short, 'Benjamin Evans, D.D. and the radical press, 1826–1871,' *Baptist Quarterly* 19 (1962): 243–52.

105. J. A. Wallace, *Lessons from the life of the late James Nisbet, publisher . . .* (Edinburgh, 1867); Taylor, *op.cit.* (1977–78), pp. 64–76.

106. Jones, *op.cit.*, pp. 135–36.

107. G. Hewitt, *Let the people read: A short history of the United Society for Christian Literature* (London: United Society for Christian literature, 1949), pp. 50–51; *Leisure Hour* (1852–1905); *Sunday at Home* (1853–1940).

108. S. N. Smith, *The house of Cassell, 1848–1958* (London: Cassell, 1958); 'Cheap literature,' *British Quarterly Review* (1859), p. 344; *Bible Christian Magazine* (1861), p. 393; *Primitive Methodist Magazine* (1862), p. 623. P. Scott, 'Victorian religious periodicals: Fragments that remain,' in D. Baker (ed.), *Studies in church history* 11 (1975): 325–29.

109. *Good Words* (Edinburgh, 1860–1906); the *Quiver* (1866–?); the *Hive* (1868–?"); *Our Own Fireside* (1864–1905); *Contemporary Review* (1872), pp. 291–390; D. Macleod, *Memoir of Norman Macleod* (1876), 2 vols; D. K. Guthrie and C. J. Guthrie, *Autobiography of Thomas Guthrie, D.D. and memoir* (1896), pp. 710–14.

110. *Sunday Magazine* (1864–1906); the *Churchmen's Family Magazine* (1863–73); the *Christian Treasury* (Edinburgh, 1845–96); I. F. Mayo, *Recollections . . .* (London: John Murray, 1910), pp. 78–150. Miss Mayo contributed to most of the new popular magazines.

111. Gillow, *op.cit.* (1895–1900), 4, pp. 298–301.

112. Gregory, *op.cit.* (1903), pp. 424–30; MS Minute Books, Book Room Committee, 5 April 1869, and following entries; Atkinson, *op.cit.* (1898), pp. 220–24.

113. *"Good Words": the theology of its editor and some of its contributors reported from the "Record" newspaper* (1863); *An experience of the "Record" newspaper in its treatment of "Good Words"* (1863); Mayo, *op.cit.* (1910), p. 145.

114. P. G. Scott, 'Richard Cope Morgan: religious periodicals and the Pontifex factor,' *Victorian Periodicals Newsletter,* no. 16 (1972), pp. 1–14.

115. *Revival Advocate* (1858–59); the *Revivalist* (1853–64); *Messenger of Life* (1859–60); *East London Evangelist,* then *Christian Mission Magazine* (1868–79).

116. Scott, *op.cit.* (1972).

117. See, for example, *Ragged School Union Magazine* (1849–75); *Ragged School Children's Magazine,* then *Our Children's Magazine* (1850–68); the *Cabman* (1874–76); the *Christian Sentinel, or Soldier's Magazine* (1857–69).

118. Ferguson and Brown, *op.cit.* (1867), pp. 278–405; J. Luke, *Sketches of the life and character of Thomas Thompson* (1868), pp. 205–10; S. T. Porter, *Lecture on the ecclesiastical system of the Independents* (1856), pp. 179–84.

119. Taylor, *op.cit.* (1977–78), pp. 72–73; Payne, *op.cit.* (1950), p. 93; T. H. Darlow, *William Robertson Nicholl* (London: Hodder and Stoughton, 1925), p. 61.

120. Darlow, *op.cit.* (1925), pp. 58–61; A. Porritt, *The best I remember,* (London: Cassell and Co., 1922); *Christian World* (1857–1961).

121. See, for example, the *Dial* (1860–64), which merged with the antiwar *Morning Star* and was promoted by David Thomas. (Information supplied by Dr Alan Lee, late of the University of Hull.) Thomas was already well known as editor of the *Homilist* (1852–92), a journal of sermons and exegesis. Samuel Morley opposed the *Morning Star* project and this newspaper died in 1869, see E. Hodder, *Life of Samuel Morley* (1887), pp. 243–46; Darlow, *op.cit.* (1925), p. 59. See Taylor, *op.cit.* (1977–78), p. 78, for the penny weekly *Christian Cabinet,* to which Spurgeon was a contributor.

122. Darlow, *op.cit.* (1925), p. 59; the *Christian Age* (1871–1917). The subtitle was *Light from across the Water.*

123. MS Minute Books, Book Room Committee, 7 November 1859 to 16 February 1860.

124. T. McCullah, *Sir William McArthur K.C.M.G.* (1891), pp. 82–84.

125. The *Methodist Recorder* (1861 to date). Ellegard, *op. cit.* (1971), p. 7 suggests a circulation of 20,000 by 1865.

126. The *Primitive Methodist* (1868–1905).

127. Beck, *op.cit.* (1950), pp. 506–97; Canon Bennett, *Father Nugent of Liverpool* (Liverpool Children's Protection Society, 1949), pp. 69–77; Darlow, *op.cit.* (1925), pp. 63–64; Balleine, *op.cit.* (1951), p. 215.

128. Darlow, *op.cit.* (1925), p. 61.

CHAPTER 6. CHILDREN AND THE PRESS, 1866–1914

1. *Child's Companion.* Quoted in M. Lang, 'Scenes from small worlds: the child, the family and society in selected children's periodicals of the 1870s (Ph.D. thesis, University of Leicester, 1980), p. 109.

2. *Girl's Own Paper,* 13 August 1887, p. 736.

3. Discussed in E. S. Turner, *Boys will be boys* (London: Michael Joseph, 1957), pp. 97–98; and P. A. Dunae, 'Penny dreadfuls: Late nineteenth century boys' literature and crime,' *Victorian Studies* 22 (1979): 133–50.

4. E. G. Salmon, 'The magazines,' in *Juvenile literature as it is* (1888), cites a variety of examples of crimes allegedly occasioned by the reading of penny dreadfuls.

5. B. G. Johns, 'The literature of the streets,' *Quarterly Review* 165 (1887): 40–65.

6. M. K. Ashby, *Joseph Ashby of Tysoe* (Cambridge: at the University Press, 1961), p. 242.

7. Discussed in Turner, *op.cit* (1951), p. 69; and S. Egoff, *Children's periodicals of the nineteenth century* (London: Library Association 1951), p. 19.

8. R. Rollington, *A brief history of boys' journals; with interesting facts about the writers of boys' stories* (Leicester: H. Simpson, 1913).

9. *Young Briton's Journal,* 1, 16 June 1888.

10. 'What people read: The growth of magazine and periodical literature,' *Publishers' Circular: Newsagents' Chronicle Supplement,* 27 November 1897, p. 8; and 'On cheap periodicals,' *Publishers' Circular,* 22 November 1898, p. 479.

11. Editorial *Boy's Friend,* 1 January 1895, p. 16. Among the characters cited below Billy Bunter is perhaps the most enduring. Stout and bespectacled, Bunter figured in a series of adventures at Greyfriars an English private school. For his impact on the English imagination see George Orwell, "Boys' Weeklies" in *Inside the whole and other essays* (London: Victor Gollancz, 1940) and for recent manifestations of continuing interest, David Green, *A White Man's Burden: the early adventures of Bunter Sahib* (London: Hodder and Stoughton, 1985) and David Hughes, *But for Bunter* (London: Heinemann, 1985).

12. L. James, 'Tom Brown's imperialist sons,' *Victorian Studies* 17 (1973): 89–99.

13. *Every Boy's Journal,* 1, 22 April 1884, p. 16.

14. G. Sturt, *A small boy in the sixties* (Cambridge: at the University Press, 1927), p. 3.

15. F. Gordon Roe, *The Victorian child* (London: Phoenix House, 1959), p. 100.

16. Quoted in P. Dunae, 'The Boy's Own Paper: Origin and editorial Policies,' *Private library,* 2d series, 9 (1976): 136.

17. J. W. Robertson Scott, *The day before yesterday* (London: Methuen and Co., 1951), p. 193.

18. J. Middleton Murry, *Between two worlds: An autobiography* (London: Jonathan Cape, 1935), p. 36.

19. *Union Jack,* (1880), 1,40 (1880), p. 640.

20. C. E. B. Russell, *Manchester Boys: Sketches of Manchester lads at work and play* (Manchester: at the University Press, 1905), pp. 107–8.

21. E. G. Salmon, *op. cit.* (1888), pp. 197–99.

22. A. Pollock, *Portrait of my Victorian youth* (London: Johnson, 1971), p. 54.

23. *Boy's Own Paper,* 24 November 1894, p. 28.

24. S. Nowell-Smith, *The house of Cassell* (London: Cassell, 1957), p. 128.

25. M. Hughes, *A London family* (London: Oxford University Press, 1946), p. 129.

26. Diana Dixon, 'English juvenile periodicals, 1870–1914: A bibliographical analysis,' (M.Phil. thesis, University of Leicester, 1978), p. 4.

27. A. Uttley, *Ambush of young days* (London: Faber & Faber, 1951), p. 165.

28. A. Bott (ed.), *Our mothers* (London: Victor Gollancz, 1932), p. 65.

29. W. Lister, 'A new year's letter for children,' *Child's Friend* 2 (1872): 3.

30. *Catholic Junior,* 1, 1 July 1913.

31. L. L. Shiman, 'The Band of Hope Movement: Respectable recreation for working class children,' *Victorian Studies* 17 (1973): 49–74.

32. *Little Wideawake* (1899).

33. *Aunt Judy's Magazine,* January 1892, pp. 189–92.

34. *Girl's Own Paper,*25 August 1888, p. 768.

35. The *Young Man,* November 1892, p. 369.

36. M. Hughes, *op. cit.* (1946), p. 130.

37. F. Gordon Roe, *op.cit.* (1959), pp. 101–2.

38. Lady Bell, *At the works: A study of a manufacturing town* (London: Edward Arnold, 1907), p. 145.

39. E. Saintsbury, *The world of Alison Uttley: A biography* (London: Howard Baker, 1980), p. 105.

40. *Sons of Britannia,* 2, 14 February 1893, p. 336.

41. *Boy's Graphic,* 2, 18 October 1890, p. 111.

42. *Boys of England,* 1, 25 November 1866, p. 16.
43. *Lads of the Village* 1 (1874): 76.
44. *Boy's World,* 1, 30 March 1905, p. 16.
45. *Bull's Eye* 1 (1898): 16.

CHAPTER 7. ADVERTISING AND EDITORIAL INTEGRITY IN THE NINETEENTH CENTURY

1. The duty was levied at the following rates:
 1800 3s.0d. (from 1789)
 1815 3s.6d.
 1833 1s.6d.
 1853 abolished.
2. For further details of these calculations see T R Nevett, 'The Development of Commercial Advertising, 1800–1914' (Ph.D. thesis, University of London, 1979), pp. 15–22.
3. 'R.K.D.', *Letter to Viscount Lord Althorp* (1831), pp. 2–3.
4. D. Dunbar, 'Estimates of Total Advertising Expenditure in the United Kingdom before 1948', *Journal of Advertising History,* 1 (1977), pp. 9–11.
5. D. Stuart, 'Anecdotes of Coleridge and of London Newspapers', *Gentleman's Magazine,* 10 (1838), p. 25.
6. Charles Knight, *The Newspaper Stamp and the Duty on Paper* (1836), pp. 19–20.
7. J. R. McCulloch, 'Newspapers' in *Dictionary of Commerce* (2nd edition, 1834), p. 828.
8. Charles Mitchell, *Newspaper Press Directory* (1846) p. 327.
9. J. Savage, *An Account of the London Daily Newspapers* (?1812), p. 14.
10. *Political Register,* 4th March 1809, cols. 347–348.
11. I. Asquith, 'James Perry and the Morning Chronicle, 1790–1821' (Ph.D. thesis, University of London, 1973), p. 356.
12. 'Inquiry into the revenue arising in Ireland &c,' *House of Commons Accounts and Papers,* 10 (1826), p. 441. Evidence of Thomas Gwynne.
13. *Newcastle Chronicle,* 2 July 1825. The copy in the British Library shows the paragraph marked in ink by a Stamp Office clerk.
14. 'Ingenious puffing,' the *Newspaper Press,* reprinted from *Leader,* 1 April 1868.
15. H. J. Palmer, 'The march of the advertiser,' *Nineteenth Century* (January 1897), pp. 135–41.
16. *Ibid.,* January 1889, p. 2.
17. Ibid., March 1888, p. 15.
18. *The ruinous tendency of auctioneering* (1812).
19. 'A paper on puffing,' *Ainsworth's Magazine* 2 (1842): 42–44.
20. T. B. Macaulay, 'Robert Montgomery's "Poems,"' *Edinburgh Review* 101 (April 1830): 196–97.
21. J. Livesey, '"Deception" Again,' *Moral Reformer* 3 (1833).
22. *Publishers' Circular,* August 1878, p. 22.
23. 'One who thinks aloud,' *The language of the walls* (Manchester, 1855), p. 91.
24. C. Barker, the *Charles Barker Records,* 25 March 1835, pp. 234–35.
25. *Publishers' Circular,* March 1888, p. 15.
26. E. Street, 'Advertising,' *Journal of the Royal Society of Arts* 61 (24 January 1913): 247–57.
27. *Publishers' Circular,* March 1888, p. 17.
28. *Advertising News,* 8 April 1904.
29. T. Russell, *Commercial advertising* (six lectures given at the London School of Economics, 1919—2d ed., 1925).
30. *Publishers' Circular,* March 1875, p. 10.

31. Ibid., December 1896, pp. 3–4.
32. Russell, *op.cit.* (1925), p. 25.
33. T. Russell, *Advertising and advertisements* (1924), p. 101.
34. Letter dated 11 November 1902 in the Archives of *The Times.*
35. In the Archives of *The Times.*
36. Russell, *op.cit.* (1925), p. 288.
37. Moberly Bell, *op.cit.*
38. Mitchell, *op.cit.* (1846), p. 326.
39. Street, *op.cit.* (1913).
40. C. Moran, *The business of advertising* (London: Methuen and Co., 1905), p. 35.
41. *Publishers' Circular,* December 1897, p. 7.

CHAPTER 8. SPORTING NEWS, 1860–1914

1. J. W. Horsley, 'Our sporting Zadkiels,' the *New Review* 9 (November 1893): 521.
2. R. H. Gretton, *A modern history of the English people, 1880–1922* (London: Martin Secker, 1930), p. 214; H. R. Fox-Bourne, *English newspapers,* 2 (1887), pp. 322–31; J. Dawson, *Practical journalism* (1885), p. 80. See also A. J. Lee, *The origins of the popular press, 1855–1914* (London: Croom Helm, 1976), pp. 127–28.
3. J. Grant, *History of the newspaper press,* 3 (1872), p. 128. The *Weekly Dispatch* also gave some prominence to sporting news in the early nineteenth century.
4. *Bell's Life,* 29 March 1886.
5. Ibid., 13 January 1822. By June 1822 the paper's title had been changed to *Bell's Life in London and Sporting Chronicle.*
6. *Sporting Life,* 28 May 1886. *Bell's Life,* 23 April 1859.
7. F. Boase, *Modern English biography,* 1, A–H (1892, 1965 ed.), col. 644.
8. 'Nimrod' was Charles James Apperley (1778–1843), the most eminent of hunting correspondents, who wrote for the *Sporting Magazine* from 1822–30. J. B. Booth, *Bits of character: a life of Henry Hall Dixon, 'The Druid'* (London: Hutchinson and Co., 1936), p. 45.
9. *Bell's Life,* 23 April 1859; *British Almanac* (1876), p. 78.
10. T. C. Sanders, 'The sporting press," *Saturday Review,* 9 February 1856, p. 275.
11. *Bell's Life,* 16 March 1872.
12. *Penny Bell's,* 13 April 1859.
13. *Sporting Life,* 18 May 1859.
14. *Penny Bell's,* 24 March 1859.
15. *Sporting Life,* 4 June 1859.
16. The observer was R. P. Watson, *Memoirs: a journalist's experience of mixed society* (1899), p. 343. The reporters who bought it were Buck and Greenwood, who both wrote the 'Hotspur' column in the *Daily Telegraph.* J. B. Booth, *Master and men: pink 'un yesterdays* (London: T. Werner Laurie, 1926), p. 77.
17. *Bell's Life,* 29 May 1886.
18. Dowling must have turned in his grave at these concessions to the new journalism. *Bell's Life,* 22 March 1884.
19. *Bell's Life,* 18 March 1885; Booth, *op. cit.* (1936), p. 77.
20. *Sporting Life,* 29 May 1886.
21. See W. Allison, *My kingdom for a horse* (London: Grant Richards, 1919), p. 344. Note the attempt by the Sporting League to discredit Burns and intervene politically against him in Battersea. W. Allison, *Memories of men and horses* (London: Grant Richards, 1922), pp. 308–10.
22. The *Sportsman,* 12 August 1865.
23. The *Sportsman* (from 1876), the *Sporting Chronicle* (from 1880), and the *Sporting Life* (from 1883).
24. *Sporting Life,* 13 June 1874.
25. For details see R. N. Rose, *The "Field" 1853–1953* (London: Michael Joseph, 1953).

26. Rose, *op. cit.* (1953), pp. 54–55.
27. Rose, *op. cit.* (1953), p. 133.
28. J. J. Bentley; see Anthony Mason, *Association football and English society, 1863–1915* (Brighton: Harvester Press, 1980), pp. 188–91.
29. See, for example, *Cricket* 17 December 1913.
30. *Daily Mail,* 11–16 May 1896.
31. *Daily Mail,* 22 September 1896.
32. See, for example, *Daily Mail,* 5, 7, 28 September 1896.
33. *Daily Herald,* 15 October 1913, for example.
34. The correspondent was G. H. West, whose obituary appeared in the paper on 7 October 1896, and whom *Cricket* called *The Times's* sporting editor. He also edited *Wisden Cricketers' Almanack,* (1880–86). *Wisden* is an annual compilation of statistics of reports concerned with cricketers and cricket matches. It first appeared under this title in 1870 and is still in publication. *Cricket* 15, 29 October 1886, p. 437.
35. See, for example, *Manchester Guardian,* 3, 6, 10, 13, 17, 20, 24, 27 January 1913. D. Ayerst, *Guardian, biography of a newspaper* (London: Collins, 1971) is dissappointingly uninformative on this side of the paper's activities.
36. *Mitchell's newspaper press directory* (1881), p. 40, and A. Wallis Myers, 'The Sunday newspaper world,' *Ludgate* 5 (January 1898): 325.
37. V. S. Berridge, 'Popular journalism and working-class attitudes: a study of *Reynolds's Newspaper, Lloyd's Weekly Newspaper* and the *Weekly Times* (Ph.D. thesis, University of London, 1976), pp. 141–42, 147.
38. It was bought by a group consisting of Emsley and Lascelles Carr, Charles Jackson, and George, later Lord, Riddell. The measurements are in columns.
39. It claimed it was the first. *Saturday Night,* 7 October 1882.
40. *Birmingham Weekly News,* 23 September 1882.
41. *Saturday Night,* 20 January 1883.
42. *Birmingham Telegram,* 24 July 1898.
43. *Blackburn Times,* 23 September 1883.
44. *Wolverhampton Express and Star,* 15 November 1884.
45. *Athletic News,* 23 January 1884.
46. Though speed could lead to mistakes. The London *Star* came out with the wrong result on Boat Race day in 1913. *Circulation Manager,* May 1913, p. 3.
47. Press Association *Evening Paper* circular, 7 December 1911.
48. *Bell's Life,* 4 January 1857. According to J. B. Booth, A. Feist, later editor of *Sporting Life,* took Ruff junior's place when he retired early, never to go near a racecourse again. Booth, *op. cit.* (1936), p. 77.
49. A photograph of the reporters' tent at the Canterbury Cricket Festival in 1871 contained, apart from King, representatives of only *Bell's,* the *Sporting Life,* the *Sportsman,* and the *Field; Cricket* 36, 11 April 1907, p. 41; the *Journalist,* 30 July 1898. See James D. Coldham, 'Some early cricket reporters,' in *The Journal of the Cricket Society* 10, no. 22 (Spring 1981): 42–46.
50. The Press Association was set up by provincial newspapers in order to privide a cheap and swift news service. See G. Scott, *Reporters anonymous* (London: Hutchinson, 1968), pp. 39, 123. On Ashley, see *Sporting Mirror* July–December 1881.
51. Booth, *op. cit.* (1936), p. 76.
52. J. C. Reid, *Buck and bruisers: Pierce Egan and Regency England* (London: Routledge and Kegan Paul, 1971), p. 92.
53. *Athletic News,* 19 March 1884.
54. *Athletic News,* 30 June 1890. B. Green (ed.), *Wisden Anthology, 1864–1900* (London: Queen Anne Press, 1976), p. 950.
55. The *Sportsman,* 14 April 1899.
56. B. Green (ed.), *Wisden Anthology, 1900–1940,* (London: Queen Anne Press, 1980), p. 827.

57. S. Galtry, *Memoirs of a racing journalist* (London: Hutchinson and Co., 1934), p. 289.

58. *Sheffield Daily Telegraph,* 9 March 1889.

59. Press Association *Report,* 38th Annual Meeting, 8 May 1908, p. 11.

60. Scott, *op. cit.* (1968), p. 127.

61. Press Association and Exchange Telegraph Company Joint Service, Football Season (1907–8), Letter to subscribers, 31 July 1907.

62. *Professional Footballers' Magazine,* 3, no. 12, November 1913.

63. *Bell's Life,* 31 October 1852. *Illustrated London News,* 13 November 1852. Boase, *op. cit.* (1965), 1, cols. 907–8.

64. *Sporting Life,* 8 July 1891.

65. See, for example, the *Sporting Life,* 28 March 1893. The 'Special Commissioner' on the *Sportsman* in the 1860s had also been an army vet. Allison, *op. cit.* (1919), p 254.

66. *Sporting Life,* 29 February 1888.

67. Watson, *op. cit.* (1899), pp. 23, 31, 40–44.

68. B. Darwin, *Green memories* (London: Hodder & Stoughton, 1928), p. 65; he admitted that even in 1928 he knew next to nothing about the technical side of journalism and rarely visited *The Times* office. See his *Pack clouds away* (London: Collins, 1941), p. 128.

69. *Sporting Life,* 28 March 1883.

70. See Wilson *op. cit.,* p. 169; V. A. S. Beanland, *Great games and great players ([London]: W. H. Allen, 1945), pp. 20–21, Watson op. cit.* (1899), p. 222.

71. Allison, *op. cit.* (1919), p. 60; J. D. Coldham, 'The Cockney sportsman,' in *The Journal of the Cricket Society* 9, no. 3 (Autumn 1979): pp. 35–6. I am grateful to Mr. Coldham for drawing my attention to his article.

72. *Sporting Times,* 11 February 1865.

73. On Egan, see Reid, *op. cit.* (1971).

74. *Bell's Life,* 11 January 1857.

75. Sanders, *op. cit.* (1856), p. 275.

76. B. Darwin, *Life is sweet, brother* (London: Collins, 1940), pp. 199–200.

77. W. H. Smith do have some records of the numbers of London sporting dailies purchased by their head office but it is not clear how reliable a guide to circulation these figures are. Letter to the author, 31 March 1981, from the archivist of W. H. Smith & Son Ltd.

78. 32,019 unstamped, 7,585 stamped. *Bell's Life,* 29 January 1860.

79. *Circulation Manager,* May 1914, gave 180,000 copies daily.

80. By 1913 the average net sale of the *Football Echo* in Sunderland was 37,840 or 800 more than that of its parent evening paper, the *Sunderland Daily Echo. Circulation Manager,* April 1914, pp. 22, 24.

81. *Athletic News,* 28 August 1893, 2 November 1896; *Circulation Manager,* May 1914, p. 18.

82. D. Wilkinson, *Rough roads* (London: Sampson Low & Co., 1912), p. 12.

83. Quoted in G. Jones 'Political and social factors in the advocacy of "free" libraries in the United Kingdom, 1801–1922 (Ph.D. thesis, University of Strathclyde, 1971), pp. 243–44.

84. *Bell's Life,* 16 March 1872.

85. *Bell's Life,* 29 May 1886.

86. *Sportsman,* 14 August 1915; *Parliamentary Papers* (hereafter PP), v (1902), Q786–87.

87. PP, v (1902), Q2853.

88. PP, v (1902), p. 449,

89. Darwin, *op. cit.* (1940), p. 218..

90. See the lament of one of them in *Westminster Review* 152 (1899): 656–64.

91. A letter to the *Athletic News,* 19 February 1876, made the point that a paper devoted to football would not only 'provide a valuable record of a grand and manly game . . . but would also enable small clubs, and particularly beginners to play the game more in accordance with specified rules, and so help to bring it nearer what our crack clubs desire to make it–i.e. a game of science. . . .' Note also the role of the *Referee* in formulating new rules for amateur boxing, Watson, *op. cit.* (1899), p. 108.

92. Galtrey, *op. cit.* (1934), p. 284.

93. PP, v (1902), Q2572–75.

94. Public Record Office, Cab. 28/84, Report on Revolutionary Organisations in the U.K. no. 13, 24 July 1919, ST 7790.

CHAPTER 9. IMPERIALISM, ILLUSTRATION AND THE *DAILY MAIL*, 1896–1914

1. C. Bolt, *Victorian attitudes to race* (London: Routledge and Kegan Paul, 1971), p. 5.

2. These ideas were further reinforced by B. Kidd, who in his *Social evolution* (1894) developed the thesis that a race becomes superior because it is willing to subordinate the interests of the individual to that of society. This idea was easily absorbed into the doctrines of imperialism.

3. F. Hardie, *The political influence of Queen Victoria, 1861–1901* (London: Frank Cass and Co., 1963), p 147.

4. R. Hyam, *Britain's imperial century, 1815–1914* (London: Batsford, 1976), p 31.

5. G. M. Young, *Victorian England: Portrait of an age* (Oxford: at the University Press, 1936), p 90.

6. When Gladstone died, part of his obituary notice included the intelligence that 'not even foreign caricaturists had seen fit to ever present him in repulsive aspect'; *Daily Mail,* 21 May 1898.

7. The *Daily Mail,* 2 July 1898, reported that it understood that the Corporation of Birmingham wished to acquire Mr. Chamberlain by Mr. Beerbohm.

8. *Daily Mail,* 16 September 1896.

9. Between 15 February 1896 and 4 May 1896 sixty-five experimental issues of the *Daily Mail* were printed. Harmsworth required these "dummy" editions to be produced with the same efficiency and have the same content as if they were actually to be put on sale the next morning.

10. There is in fact a tact in sentiment in Victorian painting with which it is rarely credited. Deep distress or strong emotion is seldom portrayed by agonized facial contortion.

11. The 'Trilby' theme obviously caught the imagination. R. Hill did a series of drawings for *Butterfly Magazine* which were illustrations to *Bab,* which plagiarized du Maurier's famous novel.

12. The *Daily Mail,* 6 January 1903, reported that when Chamberlain visited South Africa, transported with him on the *Good Hope* were no less than three hundred orchids.

13. There were ties between British and German universities. Milner, for example, completed his education in Germany.

14. The verdict was self-esteem and veneration, giving the Kaiser extraordinary—and perhaps misplaced—confidence in his own powers. *Daily Mail,* 18 November 1897.

15. Emmanuel Poire (1858–1909). The pseudonym meant lead pencil in Russian.

16. A. A. Milne declared, 'Harmsworth killed the penny dreadful by the simple process of producing a penny dreadfuller.' R. Pound and G. Harmsworth, *Northcliffe* (London: Cassell, 1959), p. 116. Harmsworth was in fact educated at the school owned by Milne's father.

17. *Daily Mail,* 3 May 1900.

18. H. W. Massingham relinquished his editorship of the *Daily Chronicle* at the end of 1899 because of his disagreement over imperial policy. He later edited the *Star* and always encouraged the use of line illustration.

19. *Morning Leader,* 31 January 1900.

20. *Daily Mail,* 9 September 1897.

21. *Daily Mail,* 6 May 1898.

22. *Daily Mail,* 5 January 1901.

23. "The Peace of Vereeniging," 31 May 1902.

24. Cecil Rhodes himself had observed that the 'Imperialism of the nineties had burst

itself out in the Mafeking bonfires.' J. Morris, *Heaven's command* (Harmondsworth: Penguin, 1979).

25. *Daily Mail,* 2 March 1896.

26. Goschen was the First Lord of the Admiralty at this time.

27. *Daily Mail,* 18 July 1898.

28. Published in 1903, ironically, the novel which described plans for an invasion of England was first thought of by Childers during the summer of 1897 at the same time as the Kaiser was conferring with Admiral von Tirpitz (head of the German Imperial Naval Office) on the very same subject. P. Kennedy, 'Riddle of the sands,' *The Times,* 3 January 1981.

29. *Daily Mail,* 18 June 1902.

30. *Daily Mail,* 19 November 1903.

31. He might have made himself marginally acceptable when he stated that he preferred British to German humor. His rival was Thomas Nast whose campaign against 'Boss' Tweed of Tammany Hall elicited a response the *Daily Mail* might well have noted. 'I don't care what they print about me,' Tweed protested, 'most of my constituents can't read anyway—but those damned pictures.' J. Geipel, *The cartoon* (Newton Abbot: David and Charles, 1972), p. 25.

32. William Kerridge Haselden (1872—1953) joined the *Daily Mirror* in 1904. In 1906 he began to contribute to *Punch,* and during the First World War he did a series of cartoons for the *Daily Mirror,* where in common with other British cartoonists he exaggerated the weasel quality of the Crown Prince. He is probably best known for his art deco caricatures of the twenties and thirties.

33. *Daily Mail,* 31 May 1904.

34. *Daily Mail,* 8 December 1903. Steevens was the *Mail's* star reporter. He died as war correspondent in the siege of Ladysmith.

35. Ferdinand Mount, 'Not quite the end of empire,' *Spectator,* 15 March 1980.

CHAPTER 10. CONTENT ANALYSIS AND HISTORICAL RESEARCH ON NEWSPAPERS

1. Quoted in B. Berelson, *Content analysis in communication research* (Glencoe, Illinois: Free Press, 1952), p. 15.

2. Ibid., p. 18.

3. T. Jeffery, 'Mass observation, part 1: The origins and development of mass observation,' *Bulletin of the society for the Social History of Medicine* 27 (1980): 8–12.

4. Q. D. Leavis, *Fiction and the reading public* (London: Chatto and Windus, 1932). For the Frankfurt School and mass culture, see J. Curran and J. Seaton, *Power without responsibility: The press and broadcasting in Britain* ([London]: Fontana, 1981), pp. 257–65.

5. *Royal Commission on the Press, 1947–1949. Investigations into the content of newspapers and their methods of presenting news in the period 1927–1947: Report presented to the Royal Commission by Mr. R. Silverman* (1949), pp. 238–359.

6. Cited in G. Philo, J. Hewitt, P. Beharrel, and H. Davis (members of the Glasgow University Media Group), *Really bad news* (London: Routledge and Kegan Paul, 1982), p. 7. See also Glasgow University Media Group, *Bad news* (London: Routledge and Kegan Paul, 1976); and idem, *More bad news* (London: Routledge and Kegan Paul, 1980).

7. J. D. Halloran, P. Elliott and G. Murdock, *Demonstrations and communications: A case study* (Harmondsworth: Penguin, 1970).

8. F. Balle, 'Les grands quotidiens français, sont-ils dépolitisés?' *Annales* (1968), pp. 296–334.

9. R. Williams, *Communications* (London: Chatto and Windus, 1966), pp. 89–90.

10. For some discussion of these issues, see Tony Bennett, 'Popular culture: Divided territory,' *Social History Society Newsletter* 6 (1981) pp. 5–6.

11. V. Berridge, 'Popular Sunday papers and mid-Victorian society,' in G. Boyce, J. Cur-

ran, and P. Wingate (eds.), *Newspaper history from the 17th Century to the present day* (London: Constable, 1978), pp. 247–64.

12. L. Galambos and B. Barrow-Spence, *The public image of big business in America, 1880–1940: A quantitative study in social change* (Baltimore: Johns Hopkins University Press, 1977).

13. H. A. Ellegard, *Darwin and the general reader* (Göteborg: Göteborg Universitets årsskrift, 1958).

14. D. McQuail, 'The influence and effects of mass media,' in J. Curran, M. Gurevitch, and J. Woollacott (eds.), *Mass communication and society* (London: Edward Arnold for the Open University Press, 1977), p. 74.

15. J. Westergaard, 'Power, class and the media,' in ibid., p. 111.

16. L. James, 'The trouble with Betsy: Periodicals and the common reader in mid-nineteenth century England,' in J. Shattock and M. Wolff (eds.), *The Victorian periodical press: Samplings and soundings* (Leicester: at the University Press, 1982), pp. 349–66.

17. A. C. H. Smith, with E. Immirzi and T. Blackwell, *Paper voices: The popular press and social change, 1935–1965* (London: Chatto and Windus, 1975).

18. For *Lloyd's* readers, see V. Berridge, *op cit.*, p. 249.

19. For details of the origin of the paper, see ibid., p. 253–54 and V. Berridge, 'Popular journalism and working class attitudes, 1854–86: A study of *Reynolds's Newspaper, Lloyd's Weekly Newspaper* and the *Weekly Times,*' (Ph.D. thesis, University of London, 1976), pp. 39–40. The content analysis which provides the percentage figures in the text is based on an analysis of all content in every tenth issue of *Reynolds's* and *Lloyd's* in every fourth year between 1854 and 1886. Column-inch and number counts were made. Some of the advertising data comes from a content analysis of a different sample of years. Tables illustrating the results of this research appear in volume 2 of my thesis.

20. J. Curran and J. Seaton, *op cit.* (1981), p. 54, sees *Reynolds's* readership as a combination of middle and working classes. However, there is no internal evidence or contemporary assessment to support this assertion.

21. For the *Northern Star* see J. Epstein, 'Feargus O'Connor and the *Northern Star,' International Review of Social History* 21 (1976): 51–97. Also, same author, *The Lion of Freedom: Feargus O'Connor and the Chartist Movement, 1832–1842* (London: Croom Helm, 1982).

22. J. Curran and J. Seaton, *op. cit.* (1981), p. 53, argues that regular features on friendly societies in *Reynolds's* were 'a ploy to attract advertising.' But average numbers of friendly society advertisements in the paper did not significantly increase until the late 1870s, and even then this increase was not maintained. Savings advertising in general declined from a peak of 12.5% of advertising material in 1854 to 2.1% in 1858 and did not rise (to 6.8%) again until 1878. See V. Berridge, *op. cit.* (thesis, 1976), 2, pp. 205–6.

23. See V. Berridge, *op. cit.* (thesis, 1976), pp. 217–31.

24. For 'Unitas' see *Reynolds's Miscellany,* 10 September 1859, p. 176.

25. *Reynolds's Newspaper,* 7 March 1886, p. 5, col. 1; 25 July 1886, p. 4, col. 7; 3 October 1886, p. 2, col. 7 and p. 4.

26. G. Best, *Mid-Victorian Britain* (London: Weidenfeld and Nicolson, 1971), pp. 200–201, also suggests that the leisure side of Victorian town life in this period had little class basis.

27. For example, reports of bouts between John Baldock and Jeremiah Regan and between Jim Mace and Joe Gos for the champion's belt and £200 a side. *Reynolds's,* 11 March 1866, and 20 May 1866.

28. *Reynolds's* carried advertisements in the fifties for 'metallic deep-toned pipes' and musical drinking glasses, e.g., *Reynolds's Newspaper,* 14 May 1854, p. 13, col. 3.

29. Hire purchase payment as a means of purchase was in fact first established in a legal case involving piano purchase, C. I. Walsh, "An Economic and Social History of the Pianoforte in Mid and Late Victorian Britain" (M.A. thesis, University of London, 1973), p. 38.

30. For example, *Reynolds's Newspaper,* 19 December 1858, p. 14, col. 2.

31. *Reynolds's Newspaper,* 18 April 1875, p. 7, col. 2.

32. *Reynolds's Newspaper,* 18 April 1875, p. 7, col. 1 even had one at 10s.6d ('the wonderful American novelty').

33. *Lloyd's Weekly Newspaper,* 18 May 1862, p. 6, col. 4.

34. On the Indian Mutiny, see *Reynolds's,* 16 June 1858, p. 1, col. 1.

35. For a more detailed analysis of patterns of reporting, see V. Berridge, *op. cit.* (thesis, 1976), 1, pp. 297–305.

36. *Reynolds's,* 25 July 1886, p. 4, col. 7.

37. There is a fuller discussion of this point in V. Berridge, *op. cit.* (1981), pp. 259–64, and in V. Berridge, 'The Language of popular and radical journalism: The case of *Reynolds's Newspaper,' Bulletin of the Society for the Study of Labour History* 44 (1982), pp. 6–7.

38. J. Curran and J. Seaton, *op. cit.,* p. 44.

39. *Reynold's,* 1 October 1854, p. 7.

40. See V. Berridge, *op. cit.* (thesis, 1976), 2, p. 295, for a similar analysis of social references in *Lloyd's* editorials. "Class" references in general were fewer, and there were no appeals to historical precedent, or attacks on the church and officeholders, as in *Reynold's.*

41. This point is expanded in V. Berridge, *op. cit.* (1982), pp. 6–7. I am grateful to Raphael Samuel for suggesting the point about popular theatre.

42. For example, M. McNeil, 'Medical theory and demographic concerns in early industrial England,' *Bulletin of the Society for the Social History of Medicine,* 25 (1979): 12–20, where the relationship between the power of the medical profession and the rise of statistical interest is examined. Medical demography, in this case, is shown to be part of the relationship between medicine and the lower classes at a period when health became identified with the ability to work.

43. Stuart Hall in his *Introduction* to Smith, Immirzi and Blackwell, *op. cit.* (1975), p. 15 assumes that content analysis cannot be used to penetrate the latent meanings of a text in this way. My analysis of *Reynolds's* and *Lloyd's* indicates that it can be useful even for aiming at some assessment of underlying perceptions and patterns of meaning, albeit in conjunction with literary presentation.

Select Bibliography

A select bibliography of modern secondary sources including books, articles, and theses with a direct bearing on the issues discussed in this volume.

Altick, R. D, *The English common reader: A social history of the mass reading public, 1800–1900.* Chicago and London: University of Chicago Press, 1957.

Aspinall, I. *Politics and the press.* London: Home and Van Thal, 1949.

Asquith, I. 'Advertising and the press in the late eighteenth and early nineteenth centuries: James Perry and the *Morning Chronicle,* 1790–1821.' *Historical Journal* 18 (1975): 703–24.

Bailey, P. *Leisure and class in Victorian England.* London: Routledge and Kegan Paul, 1978.

Berridge, V. S. 'Popular journalism and working class attitudes, 1854–86: A study of *Reynold's Newspaper, Lloyd's Weekly Newspaper* and the *Weekly Times.*' Ph.D. thesis, University of London, 1976.

Boyce, G., J. Curran, and P. Wingate (eds.). *Newspaper History: From the seventeenth century to the present day.* London: Constable/Sage, 1978.

Brewer, J. *Party ideology and popular politics at the accession of George III.* Cambridge: at the University Press, 1976.

Capp, B. *Astrology and the popular press: English almanacs, 1500–1800.* London: Faber, 1979.

Christie, I. R. *Myth and reality: Late eighteenth century British politics and other papers.* London: Macmillan, 1970.

Cranfield, G. A. *The development of the provincial newspaper, 1700–1760.* Oxford: Clarendon Press, 1962.

Cressy, D. *Literacy and the social order: Reading and writing in Tudor and Stuart England.* Cambridge: at the University Press, 1980.

Curran, J., and J. Seaton (eds.). *Power without responsibility: The Press and broadcasting in Britain.* [London]: Fontana, 1981.

Downie, J. A. *Robert Harley and the press.* Cambridge: at the University Press, 1980).

Ellyard, E. 'Readership of the periodical press: Mid-Victorian Britain.' *Victorian Periodicals Newsletter* 13 (1971): 5–22.

Elliott, B. B. *A history of English advertising.* London: Batsford, 1962.

Frank, J. *The beginnings of the English newspaper, 1620–1660.* Cambridge, Mass.: Harvard University Press, 1961.

Geifel, J. *The cartoon.* Newton Abbot: David and Charles. 1972.

Gibbs, G. C. 'Newspapers, Parliament and foreign policy in the age of Stanhope and

Walpole.' In *Mélanges offerts à G. Jacquemyns,* (Brussels: Université Libre de Bruxelles 1968), pp. 293–315.

Goldgar, B.A. *Walpole and the wits: The relation of politics to literature, 1722–1742.* Lincoln, Nebraska: Nebraska University Press, 1977.

Harris, M. 'The London newspaper press, 1725–1746.' Ph.D. thesis, University of London, 1973.

———. "Print and Politics in the Age of Walpole." In *Britain in the Age of Walpole,* ed. J. Black. London: Macmillan, 1984, pp. 189–210.

Harrison, B. '"A world of which we had no conception": Liberalism and the English temperance press, 1830–1872.' *Victorian Studies* 13 (1969–70): 125–58.

Lang, M. 'Scenes from small worlds: The child, the family and society: Selected children's periodicals of the 1870s.' Ph.D. thesis, University of Leicester, 1980.

Lee, A. J. *The origins of the popular press.* London: Croom Helm, 1976.

Mason, T. *Association football and English society, 1863–1915.* Brighton: Harvester Press, 1980.

Money, J. *Experience and identity: Birmingham and the West Midlands, 1760–1800.* Manchester: at the University Press, 1978.

Morris, J. *Pax Britannica: The climax of an empire.* Harmondsworth: Penguin, 1979.

Murphy, M. J. *Cambridge newspapers and opinion, 1780–1850.* Cambridge: at the University Press, 1977.

Neuberg, V. E. *Popular literature: A history and guide.* Harmondsworth: Penguin, 1977.

Nevett, T. R. 'The Development of Commercial Advertising, 1800–1914.' Ph.D. thesis, University of London, 1979.

———. *Advertising in Britain: A history.* London: Heinemann, 1982.

Peters, M. *Pitt and popularity.* Oxford: Clarendon Press, 1981.

Read, D. *Press and people.* London: Edward Arnold, 1961.

Shattock, J., and M. Wolff (eds.), *The Victorian periodical press: Samplings and soundings.* Leicester: at the University Press, 1982.

Siebert, F. *Freedom of the press in England, 1476–1776.* Urbana: University of Illinois Press, 1965.

The Times (London). *The history of the Times, 1785–1966.* London: Times Books, 5 vols., 1935–84.

Watson, G. (ed.) *New Cambridge bibliography of English literature.* Cambridge: At The University Press, vols. 2 and 3, 1969, 1971.

Webb, R. K. *The British working class reader, 1790–1848.* London: George Allen and Unwin, 1955.

Wiles, R. M. *Freshest advices: Early provincial newspapers in England.* Ohio: at the State University Press, 1965.

Williams, R. *Communications.* London: Chatto and Windus, 1966.

Wilson, R. G. *Gentlemen merchants.* Manchester: at the University Press, 1971.

Index